Little Oxford Dictionary of
Quotations ✳

Little Oxford Dictionary of ✲

Quotations

FOURTH EDITION

Edited by
Susan Ratcliffe

OXFORD
UNIVERSITY PRESS

OXFORD
UNIVERSITY PRESS

Great Clarendon Street, Oxford OX2 6DP

Oxford University Press is a department of the University of Oxford.
It furthers the University's objective of excellence in research, scholarship,
and education by publishing worldwide in

Oxford New York

Auckland Bangkok Buenos Aires Cape Town Chennai
Dar es Salaam Delhi Hong Kong Istanbul Karachi Kolkata
Kuala Lumpur Madrid Melbourne Mexico City Mumbai Nairobi
São Paulo Shanghai Taipei Tokyo Toronto

Oxford is a registered trade mark of Oxford University Press
in the UK and in certain other countries

Published in the United States
by Oxford University Press Inc., New York

First edition published 1994
Second edition published 2001
Third edition published 2005
Fourth edition published 2008

British Library Cataloguing in Publication Data

Data available

Library of Congress Cataloging in Publication Data

Data available

ISBN 978–0–19–954330–4

10 9 8 7 6 5 4

Typeset in Minion and Argo
by Interactive Sciences Limited, Gloucester
Printed and bound in China
by C&C Offset Printing Co., Ltd.

✳ Contents

Foreword to the Fourth Edition ✳

Nearly a hundred years ago the English critic Walter Raleigh
said that 'An anthology is like all the plums and orange peel
picked out of a cake'. The *Little Oxford Dictionary of
Quotations* picks out the best of the plums, and brings
together the perfect words for any occasion. Here you can
find the words of the great and the good, or sometimes the
bad but witty, to add colour to a speech or support for your
point of view.

The dictionary is arranged by theme, so that a variety
of quotations on each subject can be found together.
Some themes encompass special events such as **Birthdays**
('But after all, what *are* birthdays? Here today and gone
tomorrow' A. A. Milne) or **Weddings** ('The trouble with
being best man is, you don't get a chance to prove it'
Les A. Murray), some cover interests such as **Music**
(Music … can name the unnameable, and communicate
the unknowable' Leonard Bernstein) or **Football** ('… the
beautiful game' Pele), while others are more abstract such as
Character ('We are what we pretend to be' Kurt Vonnegut)
or **Idleness** ('The time you enjoy wasting is not wasted time'
Laurence Peter). New themes in this edition include **Parties**,
Punctuality ('You come most carefully upon your hour'
Shakespeare), **Relationships** ('Three things in human life are
important. The first is to be kind. The second is to be kind.
And the third is to be kind.' Henry James), and **Toasts**.

Sayings are being coined all the time, and older ones often
gain a new resonance in changed circumstances. New
arrivals in this edition from the Oxford Quotations database
include statesman Arthur Balfour: 'Nothing matters very
much and very few things matter at all', the poet William
Blake: 'No bird soars too high, if he soars with

Foreword to the Fourth Edition

his own wings', and novelist Cormac McCarthy: 'There ain't no such thing as a bargain promise'. Quotations come from all over the world, and many times and cultures: the Russian novelist Leo Tolstoy: 'The strongest of all warriors are these two—time and patience', the American writer Gertrude Stein: 'Everybody gets so much information all day long that they lose their common sense' and the Chinese philosopher Lao Tzu: 'A good traveller has no fixed plans'.

Within each theme the quotations are arranged in alphabetical order of author, and a new feature of this edition is the addition of brief author descriptions: when Martha Graham says 'The body says what words cannot' it adds interest to know that she was a dancer. Where a little more background information is necessary to understand the quotation, this is supplied after the author details. An author index is provided to help readers seeking a quotation from a particular author.

As Lucretius says, 'Nothing can be created out of nothing', and this book, like all Oxford Quotations dictionaries, would not have been possible without the work of many people. In particular I would like to thank Ben Harris, Commissioning Editor for Language Reference, for his support and advice throughout the project, Susanne Charlett, Jean Harker, and Verity Mason for their contributions to the Quotations Reading Programme, Ralph Bates for library research, and Kim Allen for proofreading.

A dictionary of quotations such as this ranges from Homer to Winston Churchill, from Jane Austen to Oprah Winfrey. In so varied a company, I think it is worth reminding the reader that while, in the words of Alan Bennett: 'You don't have to like everything', Coleridge's definition of poetry could perhaps be adapted to quotations: 'the best words in the *best* order'.

SUSAN RATCLIFFE

Oxford 2008

Foreword to the First Edition ✳

The Little Oxford Dictionary of Quotations is a collection
which casts a fresh light on even the most familiar sayings.
It is organized by themes, such as **Action**, **Liberty**, and
Memory, and within each theme the quotations are
arranged in date order, so that the interplay of ideas down
the centuries becomes apparent. It is intended for the reader
who is searching for quotations on a specific subject, the
reader who remembers the sense of a quotation but not the
precise words, and, of course, the browser.

The themes have been chosen to reflect as wide a range of
subjects as possible, concentrating on the general rather
than the specific. A few themes have a slightly different
character: thus **People** and **Places** cover quotations about
many different individual people and places, while **Political
Comment** and **Wars** include quotations relevant to specific
events. The length of the sections reflects to some extent the
preoccupations of people throughout history, ranging from
short ones such as **Advice** to the many and varied comments
on **Life** and **Love**. Where subjects overlap, the reader is
directed to related themes at the head of the section; for
example, at **Death**: see also **Epitaphs**, **Last Words**, **Murder**.
An author index is provided to help readers wishing to trace
a particular quotation or seeking quotations from specific
individuals.

Within each theme, the aim is to take in a variety of
viewpoints, including both the most familiar quotations
and some less well-known or perhaps new material. So
within **News and Journalism**, along with C. P. Scott's classic
'Comment is free, but facts are sacred', we have Tom
Stoppard's gloss 'Comment is free but facts are on expenses'
and more recently Lord MacGregor on 'journalists dabbling

Foreword to the First Edition

their fingers in the stuff of other people's souls'. This book contains some one hundred quotations which have not previously appeared in any dictionary of quotations. These new quotations appear, for example, under the themes **Environment** (…all that remains/For us will be concrete and tyres'), **Men and Women** ('Whereas nature turns girls into women, society has to make boys into men'), and **Science** ('The aim of science is not to open the door to infinite wisdom, but to set a limit to infinite error').

The chronological ordering within each theme enables the quotations to 'talk' to one another, shedding new light on each. Thus we have Samuel Johnson telling us 'Change is not made without inconvenience, even from worse to better', followed by Voltaire: 'If we do not find anything pleasant, at least we shall find something new'. Much of the cross-referencing required by an alphabetical arrangement of authors becomes redundant: Ralegh's line written on a window-pane 'Fain would I climb, yet fear I to fall' is now immediately followed by Elizabeth I's reply 'If thy heart fails thee, climb not at all.'

The quotations have been classified by their subject rather than by keywords in the text. For example, Tom Lehrer's 'It is sobering to consider that when Mozart was my age he had already been dead for a year' is essentially about **Achievement** rather than **Music** or **Death**, and has been placed accordingly. As far as possible each quotation has been included only once, but a few, such as Pope's 'To err is human, to forgive divine' plainly had a place in two sections.

A short source reference is given for each quotation, usually including its date. Where the date is uncertain or unknown, the author's date of death has been used to determine the order within a theme. The quotations themselves have been kept as short as possible: contextual information has occasionally been added to the source note, and related but less well-known and well-expressed versions have generally been excluded. Owing to constraints of space, foreign language originals have been given only where they are well-known or where translations differ. Such information, including full finding references, can be found in *The Oxford Dictionary of Quotations*.

We are always grateful to those readers who write to us with their comments, suggestions, and discoveries, and we hope this tradition will continue. *The Little Oxford Dictionary* draws largely on the work done for the fourth edition of *The Oxford Dictionary of Quotations*, and therefore owes a substantial debt to all those involved in the preparation of that volume. None the less, this book has its own identity, and the editor's chief pleasure as it took shape has been in listening to different voices speaking to each other across the ages: ' "What is the use of a book," thought Alice, "without pictures or conversations?" '

SUSAN RATCLIFFE

Oxford, March 1994

List of Subjects ✳

List of Subjects

List of Subjects

K
Knowledge

L
Language
Languages
The Law
Leadership
Leisure
Letters
Liberty
Libraries
Lies
Life
Life Sciences
Lifestyles
Literature
London
Love
Lovers
Luck

M
Madness
Management
Manners
Marriage
Mathematics
Meaning
Medicine
Meeting
Memory
Men

Men and Women
Middle Age
The Mind
Misfortune
Mistakes
Moderation
Money
Morality
Mothers
Mountains
Murder
Music

N
Names
Nature
News
Night

O
Old Age
Opinion
Optimism
Originality

P
Painting
Parents
Parties
Parting
The Past
Patience
Patriotism

Peace
Perfection
Pessimism
Philosophy
Photography
Planning
Pleasure
Poetry
Politicians
Politics
Pollution
Poverty
Power
Practicality
Praise
Prayer
Prejudice
The Present
The Presidency
Pride
Progress
Promises
Protest
Punctuality
Punishment

Q
Quotations

R
Race
Railways
Reading
Reality

List of Subjects

Quotations

Ability ✳

Natural abilities are like natural plants, that need pruning by study.
    Francis Bacon 1561–1626 English courtier

If a man write a better book, preach a better sermon, or make a better mouse-trap than his neighbour, tho' he build his house in the woods, the world will make a beaten path to his door.
    Ralph Waldo Emerson 1803–82 American writer

This very remarkable man
Commends a most practical plan:
You can do what you want
If you don't think you can't,
So don't think you can't think you can.
    Charles Inge 1868–1957, *on the French psychologist Émile Coué*

DUMBLEDORE: It is our choices, Harry, that show what we truly are, far more than our abilities.
    J. K. Rowling 1965–   English novelist

MARLON BRANDO: I could have had class. I could have been a contender.
    Budd Schulberg 1914–2009 American writer, *in the film* On the Waterfront

Non omnia possumus omnes.
We can't all do everything.
    Virgil 70–19 BC Roman poet

Intelligence is quickness to apprehend as distinct from ability, which is capacity to act wisely on the thing apprehended.
    Alfred North Whitehead 1861–1947 English philosopher

✳ Absence

The Lord watch between me and thee, when we are absent one from another.
Bible

The heart may think it knows better: the senses know that absence blots people out. We have really no absent friends.
Elizabeth Bowen 1899–1973 Anglo-Irish novelist

The absent are always in the wrong.
Philippe Néricault Destouches 1680–1754 French dramatist

Absence diminishes commonplace passions and increases great ones, as the wind extinguishes candles and kindles fire.
Duc de la Rochefoucauld 1613–80 French moralist

Absence makes the heart grow fonder.
Proverb

Most of what matters in your life takes place in your absence.
Salman Rushdie 1947– Indian-born British novelist

✳ Achievement ⇒Ambition, Effort

That's one small step for a man, one giant leap for mankind.
Neil Armstrong 1930– American astronaut, *stepping onto the moon*

We can lift ourselves out of ignorance, we can find ourselves as creatures of excellence and intelligence and skill.
Richard Bach 1936– American novelist

Achievement

The desire accomplished is sweet to the soul.
Bible

To those of you who received honours, awards and distinctions, I say well done. And to the C students, I say you, too, can be president of the United States.
George W. Bush 1946– American statesman

Give us the tools and we will finish the job.
Winston Churchill 1874–1965 British statesman

None climbs so high as he who knows not whither he is going.
Oliver Cromwell 1599–1658 English statesman

There must be a beginning of any great matter, but the continuing unto the end until it be thoroughly finished yields the true glory.
Francis Drake c.1540–96 English sailor

The distance is nothing; it is only the first step that is difficult.
Mme Du Deffand 1697–1780 French literary hostess, *commenting on the legend that St Denis, carrying his head in his hands, walked two leagues*

Nothing great was ever achieved without enthusiasm.
Ralph Waldo Emerson 1803–82 American writer

Those who believe that they are exclusively in the right are generally those who achieve something.
Aldous Huxley 1894–1963 English novelist

He has, indeed, done it very well; but it is a foolish thing well done.
Samuel Johnson 1709–84 English lexicographer

It is sobering to consider that when Mozart was my age he had already been dead for a year.
Tom Lehrer 1928– American humorist

Achievement

Fame is an accident; merit a thing absolute.
Herman Melville 1819–91 American novelist

So little done, so much to do.
Cecil Rhodes 1853–1902 South African statesman

✳ Acting ⇒The Cinema, The Theatre

To grasp the full significance of life is the actor's duty, to interpret it is his problem, and to express it his dedication.
Marlon Brando 1924–2004 American actor

Just say the lines and don't trip over the furniture.
Noël Coward 1899–1973 English dramatist

Actors are cattle.
Alfred Hitchcock 1899–1980 British-born film director

Acting is a masochistic form of exhibitionism. It is not quite the occupation of an adult.
Laurence Olivier 1907–89 English actor

She ran the whole gamut of the emotions from A to B.
Dorothy Parker 1893–1967 American critic

Acting is merely the art of keeping a large group of people from coughing.
Ralph Richardson 1902–83 English actor

Suit the action to the word, the word to the action.
William Shakespeare 1564–1616 English dramatist

O Lord, Sir—when a heroine goes mad she always goes into white satin.
Richard Brinsley Sheridan 1751–1816 Irish dramatist

They say an actor is only as good as his parts. Well, my parts have done me pretty well, darling.
Barbara Windsor 1937– English actress

Action

But men must know, that in this theatre of man's life it is reserved only for God and angels to be lookers on.
Francis Bacon 1561–1626 English courtier

Vision without action is merely a dream. Action without vision just passes the time. Vision with action can change the world.
Joel Arthur Barker American futurist

Let's roll.
Todd Beamer 1968–2001, *as Beamer and other passengers were planning to storm the cockpit of the hijacked United Airlines Flight 93, 11 September 2001*

Better to light a candle than curse the darkness.
Peter Benenson 1921–2005 English lawyer

The world can only be grasped by action, not by contemplation…The hand is the cutting edge of the mind.
Jacob Bronowski 1908–74 Polish-born scientist

Action is consolatory. It is the enemy of thought and the friend of flattering illusions.
Joseph Conrad 1857–1924 Polish-born English novelist

Progression is going forwards. Going backwards is regression. Going sideways is just aggression.
Noel Gallagher 1967– English pop singer

Oh that thou hadst like others been all words,
And no performance.
Philip Massinger 1583–1640 English dramatist

They also serve who only stand and wait.
John Milton 1608–74 English poet

Think nothing done while aught remains to do.
Samuel Rogers 1763–1855 English poet

Action

If it were done when 'tis done, then 'twere well
It were done quickly.
   William Shakespeare 1564–1616 English dramatist

✳ Advertising

Word of mouth is the best medium of all.
   Bill Bernbach 1911–82 American advertising executive

A good poster is a visual telegram.
   A. M. Cassandre 1901–68 French illustrator

Advertising is the most fun you can have with your
clothes on.
   Jerry Della Femina 1936– American advertising executive

Promise, large promise, is the soul of an advertisement.
   Samuel Johnson 1709–84 English lexicographer

Society drives people crazy with lust and calls it
advertising.
   John Lahr 1941– American critic

Advertising may be described as the science of arresting
human intelligence long enough to get money from it.
   Stephen Leacock 1869–1944 Canadian humorist

Half the money I spend on advertising is wasted, and the
trouble is I don't know which half.
   Lord Leverhulme 1851–1925 English industrialist

The consumer isn't a moron; she is your wife.
   David Ogilvy 1911–99 British-born advertising executive

Advertising is the rattling of a stick inside a swill bucket.
   George Orwell 1903–50 English novelist

Good wine needs no bush.
   Proverb

Advice ✳

Books will speak plain when counsellors blanch.
Francis Bacon 1561–1626 English courtier

Well, if you knows of a better 'ole, go to it.
Bruce Bairnsfather 1888–1959 British cartoonist

A word spoken in due season, how good is it!
Bible

Advice is seldom welcome; and those who want it the most always like it the least.
Lord Chesterfield 1694–1773 English writer

Fools need advice most, but wise men only are the better for it.
Benjamin Franklin 1706–90 American statesman and scientist

Get the advice of everybody whose advice is worth having—they are very few—and then do what you think best yourself.
Charles Stewart Parnell 1846–91 Irish nationalist leader

After all, when you seek advice from someone it's certainly not because you want them to give it. You just want them to be there while you talk to yourself.
Terry Pratchett 1948– English novelist

Look for what's missing. Many advisers can tell a president how to improve what's proposed, or what's gone amiss. Few are able to see what isn't there.
Donald Rumsfeld 1932– American politician

I always pass on good advice. It is the only thing to do with it. It is never of any use to oneself.
Oscar Wilde 1854–1900 Irish dramatist

Ambition

✳ Ambition →Achievement, Effort

No bird soars too high, if he soars with his own wings.
William Blake 1757–1827 English poet

Aut Caesar, aut nihil.
Caesar or nothing.
Cesare Borgia 1476–1507 Italian statesman

Ah, but a man's reach should exceed his grasp,
Or what's a heaven for?
Robert Browning 1812–89 English poet

Well is it known that ambition can creep as well as soar.
Edmund Burke 1729–97 Irish-born politician

[I] had rather be first in a village than second at Rome.
Julius Caesar 100–44 BC Roman statesman

All ambitions are lawful except those which climb
upwards on the miseries or credulities of mankind.
Joseph Conrad 1857–1924 Polish-born English novelist

Ambition leads me not only farther than any other man
has been before me, but as far as I think it possible for
man to go.
James Cook 1728–79 English explorer

At the age of six I wanted to be a cook. At seven I
wanted to be Napoleon. And my ambition has been
growing steadily ever since.
Salvador Dali 1904–89 Spanish painter

Hitch your wagon to a star.
Ralph Waldo Emerson 1803–82 American writer

The worst fault of the working classes is telling their
children they're not going to succeed, saying: 'There is
life, but it's not for you.'
John Mortimer 1923–2009 English lawyer

Fain would I climb, yet fear I to fall.
Walter Ralegh c.1552–1618 English courtier, *line written on a window-pane; Queen Elizabeth I (1533–1603) replied 'If thy heart fails thee, climb not at all'*

When that the poor have cried, Caesar hath wept;
Ambition should be made of sterner stuff.
William Shakespeare 1564–1616 English dramatist

The world continues to offer glittering prizes to those who have stout hearts and sharp swords.
F. E. Smith 1872–1930 British lawyer

There is always room at the top.
Daniel Webster 1782–1852 American politician

Anger ✳

Anger makes dull men witty, but it keeps them poor.
Francis Bacon 1561–1626 English courtier

A soft answer turneth away wrath.
Bible

The tigers of wrath are wiser than the horses of instruction.
William Blake 1757–1827 English poet

Anger is never without an argument, but seldom with a good one.
Lord Halifax 1633–95 English politician

Anger is a short madness.
Horace 65–8 BC Roman poet

When angry, count ten before you speak; if very angry a hundred.
Thomas Jefferson 1743–1826 American statesman

Anger

Anger in its time and place
May assume a kind of grace.
It must have some reason in it
And not last beyond a minute.
Charles Lamb 1775–1834 English writer

Never let the sun go down on your anger.
Proverb

When angry, count four; when very angry, swear.
Mark Twain 1835–1910 American writer

✳ Animals ⇒Cats, Dogs

All things bright and beautiful,
All creatures great and small,
All things wise and wonderful,
The Lord God made them all.
Cecil Frances Alexander 1818–95 Irish poet

The question is not, Can they reason? nor, Can they talk?
but, Can they suffer?
Jeremy Bentham 1748–1832 English philosopher

A righteous man regardeth the life of his beast: but the
tender mercies of the wicked are cruel.
Bible

Tiger Tiger, burning bright,
In the forests of the night;
What immortal hand or eye,
Could frame thy fearful symmetry?
William Blake 1757–1827 English poet

A four-legged friend, a four-legged friend,
He'll never let you down.
J. Brooks

Wee, sleekit, cow'rin', tim'rous beastie,
O what a panic's in thy breastie!
Robert Burns 1759–96 Scottish poet, *on a mouse*

I am fond of pigs. Dogs look up to us. Cats look down
on us. Pigs treat us as equals.
Winston Churchill 1874–1965 British statesman

Animals, whom we have made our slaves, we do not like
to consider our equal.
Charles Darwin 1809–82 English naturalist

Where in this wide world can man find nobility without
    pride,
Friendship without envy, or beauty without vanity?
Ronald Duncan 1914–82 English dramatist, *on the horse*

'Twould ring the bells of Heaven
The wildest peal for years,
If Parson lost his senses
And people came to theirs,
And he and they together
Knelt down with angry prayers
For tamed and shabby tigers
And dancing dogs and bears,
And wretched, blind, pit ponies,
And little hunted hares.
Ralph Hodgson 1871–1962 English poet

I hate a word like 'pets': it sounds so much
Like something with no living of its own.
Elizabeth Jennings 1926–2001 English poet

It ar'n't that I loves the fox less, but that I loves the
'ound more.
R. S. Surtees 1805–64 English novelist

✳ Anxiety

What's the use of worrying?
It never was worth while,
So, pack up your troubles in your old kit-bag,
And smile, smile, smile.
>**George Asaf** 1880–1951 British songwriter

In trouble to be troubled
Is to have your trouble doubled.
>**Daniel Defoe** 1660–1731 English novelist

I'm not [biting my fingernails]. I'm biting my knuckles. I finished the fingernails months ago.
>**Joseph L. Mankiewicz** 1909–93 American film director, *while directing* Cleopatra

Anxiety is love's greatest killer.
>**Anaïs Nin** 1903–77 American writer

O polished perturbation! golden care!
>**William Shakespeare** 1564–1616 English dramatist

What though care killed a cat, thou hast mettle enough in thee to kill care.
>**William Shakespeare** 1564–1616 English dramatist

Neurosis is the way of avoiding non-being by avoiding being.
>**Paul Tillich** 1886–1965 German-born theologian

✳ Apology

Very sorry can't come. Lie follows by post.
>**Lord Charles Beresford** 1846–1919 British politician, *telegraphed message to the Prince of Wales, on being summoned to dine at the eleventh hour*

Never make a defence or apology before you be accused.
>**Charles I** 1600–49 British monarch

Never complain and never explain.
Benjamin Disraeli 1804–81 British statesman

The most important thing a man can learn—the importance of three little words: 'I was wrong.' These words will get you much further than 'I love you.'
Charlton Heston 1924–2008 American actor

Several excuses are always less convincing than one.
Aldous Huxley 1894–1963 English novelist

It is a good rule in life never to apologize. The right sort of people do not want apologies, and the wrong sort take a mean advantage of them.
P. G. Wodehouse 1881–1975 English writer

Appearance →The Body

For the Lord seeth not as man seeth: for man looketh on the outward appearance, but the Lord looketh on the heart.
Bible

If everyone were cast in the same mould, there would be no such thing as beauty.
Charles Darwin 1809–82 English naturalist

I am the family face;
Flesh perishes, I live on.
Thomas Hardy 1840–1928 English novelist

At 50, everyone has the face he deserves.
George Orwell 1903–50 English novelist

Men seldom make passes
At girls who wear glasses.
Dorothy Parker 1893–1967 American critic

It costs a lot of money to look this cheap.
Dolly Parton 1946– American singer

Appearance

Had Cleopatra's nose been shorter, the whole face of the world would have changed.
Blaise Pascal 1623–62 French scientist and philosopher

Anything which says it can magically take away your wrinkles is a scandalous lie.
Anita Roddick 1942–2007 English businesswoman

There's no art
To find the mind's construction in the face.
William Shakespeare 1564–1616 English dramatist

There is no trusting appearances.
Richard Brinsley Sheridan 1751–1816 Irish dramatist

✱ Architecture

A monstrous carbuncle on the face of a much-loved and elegant friend.
Charles, Prince of Wales 1948– , *on the proposed extension to the National Gallery, London*

We shape our buildings, and afterwards our buildings shape us.
Winston Churchill 1874–1965 British statesman

Light (God's eldest daughter) is a principal beauty in building.
Thomas Fuller 1608–61 English preacher

Less is more.
Ludwig Mies van der Rohe 1886–1969 German-born architect

God is in the details.
Ludwig Mies van der Rohe 1886–1969 German-born architect

You should be able to read a building. It should be what it does.
Richard Rogers 1933–   British architect

When we build, let us think that we build for ever.
John Ruskin 1819–1900 English critic

Architecture in general is frozen music.
Friedrich von Schelling 1775–1854 German philosopher

Form follows function.
Louis Henri Sullivan 1856–1924 American architect

Well building hath three conditions. Commodity, firmness, and delight.
Henry Wotton 1568–1639 English diplomat

The physician can bury his mistakes, but the architect can only advise his client to plant vines—so they should go as far as possible from home to build their first buildings.
Frank Lloyd Wright 1867–1959 American architect

Argument ✳

It is better to dwell in a corner of the housetop, than with a brawling woman in a wide house.
Bible

It takes in reality only one to make a quarrel. It is useless for the sheep to pass resolutions in favour of vegetarianism, while the wolf remains of a different opinion.
Dean Inge 1860–1954 English writer

There is no good in arguing with the inevitable. The only argument available with an east wind is to put on your overcoat.
James Russell Lowell 1819–91 American poet

Argument

The Catholic and the Communist are alike in assuming that an opponent cannot be both honest and intelligent.
George Orwell 1903–50 English novelist

Who can refute a sneer?
William Paley 1743–1805 English theologian

The argument of the broken window pane is the most valuable argument in modern politics.
Emmeline Pankhurst 1858–1928 English suffragette leader

I am not arguing with you—I am telling you.
James McNeill Whistler 1834–1903 American-born painter

✳ The Army ⇒War

Lions led by donkeys.
Anonymous *associated with British forces during the First World War, but of earlier origin*

The sergeant is the army.
Dwight D. Eisenhower 1890–1969 American statesman

Old soldiers never die,
They simply fade away.
J. Foley 1906–70 British songwriter

The courage of a soldier is found to be the cheapest, and most common, quality of human nature.
Edward Gibbon 1737–94 English historian

How do you ask a man to be the last man to die in Vietnam? How do you ask a man to be the last man to die for a mistake?
John Kerry 1943– American politician

O it's Tommy this, an' Tommy that, an' 'Tommy, go
   away';
But it's 'Thank you, Mister Atkins,' when the band begins
   to play.

    Rudyard Kipling 1865–1936 English writer

Remember that there is not one of you who does not
carry in his cartridge-pouch the marshal's baton of the
duke of Reggio; it is up to you to bring it forth.

    Louis XVIII 1755–1824 French monarch, *to military cadets*

When I was in the military, they gave me a medal for
killing two men and a discharge for loving one.

    Leonard Matlovich 1943–88 American soldier

An army marches on its stomach.

    Napoleon I 1769–1821 French emperor

What passing-bells for these who die as cattle?
Only the monstrous anger of the guns.

    Wilfred Owen 1893–1918 English poet

Wars may be fought with weapons, but they are won by
men.

    George S. Patton 1885–1945 American general

A man who is good enough to shed his blood for the
country is good enough to be given a square deal
afterwards.

    Theodore Roosevelt 1858–1919 American statesman

When the military man approaches, the world locks up
its spoons and packs off its womankind.

    George Bernard Shaw 1856–1950 Irish dramatist

Theirs not to make reply,
Theirs not to reason why,
Theirs but to do and die:
Into the valley of Death
Rode the six hundred.

    Alfred, Lord Tennyson 1809–92 English poet

The Army

Discipline is the soul of an army. It makes small numbers formidable; procures success to the weak and esteem to all.

George Washington 1732–99 American statesman

I don't know what effect these men will have upon the enemy, but, by God, they frighten me.

Duke of Wellington 1769–1852 British general, *popular version of Wellington's remark: 'As Lord Chesterfield said of the generals of his day, "I only hope that when the enemy reads the list of their names, he trembles as I do"'*

✳ Art ⇨Painting, Sculpture

You don't have to like everything.

Alan Bennett 1934– English writer, *proposing a notice for the National Gallery*

Art is meant to disturb, science reassures.

Georges Braque 1882–1963 French painter

The history of art is the history of revivals.

Samuel Butler 1835–1902 English novelist

A product of the untalented, sold by the unprincipled to the utterly bewildered.

Al Capp 1907–79 American cartoonist, *on abstract art*

Art for art's sake, with no purpose, for any purpose perverts art. But art achieves a purpose which is not its own.

Benjamin Constant 1767–1834 French novelist

Art is vice. You don't marry it legitimately, you rape it.

Edgar Degas 1834–1917 French artist

I always said God was against art and I still believe it.

Edward Elgar 1857–1934 English composer

The artist must be in his work as God is in creation, invisible and all-powerful; one must sense him everywhere but never see him.

Gustave Flaubert 1821–80 French novelist

Art for Art's sake. Why not?
Art for Life's sake. Why not?
Art for Pleasure's sake. Why not?
What does it matter, as long as it is Art?

Paul Gauguin 1848–1903 French painter

In art the best is good enough.

Johann Wolfgang von Goethe 1749–1832 German writer

The proletarian state must bring up thousands of excellent 'mechanics of culture', 'engineers of the soul'.

Maxim Gorky 1868–1936 Russian writer

Life is short, the art long.

Hippocrates c.460–357 BC Greek physician

It's clever, but is it Art?

Rudyard Kipling 1865–1936 English writer

God help the Minister that meddles with art!

Lord Melbourne 1779–1848 English statesman

We all know that Art is not truth. Art is a lie that makes us realize truth.

Pablo Picasso 1881–1973 Spanish painter

Life without industry is guilt, and industry without art is brutality.

John Ruskin 1819–1900 English critic

The true artist will let his wife starve, his children go barefoot, his mother drudge for his living at seventy, sooner than work at anything but his art.

George Bernard Shaw 1856–1950 Irish dramatist

✳ Australia

Who knows but that England may revive in New South
Wales when it has sunk in Europe.
   Joseph Banks 1743–1820 English botanist

True patriots we; for be it understood,
We left our country for our country's good.
   Henry Carter d. 1806, *written for the opening of the
   Playhouse, Sydney, New South Wales, when the actors were
   principally convicts*

Australia is a lucky country run mainly by second-rate
people who share its luck.
   Donald Richmond Horne 1921– Australian writer

You would take Australia right back down the time
tunnel to the cultural cringe where you have always come
from.
   Paul Keating 1944– Australian statesman, *addressing
   Australian Conservative supporters of links with Great Britain*

Australia has a marvellous sky and air and blue clarity,
and a hoary sort of land beneath it, like a Sleeping
Princess on whom the dust of ages has settled.
   D. H. Lawrence 1885–1930 English writer

In joyful strains then let us sing
Advance Australia fair.
   P. D. McCormick c.1834–1916 Australian musician

Down under we send soldiers and wool abroad but keep
poets and wine at home.
   John Streeter Manifold 1915–85 Australian poet

What Great Britain calls the Far East is to us the near
north.
   Robert Gordon Menzies 1894–1978 Australian statesman

The crimson thread of kinship runs through us all.
Henry Parkes 1815–95 Australian statesman, *on Australian federation*

Autumn ✳

Early autumn—
rice field, ocean,
one green.
Matsuo Basho 1644–94 Japanese poet

Now is the time for the burning of the leaves.
Laurence Binyon 1869–1943 English poet

'What is autumn?' 'A second spring, where every leaf is a flower.'
Albert Camus 1913–60 French writer

It was one of those perfect English autumnal days which occur more frequently in memory than in life.
P. D. James 1920– English writer

Season of mists and mellow fruitfulness,
Close bosom-friend of the maturing sun;
Conspiring with him how to load and bless
With fruit the vines that round the thatch-eaves run.
John Keats 1795–1821 English poet

I want to go south, where there is no autumn, where the cold doesn't crouch over one like a snow-leopard waiting to pounce.
D. H. Lawrence 1885–1930 English writer

O wild West Wind, thou breath of Autumn's being,
Thou, from whose unseen presence the leaves dead
Are driven, like ghosts from an enchanter fleeing.
Percy Bysshe Shelley 1792–1822 English poet

Autumn

For man, autumn is a time of harvest, of gathering together. For nature, it is a time of sowing, of scattering abroad.
Edwin Way Teale 1899–1980 American journalist

In...the fall, the whole country goes to glory.
Frances Trollope 1780–1863 English writer, *of North America*

✳ Babies ⇒Birth

There is no finer investment for any community than putting milk into babies.
Winston Churchill 1874–1965 British statesman

So for the mother's sake the child was dear,
And dearer was the mother for the child.
Samuel Taylor Coleridge 1772–1834 English poet

It is a pleasant thing to reflect upon, and furnishes a complete answer to those who contend for the general degeneration of the human species, that every baby born into the world is a finer one than the last.
Charles Dickens 1812–70 English novelist

There never was a child so lovely but his mother was glad to get asleep.
Ralph Waldo Emerson 1803–82 American writer

Since you arrived, days have melted into night and back again and we are learning a new grammar, a long sentence whose punctuation marks are feeding and winding and nappy changing and these occasional moments of quiet.
Fergal Keane 1961– Irish journalist

A loud noise at one end and no sense of responsibility at the other.
Ronald Knox 1888–1957 English writer, *definition of a baby*

It is only in our advanced and synthetic civilization that mothers no longer sing to the babies they are carrying.

Yehudi Menuhin 1916–99 British violinist

A baby is God's opinion that life should go on.

Carl Sandburg 1878–1967 American poet

You know more than you think you do.

Benjamin Spock 1903–98 American paediatrician, *opening words of* Baby and Child Care

Baseball ✳

Think! How the hell are you gonna think and hit at the same time?

Yogi Berra 1925– American baseball player

A ball player's got to be kept hungry to become a big leaguer. That's why no boy from a rich family ever made the big leagues.

Joe DiMaggio 1914–99 American baseball player

Baseball is very big with my people. It figures. It's the only way we can get to shake a bat at a white man without starting a riot.

Dick Gregory 1932– American comedian

Take me out to the ball game,
Take me out with the crowd.
Buy me some peanuts and cracker-jack—
I don't care if I never get back.

Jack Norworth 1879–1959 American songwriter

All you have to do is keep the five players who hate your guts away from the five who are undecided.

Casey Stengel 1891–1975 American baseball player

Baseball

Baseball, it is said, is only a game. True. And the Grand
Canyon is only a hole in Arizona. Not all holes, or games,
are created equal.

George F. Will 1941– American columnist

✳ Beauty ⇒Good Looks

Being thought of as a beautiful woman has spared me
nothing in life. No heartache, no trouble. Beauty is
essentially meaningless.

Halle Berry 1968– American actress

Consider the lilies of the field, how they grow; they toil
not, neither do they spin:
And yet I say unto you, That even Solomon in all his
glory was not arrayed like one of these.

Bible

If you get simple beauty and naught else,
You get about the best thing God invents.

Robert Browning 1812–89 English poet

I never saw an ugly thing in my life: for let the form of an
object be what it may,—light, shade, and perspective will
always make it beautiful.

John Constable 1776–1837 English painter

Beauty is mysterious as well as terrible. God and devil are
fighting there, and the battlefield is the heart of man.

Fedor Dostoevsky 1821–81 Russian novelist

Beauty will save the world.

Fedor Dostoevsky 1821–81 Russian novelist

He was afflicted by the thought that where Beauty was,
nothing ever ran quite straight, which, no doubt, was why
so many people looked on it as immoral.

John Galsworthy 1867–1933 English novelist

All things counter, original, spare, strange;
Whatever is fickle, freckled (who knows how?)
With swift, slow; sweet, sour; adazzle, dim;
He fathers-forth whose beauty is past change:
Praise him.
    Gerard Manley Hopkins 1844–89 English poet

'Beauty is truth, truth beauty,'—that is all
Ye know on earth, and all ye need to know.
    John Keats 1795–1821 English poet

A thing of beauty is a joy for ever:
Its loveliness increases; it will never
Pass into nothingness.
    John Keats 1795–1821 English poet

At some point in life the world's beauty becomes enough.
You don't need to photograph, paint or even remember
it. It is enough.
    Toni Morrison 1931– American novelist

Remember that the most beautiful things in the world are
the most useless; peacocks and lilies for instance.
    John Ruskin 1819–1900 English critic

Beauty is all very well at first sight; but who ever looks at
it when it has been in the house three days?
    George Bernard Shaw 1856–1950 Irish dramatist

Beauty is no more than a promise of happiness.
    Stendhal 1783–1842 French novelist

Beginning →Ending

In the beginning God created the heaven and the earth.
And the earth was without form, and void; and darkness
was upon the face of the deep.
    Bible

Beginning

'Begin at the beginning,' the King said, gravely, 'and go on till you come to the end: then stop.'
Lewis Carroll 1832–98 English writer

What we call the beginning is often the end
And to make an end is to make a beginning.
The end is where we start from.
T. S. Eliot 1888–1965 American-born British poet

All this will not be finished in the first 100 days. Nor will it be finished in the first 1,000 days, nor in the life of this Administration, nor even perhaps in our lifetime on this planet. But let us begin.
John F. Kennedy 1917–63 American statesman

Are you sitting comfortably? Then I'll begin.
Julia Lang 1921– British radio presenter

A tower of nine storeys begins with a heap of earth.
The journey of a thousand *li* starts from where one
    stands.
Lao Tzu c.604–c.531 BC Chinese philosopher

I've started so I'll finish.
Magnus Magnusson 1929–2007 Icelandic broadcaster, *said when a contestant's time runs out while a question is being put on* Mastermind

☀ Behaviour ⇒Manners

When I go to Rome, I fast on Saturday, but here [Milan] I do not. Do you also follow the custom of whatever church you attend, if you do not want to give or receive scandal.
St Ambrose c.339–397 French-born bishop of Milan, *usually quoted as 'When in Rome, do as the Romans do'*

Private faces in public places
Are wiser and nicer
Than public faces in private places.
   W. H. Auden 1907–73 English poet

In necessary things, unity; in doubtful things, liberty; in
all things, charity.
   Richard Baxter 1615–91 English divine

When people are on their best behaviour they aren't
always at their best.
   Alan Bennett 1934– English writer

Caesar's wife must be above suspicion.
   Julius Caesar 100–44 BC Roman statesman

He only does it to annoy,
Because he knows it teases.
   Lewis Carroll 1832–98 English writer

He was a verray, parfit gentil knyght.
   Geoffrey Chaucer c.1343–1400 English poet

Take the tone of the company that you are in.
   Lord Chesterfield 1694–1773 English writer

O tempora, O mores!
Oh, the times! Oh, the manners!
   Cicero 106–43 BC Roman statesman

I get too hungry for dinner at eight.
I like the theatre, but never come late.
I never bother with people I hate.
That's why the lady is a tramp.
   Lorenz Hart 1895–1943 American songwriter

Be a good animal, true to your instincts.
   D. H. Lawrence 1885–1930 English writer

Behaviour

Perfect behaviour is born of complete indifference.
Cesare Pavese 1908–50 Italian writer

Go directly—see what she's doing, and tell her she mustn't.
Punch 1841–1992 English humorous periodical

The basis of all good human behaviour is kindness.
Eleanor Roosevelt 1884–1962 American diplomat

Tout comprendre rend très indulgent.
To be totally understanding makes one very indulgent.
Mme de Staël 1766–1817 French writer

❋ Belief

The Sea of Faith
Was once, too, at the full, and round earth's shore
Lay like the folds of a bright girdle furled.
But now I only hear
Its melancholy, long, withdrawing roar.
Matthew Arnold 1822–88 English poet

For what a man would like to be true, that he more readily believes.
Francis Bacon 1561–1626 English courtier

Every time a child says 'I don't believe in fairies' there is a little fairy somewhere that falls down dead.
J. M. Barrie 1860–1937 Scottish writer

A faith is something you die for; a doctrine is something you kill for: there is all the difference in the world.
Tony Benn 1925–   British politician

Lord, I believe; help thou mine unbelief.
Bible

Faith is the substance of things hoped for, the evidence of things not seen.
> **Bible**

Of course not, but I am told it works even if you don't believe in it.
> **Niels Bohr** 1885–1962 Danish physicist, *when asked whether he really believed a horseshoe hanging over his door would bring him luck*

Why, sometimes I've believed as many as six impossible things before breakfast.
> **Lewis Carroll** 1832–98 English writer

I do not believe…I know.
> **Carl Gustav Jung** 1875–1961 Swiss psychologist

Credulity is the man's weakness, but the child's strength.
> **Charles Lamb** 1775–1834 English writer

The dust of exploded beliefs may make a fine sunset.
> **Geoffrey Madan** 1895–1947 English bibliophile

We can believe what we choose. We are answerable for what we choose to believe.
> **John Henry Newman** 1801–90 English theologian

Man is a credulous animal, and must believe *something*; in the absence of good grounds for belief, he will be satisfied with bad ones.
> **Bertrand Russell** 1872–1970 British philosopher

There lives more faith in honest doubt,
Believe me, than in half the creeds.
> **Alfred, Lord Tennyson** 1809–92 English poet

Certum est quia impossibile est.
It is certain because it is impossible.
> **Tertullian** c.AD 160–c.225 Roman theologian, *often quoted as* 'Credo quia impossibile [*I believe because it is impossible*]'

✳ Bereavement ⇒Sorrow

You can shed tears that she is gone or you can smile
because she has lived.

Anonymous *preface to the Order of Service at the funeral of
Queen Elizabeth the Queen Mother*

He was my North, my South, my East and West,
My working week and my Sunday rest,
My noon, my midnight, my talk, my song;
I thought that love would last for ever: I was wrong.

W. H. Auden 1907–73 English poet

Blessed are they that mourn: for they shall be comforted.

Bible

Do not stand at my grave and weep:
I am not there. I do not sleep.
I am a thousand winds that blow.
I am the diamond glints on snow...
Do not stand at my grave and cry;
I am not there, I did not die.

Mary E. Frye 1905–2004 American poet, *quoted in letter left
by British soldier Stephen Cummins when killed by the IRA*

Bereavement is a universal and integral part of our
experience of love. It follows marriage as normally as
marriage follows courtship or as autumn follows summer.

C. S. Lewis 1898–1963 English literary scholar

A man's dying is more the survivors' affair than his own.

Thomas Mann 1875–1955 German novelist

Time does not bring relief; you all have lied
Who told me time would ease me of my pain!

Edna St Vincent Millay 1892–1950 American poet

Bereavement

I can't think of a more wonderful thanksgiving for the life I have had than that everyone should be jolly at my funeral.

Lord Mountbatten 1900–79 British statesman

The spring has gone out of the year.

Pericles c.495–429 BC Greek statesman, *funeral oration*

Widow. The word consumes itself.

Sylvia Plath 1932–63 American poet

How often are we to die before we go quite off this stage? In every friend we lose a part of ourselves, and the best part.

Alexander Pope 1688–1744 English poet

I come to bury Caesar, not to praise him.
The evil that men do lives after them,
The good is oft interrèd with their bones.

William Shakespeare 1564–1616 English dramatist

Moderate lamentation is the right of the dead, excessive grief the enemy to the living.

William Shakespeare 1564–1616 English dramatist

The bitterest tears shed over graves are for words left unsaid and deeds left undone.

Harriet Beecher Stowe 1811–96 American novelist

Beloved, come to me often in my dreams. No, not that. Live in my dreams.

Marina Tsvetaeva 1892–1941 Russian poet

Even memory is not necessary for love. There is a land of the living and a land of the dead and the bridge is love, the only survival, the only meaning.

Thornton Wilder 1897–1975 American writer

He first deceased; she for a little tried
To live without him: liked it not, and died.

Henry Wotton 1568–1639 English diplomat

✳ Biography

A well-written Life is almost as rare as a well-spent one.
Thomas Carlyle 1795–1881 Scottish historian

An autobiography is an obituary in serial form with the last instalment missing.
Quentin Crisp 1908–99 English writer

It's an excellent life of somebody else. But I've really lived inside myself, and she can't get in there.
Robertson Davies 1913–95 Canadian novelist, *on a biography of himself*

There is properly no history; only biography.
Ralph Waldo Emerson 1803–82 American writer

Nobody can write the life of a man, but those who have eat and drunk and lived in social intercourse with him.
Samuel Johnson 1709–84 English lexicographer

Lives of great men all remind us
We can make our lives sublime,
And, departing, leave behind us
Footprints on the sands of time.
Henry Wadsworth Longfellow 1807–82 American poet

To write one's memoirs is to speak ill of everybody except oneself.
Marshal Pétain 1856–1951 French statesman

Biography is the mesh through which real life escapes.
Tom Stoppard 1937– British dramatist

Discretion is not the better part of biography.
Lytton Strachey 1880–1932 English biographer

Then there is my noble and biographical friend who has added a new terror to death.
Charles Wetherell 1770–1846 English lawyer, *on Lord Campbell's* Lives of the Lord Chancellors *being written without the consent of heirs or executors*

Every great man nowadays has his disciples, and it is always Judas who writes the biography.
Oscar Wilde 1854–1900 Irish dramatist

Birds ✳

That's the wise thrush; he sings each song twice over,
Lest you should think he never could recapture
The first fine careless rapture!
Robert Browning 1812–89 English poet

The bisy larke, messager of day.
Geoffrey Chaucer c.1343–1400 English poet

It was the Rainbow gave thee birth,
And left thee all her lovely hues.
W. H. Davies 1871–1940 Welsh poet, *of the kingfisher*

I caught this morning morning's minion, kingdom of
daylight's dauphin, dapple-dawn-drawn Falcon.
Gerard Manley Hopkins 1844–89 English poet

Oh, a wondrous bird is the pelican!
His beak holds more than his belican.
He takes in his beak
Food enough for a week.
But I'll be darned if I know how the helican.
Dixon Lanier Merritt 1879–1972 American editor

I live in a city. I know sparrows from starlings. After that everything's a duck as far as I'm concerned.
Terry Pratchett 1948– English novelist

Alone and warming his five wits,
The white owl in the belfry sits.
Alfred, Lord Tennyson 1809–92 English poet

Birds

I once had a sparrow alight upon my shoulder for a moment while I was hoeing in a village garden, and I felt that I was more distinguished by that circumstance than I should have been by any epaulette I could have worn.
Henry David Thoreau 1817-62 American writer

Birth →Babies

It doesn't matter about being born in a duckyard, as long as you're hatched from a swan's egg!
Hans Christian Andersen 1805-75 Danish writer

In sorrow thou shalt bring forth children.
Bible

No phallic hero, no matter what he does to himself or to another to prove his courage, ever matches the solitary, existential courage of the woman who gives birth.
Andrea Dworkin 1946-2005 American feminist

I am not yet born; O fill me
With strength against those who would freeze my humanity.
Louis MacNeice 1907-63 British poet

Death and taxes and childbirth! There's never any convenient time for any of them.
Margaret Mitchell 1900-49 American novelist

Men should be bewailed at their birth, and not at their death.
Montesquieu 1689-1755 French political philosopher

Good work, Mary. We all knew you had it in you.
Dorothy Parker 1893-1967 American critic, *telegram to Mrs Sherwood on the arrival of her baby*

Love set you going like a fat gold watch.
The midwife slapped your footsoles, and your bald cry
Took its place among the elements.
Sylvia Plath 1932–63 American poet

What you say of the pride of giving life to an immortal
soul is very fine, dear, but I own I can not enter into that;
I think much more of our being like a cow or a dog at
such moments; when our poor nature becomes so very
animal and unecstatic.
Queen Victoria 1819–1901 British monarch

Our birth is but a sleep and a forgetting...
Not in entire forgetfulness,
And not in utter nakedness,
But trailing clouds of glory do we come.
William Wordsworth 1770–1850 English poet

Birthdays ✳

A diplomat is a man who always remembers a woman's
birthday but never remembers her age.
Robert Frost 1874–1963 American poet

Happy birthday to you.
Pattie S. Hill 1868–1946 American educationist

You know you're getting old when the candles cost more
than the cake.
Bob Hope 1903–2003 American comedian

Do you count your birthdays thankfully?
Horace 65–8 BC Roman poet

One of the sadder things, I think,
Is how our birthdays slowly sink:
Presents and parties disappear,
The cards grow fewer year by year.
Philip Larkin 1922–85 English poet

Birthdays

Believing, hear, what you deserve to hear:
Your birthday as my own to me is dear...
But yours gives most; for mine did only lend
Me to the world; yours gave to me a friend.
Martial c.AD 40–c.104 Roman epigrammatist

EEYORE: But after all, what *are* birthdays? Here today and
gone tomorrow.
A. A. Milne 1882–1956 English writer

Our birthdays are feathers in the broad wing of time.
Jean Paul Richter 1763–1825 German novelist

✳ Boats

Jolly boating weather,
And a hay harvest breeze,
Blade on the feather,
Shade off the trees
Swing, swing together
With your body between your knees.
William Cory 1823–92 English poet

A wet sheet and a flowing sea,
A wind that follows fast
And fills the white and rustling sail
And bends the gallant mast.
Allan Cunningham 1784–1842 Scottish poet

There is *nothing*—absolutely nothing—half so much
worth doing as simply messing about in boats.
Kenneth Grahame 1859–1932 Scottish-born writer

Quinquireme of Nineveh from distant Ophir
Rowing home to haven in sunny Palestine,
With a cargo of ivory,
And apes and peacocks,

Sandalwood, cedarwood, and sweet white wine.
     John Masefield 1878–1967 English poet

The Body ⇒Appearance

Entrails don't care for travel,
Entrails don't care for stress:
Entrails are better kept folded inside you
For outside, they make a mess.
     Connie Bensley 1929– English poet

I will give thanks unto thee, for I am fearfully and
wonderfully made.
     Bible

A woman watches her body uneasily, as though it were an
unreliable ally in the battle for love.
     Leonard Cohen 1934– Canadian singer

i like my body when it is with your
body. It is so quite new a thing.
Muscles better and nerves more.
     e. e. cummings 1894–1962 American poet

The leg, a source of much delight,
which carries weight and governs height.
     Ian Dury 1942–2000 British rock singer

Anatomy is destiny.
     Sigmund Freud 1856–1939 Austrian psychiatrist

The body says what words cannot.
     Martha Graham 1894–1991 American dancer

For some inexplicable reason the sense of smell does not
hold the high position it deserves among its sisters. There
is something of the fallen angel about it.
     Helen Keller 1880–1968 American writer

The Body

I'm fat, but I'm thin inside. Has it ever struck you that there's a thin man inside every fat man, just as they say there's a statue inside every block of stone?
  George Orwell 1903–50 English novelist

Every man is the builder of a temple, called his body.
  Henry David Thoreau 1817–62 American writer

Our body is a machine for living. It is organized for that, it is its nature. Let life go on in it unhindered and let it defend itself.
  Leo Tolstoy 1828–1910 Russian novelist

I sing the body electric.
  Walt Whitman 1819–92 American poet

You can never be too rich or too thin.
  Duchess of Windsor 1896–1986

The human body is the best picture of the human soul.
  Ludwig Wittgenstein 1889–1951 Austrian-born philosopher

✳ Books ⇒Libraries, Reading

Some books are undeservedly forgotten; none are undeservedly remembered.
  W. H. Auden 1907–73 English poet

Some books are to be tasted, others to be swallowed, and some few to be chewed and digested.
  Francis Bacon 1561–1626 English courtier

Books say: she did this because. Life says: she did this. Books are where things are explained to you; life is where things aren't.
  Julian Barnes 1946– English novelist

Of making many books there is no end; and much study is a weariness of the flesh.
  Bible

What literature can and should do is change the people who teach the people who don't read the books.
A. S. Byatt 1936- English novelist

A great book is like great evil.
Callimachus c.305–c.240 BC Greek poet

'What is the use of a book', thought Alice, 'without pictures or conversations?'
Lewis Carroll 1832–98 English writer

The greatest masterpiece in literature is only a dictionary out of order.
Jean Cocteau 1889–1963 French film director

I don't trust books. They're all fact, no heart.
Stephen Colbert 1964- American satirist

Another damned, thick, square book! Always scribble, scribble, scribble! Eh! Mr Gibbon?
Duke of Gloucester 1743–1805

A book must be the axe for the frozen sea within us.
Franz Kafka 1883–1924 Czech novelist

Far too many relied on the classic formula of a beginning, a muddle, and an end.
Philip Larkin 1922–85 English poet, *of novels entered for the Booker Prize*

A good book is the precious life-blood of a master spirit.
John Milton 1608–74 English poet

There is no book so bad that some good cannot be got out of it.
Pliny the Elder AD 23–79 Roman senator

The principle of procrastinated rape is said to be the ruling one in all the great best-sellers.
V. S. Pritchett 1900–97 English writer

Books

I hate books; they only teach us to talk about things we know nothing about.
Jean-Jacques Rousseau 1712–78 French philosopher

All books are divisible into two classes, the books of the hour, and the books of all time.
John Ruskin 1819–1900 English critic

No furniture so charming as books.
Sydney Smith 1771–1845 English essayist

The shelf life of the modern hardback writer is somewhere between the milk and the yoghurt.
Calvin Trillin 1935– American journalist

A good book is the best of friends, the same to-day and for ever.
Martin Tupper 1810–89 English writer

'*Classic.*' A book which people praise and don't read.
Mark Twain 1835–1910 American writer

Publish and be damned.
Duke of Wellington 1769–1852 British general, *replying to a blackmail threat*

✳ Boredom

Nothing happens, nobody comes, nobody goes, it's awful!
Samuel Beckett 1906–89 Irish writer

Life, friends, is boring. We must not say so...
And moreover my mother told me as a boy
(repeatedly) 'Ever to confess you're bored
means you have no
Inner Resources.'
John Berryman 1914–72 American poet

Everyone is a bore to someone. That is unimportant. The thing to avoid is being a bore to oneself.
Gerald Brenan 1894–1987 British writer

What's wrong with being a boring kind of guy?
George Bush 1924– American statesman

Millions long for immortality who don't know what to do with themselves on a rainy Sunday afternoon.
Susan Ertz 1894–1985 American writer

Nothing, like something, happens anywhere.
Philip Larkin 1922–85 English poet

We often forgive those who bore us, but we cannot forgive those whom we bore.
Duc de la Rochefoucauld 1613–80 French moralist

Waiting is still an occupation. It's having nothing to wait for that is terrible.
Cesare Pavese 1908–50 Italian writer

Boredom is…a vital problem for the moralist, since half the sins of mankind are caused by the fear of it.
Bertrand Russell 1872–1970 British philosopher

A healthy male adult bore consumes *each year* one and a half times his own weight in other people's patience.
John Updike 1932–2009 American writer

The secret of being a bore…is to tell everything.
Voltaire 1694–1778 French writer

Boxing ✳

Float like a butterfly, sting like a bee.
Muhammad Ali 1942– American boxer, *summary of his boxing strategy*

I'm the greatest.
Muhammad Ali 1942– American boxer

Boxing

Boxing's just showbusiness with blood.
Frank Bruno 1961– English boxer

Honey, I just forgot to duck.
Jack Dempsey 1895–1983 American boxer, *to his wife, on losing the World Heavyweight title*

The bigger they are, the further they have to fall.
Robert Fitzsimmons 1862–1917 New Zealand boxer, *prior to a boxing match*

We was robbed!
Joe Jacobs 1896–1940 American boxing manager, *after Jack Sharkey beat Max Schmeling (of whom Jacobs was manager) in a heavyweight title fight*

We're all endowed with God-given talents. Mine happens to be hitting people in the head.
Sugar Ray Leonard 1956– American boxer

He can run. But he can't hide.
Joe Louis 1914–81 American boxer, *of Billy Conn, his opponent*

I fight for money, but I am not greedy. How many steaks can one man eat?
Laszlo Papp 1926–2003 Hungarian boxer

✳ Brevity

It is a foolish thing to make a long prologue, and to be short in the story itself.
Bible

The beauty of concision…is that you can only repeat conventional thoughts.
Noam Chomsky 1928– American linguist

I strive to be brief, and I become obscure.
Horace 65–8 BC Roman poet

I have made this [letter] longer than usual, only because I have not had the time to make it shorter.
Blaise Pascal 1623–62 French scientist and philosopher

Words are like leaves; and where they most abound,
Much fruit of sense beneath is rarely found.
Alexander Pope 1688–1744 English poet

If there is anywhere a thing said in two sentences that could have been as clearly and as engagingly said in one, then it's amateur work.
Robert Louis Stevenson 1850–94 Scottish novelist

Britain ✳

Great Britain has lost an empire and has not yet found a role.
Dean Acheson 1893–1971 American politician

The land of embarrassment and breakfast.
Julian Barnes 1946– English novelist, *of Britain*

You cannot trust people who have such bad cuisine. It is the country with the worst food after Finland.
Jacques Chirac 1932– French statesman, *on the British*

The British nation is unique in this respect. They are the only people who like to be told how bad things are, who like to be told the worst.
Winston Churchill 1874–1965 British statesman

Britain is no longer totally a white place where people ride horses, wear long frocks and drink tea. The national dish is no longer fish and chips, it's curry.
Marianne Jean-Baptiste 1967– English actress

What is our task? To make Britain a fit country for heroes to live in.
David Lloyd George 1863–1945 British statesman

Britain

Fifty years on from now, Britain will still be the country of long shadows on county [cricket] grounds, warm beer, invincible green suburbs, dog lovers, and—as George Orwell said—old maids bicycling to Holy Communion through the morning mist.
John Major 1943-   British statesman

No sex, please—we're British.
Anthony Marriott 1931-   and **Alistair Foot** British dramatists

Rule, Britannia, rule the waves;
Britons never will be slaves.
James Thomson 1700-48 Scottish poet

Other nations use 'force'; we Britons alone use 'Might'.
Evelyn Waugh 1903-66 English novelist

※ Bureaucracy ⇒Management

A memorandum is written not to inform the reader but to protect the writer.
Dean Acheson 1893-1971 American politician

It is an inevitable defect, that bureaucrats will care more for routine than for results.
Walter Bagehot 1826-77 English economist

Guidelines for bureaucrats: (1) When in charge, ponder. (2) When in trouble, delegate. (3) When in doubt, mumble.
James H. Boren 1925-   American bureaucrat

Give a civil servant a good case and he'll wreck it with clichés, bad punctuation, double negatives and convoluted apology.
Alan Clark 1928-99 British politician

The Civil Service is profoundly deferential—'Yes, Minister! No, Minister! If you wish it, Minister!'
Richard Crossman 1907-74 British politician

A desk is a dangerous place from which to watch the world.
John le Carré 1931- English novelist

The truth in these matters may be stated as a scientific law: 'The persistence of public officials varies inversely with the importance of the matter on which they are persisting.'
Bernard Levin 1928-2004 British journalist

The man who is denied the opportunity of taking decisions of importance begins to regard as important the decisions he is allowed to take.
C. Northcote Parkinson 1909-93 English writer

Back in the East you can't do much without the right papers, but *with* the right papers you can do *anything*. They *believe* in papers. Papers are power.
Tom Stoppard 1937- British dramatist

Business ✳

There is nothing more requisite in business than dispatch.
Joseph Addison 1672-1719 English writer

A Company for carrying on an undertaking of Great Advantage, but no one to know what it is.
Anonymous *The South Sea Company prospectus*

A merchant shall hardly keep himself from doing wrong.
Bible (Apocrypha)

They [corporations] cannot commit treason, nor be outlawed, nor excommunicate, for they have no souls.
Edward Coke 1552-1634 English jurist

Business

Here's the rule for bargains: 'Do other men, for they would do you.' That's the true business precept.
Charles Dickens 1812–70 English novelist

Remember that time is money.
Benjamin Franklin 1706–90 American statesman and scientist

Necessity never made a good bargain.
Benjamin Franklin 1706–90 American statesman and scientist

If business always made the right decisions, business wouldn't be business.
J. Paul Getty 1892–1976 American industrialist

Only the paranoid survive.
Andrew Grove 1936– American businessman

Accountants are the witch-doctors of the modern world and willing to turn their hands to any kind of magic.
Lord Justice Harman 1894–1970 British judge

The best of all monopoly profits is a quiet life.
J. R. Hicks 1904–89 British economist

A salesman is got to dream, boy. It comes with the territory.
Arthur Miller 1915–2005 American dramatist

After a certain point money is meaningless. It ceases to be the goal. The game is what counts.
Aristotle Onassis 1906–75 Greek businessman

The customer is never wrong.
César Ritz 1850–1918 Swiss hotel proprietor

I think that business practices would improve immeasurably if they were guided by 'feminine' principles—qualities like love and care and intuition.
Anita Roddick 1942–2007 English businesswoman

People of the same trade seldom meet together, even for merriment and diversion, but the conversation ends in a conspiracy against the public, or in some contrivance to raise prices.
  Adam Smith 1723–90 Scottish economist

Deals are my art form. Other people paint beautifully on canvas or write wonderful poetry. I like making deals, preferably big deals. That's how I get my kicks.
  Donald Trump 1946– American businessman

The public be damned! I'm working for my stockholders.
  William H. Vanderbilt 1821–85 American railway magnate

[Commercialism is] doing well that which should not be done at all.
  Gore Vidal 1925– American writer

There is only one boss. The customer. And he can fire everybody in the company from the chairman on down, simply by spending his money somewhere else.
  Sam Walton 1919–92 American businessman

You cannot be a success in any business without believing that it is the greatest business in the world…You have to put your heart in the business and the business in your heart.
  Thomas Watson Snr. 1874–1956 American businessman

Canada ✳

North of the 49th parallel we value equality; south of it, they treasure freedom.
  Michael Adams Canadian writer

Dusty, cobweb-covered, maimed, and set at naught,
Beauty crieth in an attic, and no man regardeth.
O God! O Montreal!
  Samuel Butler 1835–1902 English novelist

Canada

I am rather inclined to believe that this is the land God gave to Cain.
> **Jacques Cartier** 1491–1557 French explorer

Some say that no one ever leaves Montreal, for that city, like Canada itself, is designed to preserve the past, a past that happened somewhere else.
> **Leonard Cohen** 1934– Canadian singer

I see Canada as a country torn between a very northern, rather extraordinary, mystical spirit which it fears and its desire to present itself to the world as a Scotch banker.
> **Robertson Davies** 1913–95 Canadian novelist

Vive Le Québec Libre.
Long Live Free Quebec.
> **Charles de Gaulle** 1890–1970 French statesman

Canada is ten independent personalities, united only by a common suspicion of Ottawa.
> **Allan Fotheringham** 1932– Canadian journalist

If some countries have too much history, we have too much geography.
> **William Lyon Mackenzie King** 1874–1950 Canadian statesman

That's ours—lock, stock and iceberg.
> **Brian Mulroney** 1939– Canadian statesman, *asked about Canadian sovereignty over the Arctic*

Mon pays ce n'est pas un pays, c'est l'hiver.
My country is not a country, it is winter.
> **Gilles Vigneault** 1928– Canadian singer

These two nations have been at war over a few acres of snow near Canada, and…they are spending on this fine struggle more than Canada itself is worth.
> **Voltaire** 1694–1778 French writer

O Canada! Our home and native land!
True patriot love in all thy sons command.
With glowing hearts we see thee rise,
The True North strong and free!
  Robert Stanley Weir 1856–1926 Canadian lawyer

Careers ⇨Work

I will undoubtedly have to seek what is happily known as
gainful employment, which I am glad to say does not
describe holding public office.
  Dean Acheson 1893–1971 American politician

For promotion cometh neither from the east, nor from
the west: nor yet from the south.
  Bible

McJob: A low-pay, low-prestige, low-dignity, low benefit,
no-future job in the service sector.
  Douglas Coupland 1961– Canadian writer

To do nothing and get something, formed a boy's ideal of
a manly career.
  Benjamin Disraeli 1804–81 British statesman

By working faithfully eight hours a day, you may
eventually get to be a boss and work twelve hours a day.
  Robert Frost 1874–1963 American poet

It is wonderful, when a calculation is made, how little the
mind is actually employed in the discharge of any
profession.
  Samuel Johnson 1709–84 English lexicographer

I didn't get where I am today without….
  David Nobbs 1935– British novelist, *catchphrase used by
  Reginald Perrin's manager C. J.*

Careers

I have that normal male thing of valuing myself
according to the job I do. When I can't tell someone in
one word what I am, then something is missing. I don't
represent anything any more.
Michael Portillo 1953– British politician

Thou art not for the fashion of these times,
Where none will sweat but for promotion.
William Shakespeare 1564–1616 English dramatist

It is difficult to get a man to understand something when
his salary depends on his not understanding it.
Upton Sinclair 1878–1968 American novelist

The test of a vocation is the love of the drudgery it
involves.
Logan Pearsall Smith 1865–1946 American writer

Cars

Take it easy driving—the life you save may be mine.
James Dean 1931–55 American actor

[There are] only two classes of pedestrians in these days
of reckless motor traffic—the quick, and the dead.
Lord Dewar 1864–1930 British industrialist

The poetry of motion! The *real* way to travel! The *only*
way to travel! Here today—in next week tomorrow!
Kenneth Grahame 1859–1932 Scottish-born writer

O bliss! O poop-poop! O my!
Kenneth Grahame 1859–1932 Scottish-born writer

Cyclists see motorists as tyrannical and uncaring.
Motorists believe cyclists are afflicted by a perversion.
Boris Johnson 1964– British politician

What good is speed if the brain has oozed out on the way?

Karl Kraus 1874–1936 Austrian satirist

The car has become an article of dress without which we feel uncertain, unclad and incomplete in the urban compound.

Marshall McLuhan 1911–80 Canadian communications scholar

Beneath this slab
John Brown is stowed.
He watched the ads,
And not the road.

Ogden Nash 1902–71 American humorist

No other man-made device since the shields and lances of ancient knights fulfils a man's ego like an automobile.

Lord Rootes 1894–1964 British automobile manufacturer

Cats

Macavity, Macavity, there's no one like Macavity,
There never was a Cat of such deceitfulness and suavity.
He always has an alibi, and one or two to spare:
At whatever time the deed took place—MACAVITY WASN'T THERE!

T. S. Eliot 1888–1965 American-born British poet

He walked by himself, and all places were alike to him.

Rudyard Kipling 1865–1936 English writer

Cats seem to go on the principle that it never does any harm to ask for what you want.

Joseph Wood Krutch 1893–1970 American critic and naturalist

If a fish is the movement of water embodied, given shape, then cat is a diagram and pattern of subtle air.

Doris Lessing 1919- English writer

When I play with my cat, who knows whether she isn't amusing herself with me more than I am with her?

Montaigne 1533–92 French moralist

The trouble with a kitten is
THAT
Eventually it becomes a
CAT.

Ogden Nash 1902–71 American humorist

For I will consider my Cat Jeoffry...
For he counteracts the powers of darkness by his electrical skin and glaring eyes.
For he counteracts the Devil, who is death, by brisking about the life.

Christopher Smart 1722–71 English poet

Censorship

The reading or non-reading a book—will never keep down a single petticoat.

Lord Byron 1788–1824 English poet

One does not put Voltaire in the Bastille.

Charles de Gaulle 1890–1970 French statesman, *when asked to arrest Sartre*

Is it a book you would even wish your wife or your servants to read?

Mervyn Griffith-Jones 1909–79 British lawyer, *of D. H. Lawrence's* Lady Chatterley's Lover

Wherever books will be burned, men also, in the end, are burned.

Heinrich Heine 1797–1856 German poet

One has to multiply thoughts to the point where there aren't enough policemen to control them.
Stanislaw Lec 1909–66 Polish writer

The power of the press is very great, but not so great as the power of suppress.
Lord Northcliffe 1865–1922 British newspaper proprietor

If these writings of the Greeks agree with the book of God, they are useless and need not be preserved; if they disagree, they are pernicious and ought to be destroyed.
Caliph Omar c.581–644, *on burning the library of Alexandria*

Don't you see that the whole aim of Newspeak is to narrow the range of thought? In the end we shall make thoughtcrime literally impossible, because there will be no words in which to express it.
George Orwell 1903–50 English novelist

It is obvious that 'obscenity' is not a term capable of exact legal definition; in the practice of the Courts, it means 'anything that shocks the magistrate'.
Bertrand Russell 1872–1970 British philosopher

If decade after decade the truth cannot be told, each person's mind begins to roam irretrievably. One's fellow countrymen become harder to understand than Martians.
Alexander Solzhenitsyn 1918–2008 Russian novelist

The state has no place in the nation's bedrooms.
Pierre Trudeau 1919–2000 Canadian statesman

I disapprove of what you say, but I will defend to the death your right to say it.
Voltaire 1694–1778 French writer, *a later summary of his attitude towards Helvétius following the burning of the latter's De l'esprit*

✳ Certainty ⇒Doubt

My mind is not a bed to be made and re-made.
James Agate 1877–1947 British writer

If a man will begin with certainties, he shall end in
doubts; but if he will be content to begin with doubts, he
shall end in certainties.
Francis Bacon 1561–1626 English courtier

We often call a certainty a hope, to bring it luck.
Elizabeth Bibesco 1897–1945 British writer

The archbishop is usually to be found nailing his colours
to the fence.
Frank Field 1942– British politician, *of Archbishop Runcie*

What, never?
No, never!
What, *never*?
Hardly ever!
W. S. Gilbert 1836–1911 English writer

I'll give you a definite maybe.
Sam Goldwyn 1882–1974 American film producer

It's one thing to be certain, but you can be certain and
you can be wrong.
John Kerry 1943– American politician

I wish I was as cocksure of anything as Tom Macaulay is
of everything.
Lord Melbourne 1779–1848 English statesman

Ah, what a dusty answer gets the soul
When hot for certainties in this our life!
George Meredith 1828–1909 English writer

Minds like beds always made up,
(more stony than a shore)
unwilling or unable.
  William Carlos Williams 1883–1963 American poet

Chance ⇒Luck ✶

Cast thy bread upon the waters: for thou shalt find it
after many days.
  Bible

But for the grace of God there goes John Bradford.
  John Bradford c.1510–55 English martyr, *on seeing a group of
  criminals being led to their execution; usually quoted as 'There
  but for the grace of God go I'*

The best laid schemes o' mice an' men
Gang aft a-gley.
  Robert Burns 1759–96 Scottish poet

The chapter of knowledge is a very short, but the chapter
of accidents is a very long one.
  Lord Chesterfield 1694–1773 English writer

At this moment he was unfortunately called out by a
person on business from Porlock.
  Samuel Taylor Coleridge 1772–1834 English poet, *preliminary
  note to 'Kubla Khan', explaining why the poem remained
  unfinished*

Accidents will occur in the best-regulated families.
  Charles Dickens 1812–70 English novelist

If an army of monkeys were strumming on typewriters
they *might* write all the books in the British Museum.
  Arthur Eddington 1882–1944 British astrophysicist

I am convinced that *He* [God] does not play dice.
  Albert Einstein 1879–1955 German-born theoretical physicist

Chance

Mr Bond, they have a saying in Chicago: 'Once is happenstance. Twice is coincidence. The third time it's enemy action.'

Ian Fleming 1908–64 English writer, *Goldfinger to James Bond*

Predictability: Does the flap of a butterfly's wings in Brazil set off a tornado in Texas?

Edward N. Lorenz 1917–2008 American meteorologist

O! many a shaft, at random sent,
Finds mark the archer little meant!
And many a word, at random spoken,
May soothe or wound a heart that's broken.

Sir Walter Scott 1771–1832 Scottish novelist

There is a tide in the affairs of men,
Which, taken at the flood, leads on to fortune.

William Shakespeare 1564–1616 English dramatist

✹ Change ⇒Beginning, Ending

He that will not apply new remedies must expect new evils; for time is the greatest innovator.

Francis Bacon 1561–1626 English courtier

Can the Ethiopian change his skin, or the leopard his spots?

Bible

Variety's the very spice of life,
That gives it all its flavour.

William Cowper 1731–1800 English poet

Change is inevitable in a progressive country. Change is constant.

Benjamin Disraeli 1804–81 British statesman

He not busy being born
Is busy dying.

Bob Dylan 1941– American singer

When it is not necessary to change, it is necessary not to change.
> **Lucius Cary, Viscount Falkland** 1610–43 English politician

Most of the change we think we see in life
Is due to truths being in and out of favour.
> **Robert Frost** 1874–1963 American poet

You can't step twice into the same river.
> **Heraclitus** c.540–c.480 BC Greek philosopher

Consistency is contrary to nature, contrary to life. The only completely consistent people are the dead.
> **Aldous Huxley** 1894–1963 English novelist

Change is not made without inconvenience, even from worse to better.
> **Samuel Johnson** 1709–84 English lexicographer

Plus ça change, plus c'est la même chose.
The more things change, the more they are the same.
> **Alphonse Karr** 1808–90 French writer

If we want things to stay as they are, things will have to change.
> **Giuseppe di Lampedusa** 1896–1957 Italian writer

It is best not to swap horses when crossing streams.
> **Abraham Lincoln** 1809–65 American statesman

Change and decay in all around I see;
O Thou, who changest not, abide with me.
> **Henry Francis Lyte** 1793–1847 English hymn-writer

Tomorrow to fresh woods, and pastures new.
> **John Milton** 1608–74 English poet

And now for something completely different.
> **Monty Python's Flying Circus** 1969–74 British television programme

Change

God, give us the serenity to accept what cannot be
    changed;
Give us the courage to change what should be changed;
Give us the wisdom to distinguish one from the other.
     Reinhold Niebuhr 1892–1971 American theologian

             Forward, forward let us range,
Let the great world spin for ever down the ringing
    grooves of change.
     Alfred, Lord Tennyson 1809–92 English poet

If we do not find anything pleasant, at least we shall find
something new.
     Voltaire 1694–1778 French writer

All changed, changed utterly:
A terrible beauty is born.
     W. B. Yeats 1865–1939 Irish poet

✳ Character

It is not in the still calm of life, or the repose of a pacific
station, that great characters are formed…Great
necessities call out great virtues.
     Abigail Adams 1744–1818 American letter writer

A thick skin is a gift from God.
     Konrad Adenauer 1876–1967 German statesman

You will never make a crab walk straight.
     Aristophanes c.450–c.385 BC Greek comic dramatist

In one and the same fire, clay grows hard and wax melts.
     Francis Bacon 1561–1626 English courtier

It is the nature, and the advantage, of strong people that
they can bring out the crucial questions and form a clear
opinion about them. The weak always have to decide

between alternatives that are not their own.
Dietrich Bonhoeffer 1906–45 German theologian

If you have bright plumage, people will take pot shots at you.
Alan Clark 1928–99 British politician

Claudia's the sort of person who goes through life holding on to the sides.
Alice Thomas Ellis 1932–2005 English novelist

Talent develops in quiet places, character in the full current of human life.
Johann Wolfgang von Goethe 1749–1832 German writer

Those who stand for nothing fall for anything.
Alex Hamilton 1936–

A man's character is his fate.
Heraclitus c.540–c.480 BC Greek philosopher

A propensity to hope and joy is real riches: one to fear and sorrow, real poverty.
David Hume 1711–76 Scottish philosopher

If you can fill the unforgiving minute
With sixty seconds' worth of distance run,
Yours is the Earth and everything that's in it,
And—which is more—you'll be a Man, my son!
Rudyard Kipling 1865–1936 English writer

I see the better things, and approve; I follow the worse.
Ovid 43 BC–c.AD 17 Roman poet

He's so wet you could shoot snipe off him.
Anthony Powell 1905–2000 English novelist

You can tell a lot about a fellow's character by his way of eating jellybeans.
Ronald Reagan 1911–2004 American statesman

Character

> My nature is subdued
> To what it works in, like the dyer's hand.
> **William Shakespeare** 1564–1616 English dramatist

> If you can't stand the heat, get out of the kitchen.
> **Harry Vaughan** 1893–1981 American military aide, *associated with Harry S. Truman*

> We are what we pretend to be.
> **Kurt Vonnegut** 1922–2007 American novelist

✳ Charity ⇒Gifts

> God loveth a cheerful giver.
> **Bible**

> CHAIRMAN: What is service?
> CANDIDATE: The rent we pay for our room on earth.
> **Tubby Clayton** 1885–1972 British clergyman, *admission ceremony of Toc H*

> The best form of charity I know is the art of meeting a payroll.
> **J. Paul Getty** 1892–1976 American industrialist

> You cannot feed the hungry on statistics.
> **David Lloyd George** 1863–1945 British statesman

> People often feed the hungry so that nothing may disturb their own enjoyment of a good meal.
> **W. Somerset Maugham** 1874–1965 English novelist

> Do good by stealth, and blush to find it fame.
> **Alexander Pope** 1688–1744 English poet

> He gives the poor man twice as much good who gives quickly.
> **Publilius Syrus** 1st century BC Roman writer

'Tis not enough to help the feeble up,
But to support him after.
William Shakespeare 1564–1616 English dramatist

Thy necessity is yet greater than mine.
Philip Sidney 1554–86 English writer, *on giving his water-bottle to a dying soldier on the battle-field of Zutphen; commonly quoted as 'thy need is greater than mine'*

Charity begins today. Today somebody is suffering, today somebody is in the street, today somebody is hungry.
Mother Teresa 1910–97 Roman Catholic nun

No one would remember the Good Samaritan if he'd only had good intentions. He had money as well.
Margaret Thatcher 1925– British stateswoman

Friends, I have lost a day.
Titus AD 39–81 Roman emperor, *on reflecting that he had done nothing to help anybody all day*

Behold, I do not give lectures or a little charity,
When I give I give myself.
Walt Whitman 1819–92 American poet

Charm ✳

Charm…it's a sort of bloom on a woman. If you have it, you don't need to have anything else; and if you don't have it, it doesn't much matter what else you have.
J. M. Barrie 1860–1937 Scottish writer

You know what charm is: a way of getting the answer yes without having asked any clear question.
Albert Camus 1913–60 French writer

All charming people have something to conceal, usually their total dependence on the appreciation of others.
Cyril Connolly 1903–74 English writer

Charm

Oozing charm from every pore,
He oiled his way around the floor.
Alan Jay Lerner 1918–86 American songwriter

✳ Children ⇒ Babies, The Family, Youth

Children sweeten labours, but they make misfortunes
more bitter.
Francis Bacon 1561–1626 English courtier

Quality time? There's always another load of washing.
Julian Barnes 1946– English novelist

Suffer the little children to come unto me, and forbid
them not: for of such is the kingdom of God.
Bible

When I was a child, I spake as a child, I understood as a
child, I thought as a child: but when I became a man, I
put away childish things.
Bible

There is no such thing as other people's children.
Hillary Rodham Clinton 1947– American lawyer

Our greatest natural resource is the minds of our
children.
Walt Disney 1901–66 American film producer

Alas, regardless of their doom,
The little victims play!
No sense have they of ills to come,
Nor care beyond to-day.
Thomas Gray 1716–71 English poet

Allow them [children] to be happy their own way, for
what better way will they ever find?
Samuel Johnson 1709–84 English lexicographer

If there is anything that we wish to change in the child, we should first examine it and see whether it is not something that could better be changed in ourselves.
Carl Gustav Jung 1875–1961 Swiss psychologist

A child is owed the greatest respect; if you ever have something disgraceful in mind, don't ignore your son's tender years.
Juvenal c.AD 60–c.130 Roman satirist

Literature is mostly about having sex and not much about having children. Life is the other way round.
David Lodge 1935– English novelist

It should be noted that children at play are not playing about; their games should be seen as their most serious-minded activity.
Montaigne 1533–92 French moralist

But all children matures,
Maybe even yours.
Ogden Nash 1902–71 American humorist

The affection you get back from children is sixpence given as change for a sovereign.
Edith Nesbit 1858–1924 English writer

Behold the child, by Nature's kindly law
Pleased with a rattle, tickled with a straw.
Alexander Pope 1688–1744 English poet

A child is not a vase to be filled, but a fire to be lit.
François Rabelais c.1494–c.1553 French humanist

Any man who hates dogs and babies can't be all bad.
Leo Rosten 1908–97 American writer, *of W. C. Fields, and often attributed to him*

Grown-ups never understand anything for themselves, and it is tiresome for children to be always and forever explaining things to them.
Antoine de Saint-Exupéry 1900–44 French novelist

Children

You will find as the children grow up that as a rule children are a bitter disappointment—their greatest object being to do precisely what their parents do not wish and have anxiously tried to prevent.
Queen Victoria 1819–1901 British monarch

I have four sons and three stepsons. I have learnt what it is like to step on Lego with bare feet.
Fay Weldon 1931– British novelist

The Child is father of the Man.
William Wordsworth 1770–1850 English poet

☀ Choice

White shall not neutralize the black, nor good
Compensate bad in man, absolve him so:
Life's business being just the terrible choice.
Robert Browning 1812–89 English poet

The die is cast.
Julius Caesar 100–44 BC Roman statesman, *at the crossing of the Rubicon*

Any customer can have a car painted any colour that he wants so long as it is black.
Henry Ford 1863–1947 American car manufacturer, *of the Model T Ford*

Two roads diverged in a wood, and I—
I took the one less travelled by,
And that has made all the difference.
Robert Frost 1874–1963 American poet

How happy could I be with either,
Were t'other dear charmer away!
John Gay 1685–1732 English writer

Which do you want? A whipping and no turnips or turnips and no whipping?
Toni Morrison 1931- American novelist

You pays your money and you takes your choice.
Punch 1841–1992 English humorous periodical

I'll make him an offer he can't refuse.
Mario Puzo 1920–99 American novelist

To be, or not to be: that is the question.
William Shakespeare 1564–1616 English dramatist

Take care to get what you like or you will be forced to like what you get.
George Bernard Shaw 1856–1950 Irish dramatist

There is no real alternative.
Margaret Thatcher 1925- British stateswoman

Between two evils, I always pick the one I never tried before.
Mae West 1892–1980 American film actress

Christmas ✳

Christmas won't be Christmas without any presents.
Louisa May Alcott 1832–88 American novelist

I'm dreaming of a white Christmas,
Just like the ones I used to know.
Irving Berlin 1888–1989 American songwriter

And girls in slacks remember Dad,
And oafish louts remember Mum,
And sleepless children's hearts are glad,

Christmas

And Christmas-morning bells say 'Come!'
John Betjeman 1906–84 English poet

She brought forth her firstborn son, and wrapped him in swaddling clothes, and laid him in a manger; because there was no room for them in the inn.
Bible

Yes, Virginia, there is a Santa Claus.
Francis Pharcellus Church 1839–1906 American editor, *newspaper editorial replying to a letter from eight-year-old Virginia O'Hanlon*

Christmas is the Disneyfication of Christianity.
Don Cupitt 1934– British theologian

'Bah,' said Scrooge. 'Humbug!'
Charles Dickens 1812–70 English novelist, *responding to the greeting 'Merry Christmas'*

A lovely thing about Christmas is that it's compulsory, like a thunderstorm, and we all go through it together.
Garrison Keillor 1942– American writer

'Twas the night before Christmas, when all through the house
Not a creature was stirring, not even a mouse.
Clement C. Moore 1779–1863 American writer

Still xmas is a good time with all those presents and good food and i hope it will never die out or at any rate not until i am grown up and hav to pay for it all.
Geoffrey Willans 1911–58 and **Ronald Searle** 1920– English writers

Be nice to yu turkeys dis Christmas
Cos' turkeys just wanna hav fun.
Benjamin Zephaniah 1958– British poet

The Church →Religion

The nearer the Church the further from God.
Bishop Lancelot Andrewes 1555–1626 English preacher

He cannot have God for his father who has not the church for his mother.
St Cyprian C.AD 200–258 Roman writer and martyr

Our cathedrals are like abandoned computers now, but they used to be prayer factories once.
Lawrence Durrell 1912–90 English writer

I want to throw open the windows of the Church so that we can see out and the people can see in.
Pope John XXIII 1881–1963 Italian cleric

We are an Easter people and Alleluia is our song.
Pope John Paul II 1920–2005 Polish cleric

'The Church is an anvil which has worn out many hammers', and the story of the first collision is, in essentials, the story of all.
Alexander Maclaren 1826–1910 Scottish divine

The Church [of England] should go forward along the path of progress and be no longer satisfied only to represent the Conservative Party at prayer.
Maude Royden 1876–1956 English writer

The Church can no longer contain the fizzy, explosive stuff that the true wine of the bottle ought to be.
Donald Soper 1903–98 British Methodist minister

I never saw, heard, nor read, that the clergy were beloved in any nation where Christianity was the religion of the country. Nothing can render them popular, but some degree of persecution.
Jonathan Swift 1667–1745 Irish poet and satirist

The Church

As often as we are mown down by you, the more we grow in numbers; the blood of Christians is the seed.

> **Tertullian** c.AD 160–c.225 Roman theologian, *traditionally 'The blood of the martyrs is the seed of the Church'*

I look upon all the world as my parish.

> **John Wesley** 1703–91 English preacher

The Catholic Church has never really come to terms with women. What I object to is being treated either as Madonnas or Mary Magdalenes.

> **Shirley Williams** 1930– British politician

✳ The Cinema →Acting

WILLIAM HOLDEN: You used to be in pictures. You used to be big.

GLORIA SWANSON: I am big. It's the pictures that got small.

> **Charles Brackett** 1892–1969 and **Billy Wilder** 1906–2002 American screenwriters, *in the film* Sunset Boulevard

There are no rules in film-making. Only sins. And the cardinal sin is dullness.

> **Frank Capra** 1897–1991 American film director

All I need to make a comedy is a park, a policeman and a pretty girl.

> **Charlie Chaplin** 1889–1977 English film actor

GEORGES FRANJU: Movies should have a beginning, a middle and an end.

GODARD: Certainly, but not necessarily in that order.

> **Jean-Luc Godard** 1930– French film director

Photography is truth. The cinema is truth 24 times per second.

> **Jean-Luc Godard** 1930– French film director

Nobody knows anything.
> **William Goldman** 1931– American writer, *on the film industry*

Pictures are for entertainment, messages should be delivered by Western Union.
> **Sam Goldwyn** 1882–1974 American film producer

Why should people go out and pay to see bad movies when they can stay at home and see bad television for nothing?
> **Sam Goldwyn** 1882–1974 American film producer

If I made Cinderella, the audience would immediately be looking for a body in the coach.
> **Alfred Hitchcock** 1899–1980 British-born film director

If you gave him a good script, actors and technicians, Mickey Mouse could direct a movie.
> **Nicholas Hytner** 1956– English film director

We've got more stars than there are in the heavens, all of them except for that damned Mouse over at Disney.
> **Louis B. Mayer** 1885–1957 American film executive

The trouble, Mr Goldwyn, is that you are only interested in art and I am only interested in money.
> **George Bernard Shaw** 1856–1950 Irish dramatist

This is the biggest electric train a boy ever had!
> **Orson Welles** 1915–85 American film director, *of the RKO studios*

It is like writing history with lightning. And my only regret is that it is all so terribly true.
> **Woodrow Wilson** 1856–1924 American statesman, *on seeing D. W. Griffith's film* The Birth of a Nation

✳ Civilization

The three great elements of modern civilization,
Gunpowder, Printing, and the Protestant Religion.
Thomas Carlyle 1795–1881 Scottish historian

Civilization and profits go hand in hand.
Calvin Coolidge 1872–1933 American statesman

JOURNALIST: Mr Gandhi, what do you think of modern
civilization?
GANDHI: That would be a good idea.
Mahatma Gandhi 1869–1948 Indian statesman

If a nation expects to be ignorant and free, in a state of
civilization, it expects what never was and never will be.
Thomas Jefferson 1743–1826 American statesman

Whenever I hear the word culture…I release the safety-
catch of my Browning!
Hanns Johst 1890–1978 German dramatist, *often attributed to
Hermann Goering, and quoted as 'Whenever I hear the word
culture, I reach for my pistol!'*

If civilization had been left in female hands, we would
still be living in grass huts.
Camille Paglia 1947– American writer

You can't say civilization don't advance, however, for in
every war they kill you in a new way.
Will Rogers 1879–1935 American actor

Civilization has made the peasantry its pack animal. The
bourgeoisie in the long run only changed the form of the
pack.
Leon Trotsky 1879–1940 Russian revolutionary

In Italy for thirty years under the Borgias they had
warfare, terror, murder, bloodshed—they produced
Michelangelo, Leonardo da Vinci and the Renaissance. In

Switzerland they had brotherly love, five hundred years of
democracy and peace and what did that produce…? The
cuckoo clock.
  Orson Welles 1915–85 American film director

Class ✳

The rich man in his castle,
The poor man at his gate,
God made them, high or lowly,
And ordered their estate.
  Cecil Frances Alexander 1818–95 Irish poet

Il faut épater le bourgeois.
One must astonish the bourgeois.
  Charles Baudelaire 1821–67 French poet

Like many of the Upper Class
He liked the Sound of Broken Glass.
  Hilaire Belloc 1870–1953 British writer

Just because I have made a point of never losing my
accent it doesn't mean I am an eel-and-pie yob.
  Michael Caine 1933– English film actor

The Stately Homes of England,
How beautiful they stand,
To prove the upper classes
Have still the upper hand.
  Noël Coward 1899–1973 English dramatist

O let us love our occupations,
Bless the squire and his relations,
Live upon our daily rations,
And always know our proper stations.
  Charles Dickens 1812–70 English novelist

Class

The proletarians have nothing to lose but their chains.
They have a world to win. WORKING MEN OF ALL
COUNTRIES, UNITE!

Karl Marx 1818–83 and **Friedrich Engels** 1820–95 German
philosopher and German socialist, *commonly rendered 'Workers
of the world, unite!'*

First you take their faces from 'em by calling 'em the
masses and then you accuse 'em of not having any faces.

J. B. Priestley 1894–1984 English writer

When Adam dalfe and Eve spane...
Where was than the pride of man?

Richard Rolle de Hampole c.1290–1349 English mystic, *taken
in the form 'When Adam delved and Eve span, who was then the
gentleman?' by John Ball as the text of his revolutionary sermon
on the outbreak of the Peasants' Revolt, 1381*

The State is an instrument in the hands of the ruling
class, used to break the resistance of the adversaries of
that class.

Joseph Stalin 1879–1953 Soviet dictator

The French want no-one to be their *superior*. The English
want *inferiors*. The Frenchman constantly raises his eyes
above him with anxiety. The Englishman lowers his
beneath him with satisfaction.

Alexis de Tocqueville 1805–59 French historian

✳ Clothes

It is totally impossible to be well dressed in cheap shoes.

Hardy Amies 1909–2003 English couturier

From the cradle to the grave, underwear first, last and all
the time.

Bertolt Brecht 1898–1956 German dramatist

No perfumes, but very fine linen, plenty of it, and country washing.
Beau Brummell 1778–1840 English dandy

Look for the woman in the dress. If there is no woman, there is no dress.
Coco Chanel 1883–1971 French couturière

The sense of being well-dressed gives a feeling of inward tranquillity which religion is powerless to bestow.
Miss C. F. Forbes 1817–1911 English writer

A sweet disorder in the dress
Kindles in clothes a wantonness.
Robert Herrick 1591–1674 English poet

You should never have your best trousers on when you go out to fight for freedom and truth.
Henrik Ibsen 1828–1906 Norwegian dramatist

A tie is a noose, and inverted though it is, it will hang a man nonetheless if he's not careful.
Yann Martel 1963– Canadian writer

I have often said that I wish I had invented blue jeans.
Yves Saint Laurent 1936–2008 French couturier

His socks compelled one's attention without losing one's respect.
Saki 1870–1916 Scottish writer

The apparel oft proclaims the man.
William Shakespeare 1564–1616 English dramatist

Beware of all enterprises that require new clothes.
Henry David Thoreau 1817–62 American writer

Life is an adventure, so I make clothes to have adventures in.
Vivienne Westwood 1941– British fashion designer

☀ Computers

To err is human but to really foul things up requires a computer.
Anonymous

A modern computer hovers between the obsolescent and the nonexistent.
Sydney Brenner 1927- British scientist

The Internet is an elite organisation; most of the population of the world has never even made a phone call.
Noam Chomsky 1928- American linguist

The email of the species is deadlier than the mail.
Stephen Fry 1957- English comedian

I think computer viruses should count as life. Maybe it says something about human nature, that the only form of life we have created so far is purely destructive.
Stephen Hawking 1942- English theoretical physicist

The symbol of the atomic age, which tended to centralise power, was a nucleus with electrons held in tight orbit; the symbol of the digital age is the Web, with countless centres of power all equally networked.
Walter Isaacson 1952- American writer

The PC is the LSD of the '90s.
Timothy Leary 1920-96 American psychologist

Computer says No.
Matt Lucas 1974- and **David Walliams** 1971- British comedians

You have zero privacy anyway. Get over it.
Scott McNealy 1954- American businessman, *on the introduction of Jini networking technology*

On the Internet, nobody knows you're a dog.
Peter Steiner 1940– American cartoonist, *cartoon caption*

We used to have lots of questions to which there were no answers. Now with the computer there are lots of answers to which we haven't thought up the questions.
Peter Ustinov 1921–2004 British actor

We've all heard that a million monkeys banging on a million typewriters will eventually reproduce the entire works of Shakespeare. Now, thanks to the Internet, we know this is not true.
Robert Wilensky 1951– American academic

Conscience ✳

We have erred, and strayed from thy ways like lost sheep. We have followed too much the devices and desires of our own hearts.
Book of Common Prayer 1662

Conscience is thoroughly well-bred and soon leaves off talking to those who do not wish to hear it.
Samuel Butler 1835–1902 English novelist

O dignitosa coscienza e netta,
Come t'è picciol fallo amaro morso!
O pure and noble conscience, how bitter a sting to thee is a little fault!
Dante Alighieri 1265–1321 Italian poet

In many walks of life, a conscience is a more expensive encumbrance than a wife or a carriage.
Thomas De Quincey 1785–1859 English essayist

A good conscience is a continual Christmas.
Benjamin Franklin 1706–90 American statesman and scientist

Conscience

I cannot and will not cut my conscience to fit this year's fashions.
Lillian Hellman 1905–84 American dramatist

Conscience: the inner voice which warns us that someone may be looking.
H. L. Mencken 1880–1956 American journalist

Thus conscience doth make cowards of us all.
William Shakespeare 1564–1616 English dramatist

Corporations have neither bodies to be punished, nor souls to be condemned, they therefore do as they like.
Edward, 1st Baron Thurlow 1731–1806 English jurist, *usually quoted as 'Did you ever expect a corporation to have a conscience, when it has no soul to be damned, and no body to be kicked?'*

✳ Conversation ⇨Speechmaking

On every formal visit a child ought to be of the party, by way of provision for discourse.
Jane Austen 1775–1817 English novelist

Although there exist many thousand subjects for elegant conversation, there are persons who cannot meet a cripple without talking about feet.
Ernest Bramah 1868–1942 English writer

'The time has come,' the Walrus said,
'To talk of many things:
Of shoes—and ships—and sealing wax—
Of cabbages—and kings.'
Lewis Carroll 1832–98 English writer

Religion is by no means a proper subject of conversation in a mixed company.
Lord Chesterfield 1694–1773 English writer

Too much agreement kills a chat.
Eldridge Cleaver 1935-98 American political activist

Someone to tell it to is one of the fundamental needs of
human beings.
Miles Franklin 1879-1954 Australian writer

And, when you stick on conversation's burrs,
Don't strew your pathway with those dreadful *urs*.
Oliver Wendell Holmes 1809-94 American physician

A...sharp tongue is the only edged tool that grows keener
with constant use.
Washington Irving 1783-1859 American writer

Questioning is not the mode of conversation among
gentlemen. It is assuming a superiority.
Samuel Johnson 1709-84 English lexicographer

Must I always be a mere listener?
Juvenal c.AD 60-c.130 Roman satirist

The opposite of talking isn't listening. The opposite of
talking is waiting.
Fran Lebowitz 1946- American writer

Speech is civilisation itself. The word, even the most
contradictory word, preserves contact—it is silence which
isolates.
Thomas Mann 1875-1955 German novelist

With thee conversing I forget all time.
John Milton 1608-74 English poet

The feast of reason and the flow of soul.
Alexander Pope 1688-1744 English poet

I am not bound to please thee with my answer.
William Shakespeare 1564-1616 English dramatist

�֍ Cookery ⇒Eating, Food

Anyone who tells a lie has not a pure heart, and cannot make a good soup.
> **Ludwig van Beethoven** 1770–1827 German composer

Be content to remember that those who can make omelettes properly can do nothing else.
> **Hilaire Belloc** 1870–1953 British writer

Cooking is the most ancient of the arts, for Adam was born hungry.
> **Anthelme Brillat-Savarin** 1755–1826 French gourmet

Good food is always a trouble and its preparation should be regarded as a labour of love.
> **Elizabeth David** 1913–92 British cook

Heaven sends us good meat, but the Devil sends cooks.
> **David Garrick** 1717–79 English actor-manager

Kissing don't last: cookery do!
> **George Meredith** 1828–1909 English writer

I never see any home cooking. All I get is fancy stuff.
> **Philip, Duke of Edinburgh** 1921– Greek-born husband of Elizabeth II

The cook was a good cook, as cooks go; and as cooks go, she went.
> **Saki** 1870–1916 Scottish writer

✖ Cooperation

If a house be divided against itself, that house cannot stand.
> **Bible**

When bad men combine, the good must associate; else they will fall, one by one, an unpitied sacrifice in a contemptible struggle.

Edmund Burke 1729–97 Irish-born politician

All for one, one for all.

Alexandre Dumas 1802–70 French novelist

We must indeed all hang together, or, most assuredly, we shall all hang separately.

Benjamin Franklin 1706–90 American statesman and scientist

If someone claps his hand a sound arises. Listen to the sound of the single hand!

Hakuin 1686–1769 Japanese monk

If we cannot end now our differences, at least we can help make the world safe for diversity.

John F. Kennedy 1917–63 American statesman

We must learn to live together as brothers or perish together as fools.

Martin Luther King 1929–68 American civil rights leader

When Hitler attacked the Jews I was not a Jew, therefore, I was not concerned. And when Hitler attacked the Catholics, I was not a Catholic, and therefore, I was not concerned. And when Hitler attacked the unions and the industrialists, I was not a member of the unions and I was not concerned. Then, Hitler attacked me and the Protestant church—and there was nobody left to be concerned.

Martin Niemöller 1892–1984 German theologian

Government and cooperation are in all things the laws of life; anarchy and competition the laws of death.

John Ruskin 1819–1900 English critic

✳ The Country →Environment

'Tis distance lends enchantment to the view,
And robes the mountain in its azure hue.
Thomas Campbell 1777–1844 Scottish poet

God made the country, and man made the town.
William Cowper 1731–1800 English poet

It is my belief, Watson, founded upon my experience, that
the lowest and vilest alleys in London do not present a
more dreadful record of sin than does the smiling and
beautiful countryside.
Arthur Conan Doyle 1859–1930 Scottish-born writer

Green belts should be the start of the countryside, not a
ditch between Subtopias.
Hugh Gaitskell 1906–63 British politician

Our salvation can only come through the farmer. Neither
the lawyers, nor the doctors, nor the rich landlords are
going to secure it.
Mahatma Gandhi 1869–1948 Indian statesman

Agriculture is the foundation of manufactures; since the
productions of nature are the materials of art.
Edward Gibbon 1737–94 English historian

There is nothing good to be had in the country, or if
there is, they will not let you have it.
William Hazlitt 1778–1830 English essayist

The Farmer will never be happy again;
He carries his heart in his boots;
For either the rain is destroying his grain
Or the drought is destroying his roots.
A. P. Herbert 1890–1971 English writer

Oh, give me land, lots of land under starry skies above,
Don't fence me in.
Cole Porter 1891–1964 American songwriter

I have no relish for the country; it is a kind of healthy
grave.
Sydney Smith 1771–1845 English essayist

Anybody can be good in the country.
Oscar Wilde 1854–1900 Irish dramatist

Courage ✳

No coward soul is mine,
No trembler in the world's storm-troubled sphere:
I see Heaven's glories shine,
And faith shines equal, arming me from fear.
Emily Brontë 1818–48 English writer

Courage is rightly esteemed the first of human qualities
because as has been said, it is the quality which
guarantees all others.
Winston Churchill 1874–1965 British statesman

Boldness, and again boldness, and always boldness!
Georges Jacques Danton 1759–94 French revolutionary

Courage is the price that Life exacts for granting peace,
The soul that knows it not, knows no release
From little things.
Amelia Earhart 1898–1937 American aviator

Grace under pressure.
Ernest Hemingway 1899–1961 American novelist, *when asked
what he meant by 'guts'*

Tender-handed stroke a nettle,
And it stings you for your pains;
Grasp it like a man of mettle,

Courage

And it soft as silk remains.
Aaron Hill 1685–1750 English writer

Courage is not simply *one* of the virtues but the form of every virtue at the testing point.
C. S. Lewis 1898–1963 English literary scholar

As to moral courage, I have very rarely met with two o'clock in the morning courage: I mean instantaneous courage.
Napoleon I 1769–1821 French emperor

All men would be cowards if they durst.
John Wilmot, Earl of Rochester 1647–80 English poet

Cowards die many times before their deaths;
The valiant never taste of death but once.
William Shakespeare 1564–1616 English dramatist

Fortune assists the bold.
Virgil 70–19 BC Roman poet, *often quoted as 'Fortune favours the brave'*

✳ Creativity

The more you reason, the less you create.
Raymond Chandler 1888–1959 American writer

Think before you speak is criticism's motto; speak before you think creation's.
E. M. Forster 1879–1970 English novelist

That which is creative must create itself.
John Keats 1795–1821 English poet

Poems are made by fools like me,
But only God can make a tree.
Joyce Kilmer 1886–1918 American poet

Nothing can be created out of nothing.
Lucretius c.94–55 BC Roman poet

Why does my Muse only speak when she is unhappy?
She does not, I only listen when I am unhappy
When I am happy I live and despise writing
For my Muse this cannot but be dispiriting.
  Stevie Smith 1902–71 English poet

The worst crime is to leave a man's hands empty.
Men are born makers, with that primal simplicity
In every maker since Adam.
  Derek Walcott 1930– West Indian writer

Urge and urge and urge,
Always the procreant urge of the world.
  Walt Whitman 1819–92 American poet

Cricket ✳

Bowl fast, bowl faster. When you play Test cricket you
don't give Englishmen an inch. Play it tough, all the way.
Grind them into the dust.
  Don Bradman 1908–2001 Australian cricketer

Never read print, it spoils one's eye for the ball.
  W. G. Grace 1848–1915 English cricketer, *habitual advice to his
  players*

It's more than a game. It's an institution.
  Thomas Hughes 1822–96 English lawyer and writer

Cricket—a game which the English, not being a spiritual
people, have invented in order to give themselves some
conception of eternity.
  Lord Mancroft 1914–87 British politician

Cricket civilizes people and creates good gentlemen. I
want everyone to play cricket in Zimbabwe; I want ours
to be a nation of gentlemen.
  Robert Mugabe 1924– African stateman

Cricket

There's a breathless hush in the Close to-night—
Ten to make and the match to win—
A bumping pitch and a blinding light,
An hour to play and the last man in.
Henry Newbolt 1862–1938 English writer

Personally, I have always looked on cricket as organized loafing.
William Temple 1881–1944 English theologian

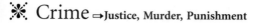 Crime ⇒Justice, Murder, Punishment

Labour is the party of law and order in Britain today. Tough on crime and tough on the causes of crime.
Tony Blair 1953– British statesman

Once in the racket you're always in it.
Al Capone 1899–1947 American gangster

Crime isn't a disease, it's a symptom. Cops are like a doctor that gives you aspirin for a brain tumour.
Raymond Chandler 1888–1959 American writer

Thieves respect property. They merely wish the property to become their property that they may more perfectly respect it.
G. K. Chesterton 1874–1936 English writer

Thou shalt not steal; an empty feat,
When it's so lucrative to cheat.
Arthur Hugh Clough 1819–61 English poet

Singularity is almost invariably a clue. The more featureless and commonplace a crime is, the more difficult is it to bring it home.
Arthur Conan Doyle 1859–1930 Scottish-born writer

For de little stealin' dey gits you in jail soon or late. For de big stealin' dey makes you Emperor and puts you in de Hall o' Fame when you croaks.
Eugene O'Neill 1888–1953 American dramatist

Crime doesn't pay.
Proverb

A clever theft was praiseworthy amongst the Spartans; and it is equally so amongst Christians, provided it be on a sufficiently large scale.
Herbert Spencer 1820–1903 English philosopher

Crises ✳

Don't panic.
Douglas Adams 1952–2001 English writer, *on the cover of* The Hitch Hiker's Guide to the Galaxy

Comin' in on a wing and a pray'r.
Harold Adamson 1906–80 American songwriter

Crisis? What Crisis?
Anonymous Sun *headline, summarizing James Callaghan on the winter of discontent: 'I don't think other people in the world would share the view [that] there is mounting chaos'*

We do not experience and thus we have no measure of the disasters we prevent.
J. K. Galbraith 1908–2006 American economist

Swimming for his life, a man does not see much of the country through which the river winds.
W. E. Gladstone 1809–98 British statesman

The illustrious bishop of Cambrai was of more worth than his chambermaid, and there are few of us that would hesitate to pronounce, if his palace were in flames, and the life of only one of them could be preserved,

which of the two ought to be preferred.
William Godwin 1756–1836 English philosopher

For it is your business, when the wall next door catches fire.
Horace 65-8 BC Roman poet

If you can keep your head when all about you
Are losing theirs and blaming it on you.
Rudyard Kipling 1865–1936 English writer

A trifle consoles us because a trifle upsets us.
Blaise Pascal 1623–62 French scientist and philosopher

We're eyeball to eyeball, and I think the other fellow just blinked.
Dean Rusk 1909– American politician

I myself have always deprecated…in crisis after crisis, appeals to the Dunkirk spirit as an answer to our problems.
Harold Wilson 1916–95 British statesman

I'm at my best in a messy, middle-of-the-road muddle.
Harold Wilson 1916–95 British statesman

✳ Criticism

A man must serve his time to every trade
Save censure—critics all are ready made.
Lord Byron 1788–1824 English poet

Everything must be like something, so what is this like?
E. M. Forster 1879–1970 English novelist

No theoretician, no writer on art, however interesting he or she might be, could be as interesting as Picasso. A good writer on art may give you an insight to Picasso, but, after all, Picasso was there first.
David Hockney 1937– British artist

Parodies and caricatures are the most penetrating of criticisms.
> **Aldous Huxley** 1894–1963 English novelist

I don't care anything about reasons, but I know what I like.
> **Henry James** 1843–1916 American novelist

This will never do.
> **Francis, Lord Jeffrey** 1773–1850 Scottish critic, *on Wordsworth's* The Excursion

You *may* abuse a tragedy, though you cannot write one. You may scold a carpenter who has made you a bad table, though you cannot make a table. It is not your trade to make tables.
> **Samuel Johnson** 1709–84 English lexicographer, *on literary criticism*

I cry all the way to the bank.
> **Liberace** 1919–87 American showman, *on bad reviews*

People who like this sort of thing will find this the sort of thing they like.
> **Abraham Lincoln** 1809–65 American statesman, *judgement of a book*

One should look long and carefully at oneself before one considers judging others.
> **Molière** 1622–73 French comic dramatist

I am sitting in the smallest room of my house. I have your review before me. In a moment it will be behind me.
> **Max Reger** 1873–1916 German composer, *responding to a savage review*

If you are not criticized, you may not be doing much.
> **Donald Rumsfeld** 1932– American politician

Criticism

Remember, a statue has never been set up in honour of a
critic!

Jean Sibelius 1865–1957 Finnish composer

I never read a book before reviewing it; it prejudices a
man so.

Sydney Smith 1771–1845 English essayist

As learned commentators view
In Homer more than Homer knew.

Jonathan Swift 1667–1745 Irish poet and satirist

A critic is a man who knows the way but can't drive the
car.

Kenneth Tynan 1927–80 English critic

I maintain that two and two would continue to make
four, in spite of the whine of the amateur for three, or
the cry of the critic for five.

James McNeill Whistler 1834–1903 American-born painter

✳ Cruelty

Boys throw stones at frogs for fun, but the frogs don't die
for 'fun', but in sober earnest.

Bion c.325–c.255 BC Greek philosopher

A robin red breast in a cage
Puts all Heaven in a rage.

William Blake 1757–1827 English poet

It is cruel to break people's legs, even if the statement is
made by someone in the habit of breaking their arms.

Brigid Brophy 1929–95 English novelist

Man's inhumanity to man
Makes countless thousands mourn!

Robert Burns 1759–96 Scottish poet

Cruelty, like every other vice, requires no motive outside itself—it only requires opportunity.
George Eliot 1819–80 English novelist

The healthy man does not torture others—generally it is the tortured who turn into torturers.
Carl Gustav Jung 1875–1961 Swiss psychologist

Our language lacks words to express this offence, the demolition of a man.
Primo Levi 1919–87 Italian writer, *of a year spent in Auschwitz*

Death may be inevitable but cruelty is not. If we must eat meat, then we must ensure that the animals we kill for our food live the best possible lives before they die.
Desmond Morris 1928– English anthropologist

I must be cruel only to be kind.
William Shakespeare 1564–1616 English dramatist

This was the most unkindest cut of all.
William Shakespeare 1564–1616 English dramatist

Custom ✳

One can't carry one's father's corpse about everywhere.
Guillaume Apollinaire 1880–1918 French poet, *on tradition*

Custom reconciles us to everything.
Edmund Burke 1729–97 Irish-born politician

Tradition means giving votes to the most obscure of all classes, our ancestors. It is the democracy of the dead.
G. K. Chesterton 1874–1936 English writer

I confess myself to be a great admirer of tradition. The longer you can look back, the farther you can look forward.
Winston Churchill 1874–1965 British statesman

Custom

Actions receive their tincture from the times,
And as they change are virtues made or crimes.
   Daniel Defoe 1660–1731 English novelist

Custom, then, is the great guide of human life.
   David Hume 1711–76 Scottish philosopher

The tradition of all the dead generations weighs like a
nightmare on the brain of the living.
   Karl Marx 1818–83 German philosopher

Everyone calls barbarism what is not customary to him.
   Molière 1622–73 French comic dramatist

But to my mind,—though I am native here,
And to the manner born,—it is a custom
More honoured in the breach than the observance.
   William Shakespeare 1564–1616 English dramatist

Laws are sand, customs are rock. Laws can be evaded and
punishment escaped, but an openly transgressed custom
brings sure punishment.
   Mark Twain 1835–1910 American writer

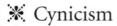 Cynicism

Kill them all; God will recognize his own.
   Arnald-Amaury d. 1225 French abbot, *when asked how the
   true Catholics could be distinguished from the heretics at the
   massacre of Béziers*

Nothing matters very much and very few things matter at
all.
   Arthur James Balfour 1848–1930 British statesman

Never glad confident morning again!
   Robert Browning 1812–89 English poet

What makes all doctrines plain and clear?
About two hundred pounds a year.
And that which was proved true before,

Prove false again? Two hundred more.
Samuel Butler 1612–80 English poet

To get practice in being refused.
Diogenes c.400–c.325 BC Greek philosopher, *reply when asked why he was begging for alms from a statue*

Pathos, piety, courage—they exist, but are identical, and so is filth. Everything exists, nothing has value.
E. M. Forster 1879–1970 English novelist

Cynicism is an unpleasant way of saying the truth.
Lillian Hellman 1905–84 American dramatist

Paris is well worth a mass.
Henri IV 1553–1610 French monarch

Cynicism is our shared common language, the Esperanto that actually caught on.
Nick Hornby 1957– British writer

A man who knows the price of everything and the value of nothing.
Oscar Wilde 1854–1900 Irish dramatist, *definition of a cynic*

Dance ✳

A dance is a measured pace, as a verse is a measured speech.
Francis Bacon 1561–1626 English courtier

There may be trouble ahead,
But while there's moonlight and music and love and
    romance,
Let's face the music and dance.
Irving Berlin 1888–1989 American songwriter

Dance

On with the dance! let joy be unconfined;
No sleep till morn, when Youth and Pleasure meet
To chase the glowing Hours with flying feet.
Lord Byron 1788–1824 English poet

This wondrous miracle did Love devise,
For dancing is love's proper exercise.
John Davies 1569–1626 English poet

The truest expression of a people is in its dances and its
music. Bodies never lie.
Agnes de Mille 1908–93 American dancer

Dance is the hidden language of the soul.
Martha Graham 1894–1991 American dancer

Come, and trip it as ye go
On the light fantastic toe.
John Milton 1608–74 English poet

[Dancing is] a perpendicular expression of a horizontal
desire.
George Bernard Shaw 1856–1950 Irish dramatist

Everyone knows that the real business of a ball is either
to look out for a wife, to look after a wife, or to look
after somebody else's wife.
R. S. Surtees 1805–64 English novelist

※ Danger

You can put up a sign on the door, 'beware of the dog',
without having a dog.
Hans Blix 1928– Swedish diplomat

Dangers by being despised grow great.
Edmund Burke 1729–97 Irish-born politician

When there is no peril in the fight, there is no glory in the triumph.
Pierre Corneille 1606–84 French dramatist

In skating over thin ice, our safety is in our speed.
Ralph Waldo Emerson 1803–82 American writer

Out of this nettle, danger, we pluck this flower, safety.
William Shakespeare 1564–1616 English dramatist

Considering how dangerous everything is nothing is really very frightening.
Gertrude Stein 1874–1946 American writer

Day ⇒Night ☀️

This is the day which the Lord hath made: we will rejoice and be glad in it.
Bible

Morning has broken
Like the first morning.
Eleanor Farjeon 1881–1965 English writer

Awake! for Morning in the bowl of night
Has flung the stone that puts the stars to flight.
Edward Fitzgerald 1809–83 English poet

What are days for?
Days are where we live.
Philip Larkin 1922–85 English poet

I have a horror of sunsets, they're so romantic, so operatic.
Marcel Proust 1871–1922 French novelist

Night's candles are burnt out, and jocund day
Stands tiptoe on the misty mountain tops.
William Shakespeare 1564–1616 English dramatist

Death

※ Death →Bereavement

It's not that I'm afraid to die. I just don't want to be there when it happens.
> **Woody Allen** 1935- American film director

To die will be an awfully big adventure.
> **J. M. Barrie** 1860–1937 Scottish writer

For dust thou art, and unto dust shalt thou return.
> **Bible**

O death, where is thy sting? O grave, where is thy victory?
> **Bible**

In the midst of life we are in death.
> **Book of Common Prayer** 1662

Forasmuch as it hath pleased Almighty God of his great mercy to take unto himself the soul of our dear brother here departed, we therefore commit his body to the ground; earth to earth, ashes to ashes, dust to dust; in sure and certain hope of the Resurrection to eternal life.
> **Book of Common Prayer** 1662

If I should die, think only this of me:
That there's some corner of a foreign field
That is for ever England.
> **Rupert Brooke** 1887–1915 English poet

However many ways there may be of being alive, it is certain that there are vastly more ways of being dead.
> **Richard Dawkins** 1941- English biologist

Any man's death diminishes me, because I am involved in Mankind; And therefore never send to know for whom the bell tolls; it tolls for thee.
> **John Donne** 1572–1631 English poet

Death be not proud, though some have called thee
Mighty and dreadful, for thou art not so.
John Donne 1572–1631 English poet

The bodies of those that made such a noise and tumult
when alive, when dead, lie as quietly among the graves of
their neighbours as any others.
Jonathan Edwards 1703–58 American theologian

Webster was much possessed by death
And saw the skull beneath the skin.
T. S. Eliot 1888–1965 American-born British poet

Death, therefore, the most awful of evils, is nothing to us,
seeing that, when we are death is not come, and when
death is come, we are not.
Epicurus 341–271 BC Greek philosopher

Death is nothing if one can approach it as such. I was
just a tiny night-light, suffocated in its own wax, and on
the point of expiring.
E. M. Forster 1879–1970 English novelist

Death is nothing at all; it does not count. I have only
slipped away into the next room.
Henry Scott Holland 1847–1918 English theologian

I would rather be tied to the soil as another man's serf,
even a poor man's, who hadn't much to live on himself,
than be King of all these the dead and destroyed.
Homer 8th century BC Greek poet

Non omnis moriar.
I shall not altogether die.
Horace 65–8 BC Roman poet

Depend upon it, Sir, when a man knows he is to be
hanged in a fortnight, it concentrates his mind
wonderfully.
Samuel Johnson 1709–84 English lexicographer

Death

Now more than ever seems it rich to die,
To cease upon the midnight with no pain.
> **John Keats** 1795–1821 English poet

This parrot is no more! It has ceased to be! It's expired
and gone to meet its maker! This is a late parrot! It's a
stiff! Bereft of life it rests in peace—if you hadn't nailed
it to the perch it would be pushing up the daisies! It's
rung down the curtain and joined the choir invisible! It's
THIS IS AN EX–PARROT!
> **Monty Python's Flying Circus** 1969–74 British television
> programme

And all our calm is in that balm—
Not lost but gone before.
> **Caroline Norton** 1808–77 English poet

Die, my dear Doctor, that's the last thing I shall do!
> **Lord Palmerston** 1784–1865 British statesman

Guns aren't lawful;
Nooses give;
Gas smells awful;
You might as well live.
> **Dorothy Parker** 1893–1967 American critic

We shall die alone.
> **Blaise Pascal** 1623–62 French scientist and philosopher

Abiit ad plures.
He's gone to join the majority [the dead].
> **Petronius** d. 65 Roman satirist

Anyone can stop a man's life, but no one his death; a
thousand doors open on to it.
> **Seneca ('the Younger')** c.4 BC–AD 65 Roman philosopher

Nothing in his life
Became him like the leaving it.
William Shakespeare 1564–1616 English dramatist

To die, to sleep;
To sleep: perchance to dream: ay, there's the rub;
For in that sleep of death what dreams may come
When we have shuffled off this mortal coil,
Must give us pause.
William Shakespeare 1564–1616 English dramatist

If there wasn't death, I think you couldn't go on.
Stevie Smith 1902–71 English poet

Death must be distinguished from dying, with which it is
often confused.
Sydney Smith 1771–1845 English essayist

One death is a tragedy, a million deaths a statistic.
Joseph Stalin 1879–1953 Soviet dictator

For though from out our bourne of time and place
The flood may bear me far,
I hope to see my pilot face to face
When I have crossed the bar.
Alfred, Lord Tennyson 1809–92 English poet

Though lovers be lost love shall not;
And death shall have no dominion.
Dylan Thomas 1914–53 Welsh poet

So it goes.
Kurt Vonnegut 1922–2007 American novelist

I know death hath ten thousand several doors
For men to take their exits.
John Webster c.1580–c.1625 English dramatist

Death

> The good die first,
> And they whose hearts are dry as summer dust
> Burn to the socket.
> **William Wordsworth** 1770–1850 English poet

> Nor dread nor hope attend
> A dying animal;
> A man awaits his end
> Dreading and hoping all.
> **W. B. Yeats** 1865–1939 Irish poet

✳ Debt

> I don't borrow on credit cards because it is too expensive.
> **Matt Barrett** 1944– Irish-Canadian banker, *view of the chief executive of Barclays Bank*

> Be not made a beggar by banqueting upon borrowing.
> **Bible**

> Rather go to bed supperless than rise in debt.
> **Benjamin Franklin** 1706–90 American statesman and scientist

> The human species, according to the best theory I can form of it, is composed of two distinct races, *the men who borrow*, and *the men who lend*.
> **Charles Lamb** 1775–1834 English writer

> Should we really let our people starve so we can pay our debts?
> **Julius Nyerere** 1922–99 Tanzanian statesman

> You can't put your VISA bill on your American Express card.
> **P. J. O'Rourke** 1947– American writer

> Neither a borrower, nor a lender be.
> **William Shakespeare** 1564–1616 English dramatist

Deceit →Lies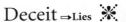

Propaganda is a soft weapon: hold it in your hands too long, and it will move about like a snake, and strike the other way.
Jean Anouilh 1910–87 French dramatist

An open foe may prove a curse,
But a pretended friend is worse.
John Gay 1685–1732 English writer

It was beautiful and simple as all truly great swindles are.
O. Henry 1862–1910 American short-story writer

You may fool all the people some of the time; you can even fool some of the people all the time; but you can't fool all of the people all the time.
Abraham Lincoln 1809–65 American statesman

A deception that elevates us is dearer than a host of low truths.
Alexander Pushkin 1799–1837 Russian poet

O what a tangled web we weave,
When first we practise to deceive!
Sir Walter Scott 1771–1832 Scottish novelist

Democracy →Elections, Politics

The cure for the ills of Democracy is more Democracy.
John Adams 1735–1826 American statesman

The basis of a democratic state is liberty.
Aristotle 384–322 BC Greek philosopher

Democracy means government by discussion, but it is only effective if you can stop people talking.
Clement Attlee 1883–1967 British statesman

Democracy

One man shall have one vote.
John Cartwright 1740–1824 English political reformer

Democracy is the worst form of Government except all those other forms that have been tried from time to time.
Winston Churchill 1874–1965 British statesman

As for our majority...one is enough.
Benjamin Disraeli 1804–81 British statesman

So Two cheers for Democracy: one because it admits variety and two because it permits criticism. Two cheers are quite enough: there is no occasion to give three. Only Love the Beloved Republic deserves that.
E. M. Forster 1879–1970 English novelist

All the world over, I will back the masses against the classes.
W. E. Gladstone 1809–98 British statesman

We here highly resolve that the dead shall not have died in vain, that this nation, under God, shall have a new birth of freedom; and that government of the people, by the people, and for the people, shall not perish from the earth.
Abraham Lincoln 1809–65 American statesman

I never could believe that Providence had sent a few men into the world, ready booted and spurred to ride, and millions ready saddled and bridled to be ridden.
Richard Rumbold c.1622–85 English republican conspirator

Democracy substitutes election by the incompetent many for appointment by the corrupt few.
George Bernard Shaw 1856–1950 Irish dramatist

Democracy is not worth a brass farthing if it is being installed by bayonets.
Alexander Solzhenitsyn 1918–2008 Russian novelist

If one must serve, I hold it better to serve a well-bred lion, who is naturally stronger than I am, than two hundred rats of my own breed.

Voltaire 1694–1778 French writer

The world must be made safe for democracy.

Woodrow Wilson 1856–1924 American statesman

Despair ⇒Hope, Pessimism

My God, my God, look upon me; why hast thou forsaken me?

Bible

There is no despair so absolute as that which comes with the first moments of our first great sorrow, when we have not yet known what it is to have suffered and be healed, to have despaired and have recovered hope.

George Eliot 1819–80 English novelist

In a real dark night of the soul it is always three o'clock in the morning.

F. Scott Fitzgerald 1896–1940 American novelist

Not, I'll not, carrion comfort, Despair, not feast on thee;
Not untwist—slack they may be—these last strands
   of man
In me or, most weary, cry *I can no more.* I can;
Can something, hope, wish day come, not choose not
   to be.

Gerard Manley Hopkins 1844–89 English poet

Don't despair, not even over the fact that you don't despair.

Franz Kafka 1883–1924 Czech novelist

Human life begins on the far side of despair.

Jean-Paul Sartre 1905–80 French philosopher

✳ Determination

Ils ne passeront pas.

They shall not pass.

> **Anonymous** *slogan of the French army at the defence of Verdun, 1916*

Nil carborundum illegitimi.

Don't let the bastards grind you down.

> **Anonymous** *cod Latin saying, in circulation during the Second World War, though possibly of earlier origin*

Thought shall be the harder, heart the keener, courage the greater, as our might lessens.

> **The Battle of Maldon** c.1000

I can only go one way. I've not got a reverse gear.

> **Tony Blair** 1953- British statesman

I was ever a fighter, so—one fight more,
The best and the last!
I would hate that death bandaged my eyes, and forbore,
And bade me creep past.

> **Robert Browning** 1812–89 English poet

Obstinacy, Sir, is certainly a great vice…It happens, however, very unfortunately, that almost the whole line of the great and masculine virtues, constancy, gravity, magnanimity, fortitude, fidelity, and firmness are closely allied to this disagreeable quality.

> **Edmund Burke** 1729–97 Irish-born politician

I will fight for what I believe in until I drop dead. And that's what keeps you alive.

> **Barbara Castle** 1910–2002 British politician

Never give in. Never give in, *never, never, never, never*—in nothing, great or small, large or petty—never give in, except to convictions of honour and good sense. Never

yield to force: never yield to the apparently overwhelming might of the enemy.
    Winston Churchill 1874–1965 British statesman

Say not the struggle naught availeth,
The labour and the wounds are vain,
The enemy faints not, nor faileth,
And as things have been, things remain.
    Arthur Hugh Clough 1819–61 English poet

Nothing in the world can take the place of persistence. Talent will not; nothing is more common than unsuccessful men with talent. Genius will not; unrewarded genius is almost a proverb. Education will not; the world is full of educated derelicts. Persistence and determination are omnipotent. The slogan 'press on' has solved and always will solve the problems of the human race.
    Calvin Coolidge 1872–1933 American statesman

Pick yourself up,
Dust yourself off,
Start all over again.
    Dorothy Fields 1905–74 American songwriter

The best way out is always through.
    Robert Frost 1874–1963 American poet

Under the bludgeonings of chance
My head is bloody, but unbowed.
    W. E. Henley 1849–1903 English poet

When the going gets tough, the tough get going.
    Joseph P. Kennedy 1888–1969 American financier

The drop of rain maketh a hole in the stone, not by violence, but by oft falling.
    Hugh Latimer c.1485–1555 English martyr

Determination

With malice toward none; with charity for all; with firmness in the right, as God gives us to see the right, let us strive on to finish the work we are in.
Abraham Lincoln 1809–65 American statesman

> Perseverance, dear my lord,
Keeps honour bright.
William Shakespeare 1564–1616 English dramatist

One man that has a mind and knows it can always beat ten men who haven't and don't.
George Bernard Shaw 1856–1950 Irish dramatist

Do not underestimate the determination of a quiet man.
Iain Duncan Smith 1954– British politician

'Tis known by the name of perseverance in a good cause,—and of obstinacy in a bad one.
Laurence Sterne 1713–68 English novelist

> That which we are, we are;
One equal temper of heroic hearts,
Made weak by time and fate, but strong in will
To strive, to seek, to find, and not to yield.
Alfred, Lord Tennyson 1809–92 English poet

We shall not be diverted from our course. To those waiting with bated breath for that favourite media catch-phrase, the U-turn, I have only this to say. 'You turn if you want; the lady's not for turning.'
Margaret Thatcher 1925– British stateswoman

✳ Diaries

What is more dull than a discreet diary? One might just as well have a discreet soul.
Henry 'Chips' Channon 1897–1958 British politician

I want to go on living even after death!
Anne Frank 1929–45 German-born Jewish diarist

To be a good diarist one must have a little snouty, sneaky mind.
Harold Nicolson 1886–1968 English diplomat

One need not write in a diary what one is to remember for ever.
Sylvia Townsend Warner 1893–1978 English writer

I always say, keep a diary and some day it'll keep you.
Mae West 1892–1980 American film actress

I never travel without my diary. One should always have something sensational to read in the train.
Oscar Wilde 1854–1900 Irish dramatist

Diplomacy ✳

In things that are tender and unpleasing, it is good to break the ice by some whose words are of less weight, and to reserve the more weighty voice to come in as by chance.
Francis Bacon 1561–1626 English courtier

To jaw-jaw is always better than to war-war.
Winston Churchill 1874–1965 British statesman

Euphemisms are unpleasant truths wearing diplomatic cologne.
Quentin Crisp 1908–99 English writer

Treaties, you see, are like girls and roses: they last while they last.
Charles de Gaulle 1890–1970 French statesman

Diplomacy

I feel happier now that we have no allies to be polite to and to pamper.

George VI 1895–1952 British monarch

Let us never negotiate out of fear. But let us never fear to negotiate.

John F. Kennedy 1917–63 American statesman

One of the things I learnt when I was negotiating was that until I changed myself I could not change others.

Nelson Mandela 1918– South African statesman

We are prepared to go to the gates of Hell—but no further.

Pope Pius VII 1742–1823 Italian cleric, *attempting to reach an agreement with Napoleon*

I'm afraid you've got a bad egg, Mr Jones.
Oh no, my Lord, I assure you! Parts of it are excellent!

Punch 1841–1992 English humorous periodical

Speak softly and carry a big stick; you will go far.

Theodore Roosevelt 1858–1919 American statesman

You can no more make an agreement with those leaders of Colombia than you can nail currant jelly to the wall. And the failure to nail currant jelly to the wall is not due to the nail. It's due to the currant jelly.

Theodore Roosevelt 1858–1919 American statesman

By indirections find directions out.

William Shakespeare 1564–1616 English dramatist

An ambassador is an honest man sent to lie abroad for the good of his country.

Henry Wotton 1568–1639 English diplomat

Discontent ⇒Satisfaction

When you don't have any money, the problem is food.
When you have money, it's sex. When you have both it's
health.
    J. P. Donleavy 1926– Irish-American novelist

We loathe our manna, and we long for quails.
    John Dryden 1631–1700 English poet

It is an uneasy lot at best, to be what we call highly
taught and yet not to enjoy: to be present at this great
spectacle of life and never to be liberated from a small
hungry shivering self.
    George Eliot 1819–80 English novelist

            It is a flaw
In happiness, to see beyond our bourn—
It forces us in summer skies to mourn:
It spoils the singing of the nightingale.
    John Keats 1795–1821 English poet

It is better to be a human being dissatisfied than a pig
satisfied; better to be Socrates dissatisfied than a fool
satisfied.
    John Stuart Mill 1806–73 English philosopher

Whoever is dissatisfied with himself is continually ready
for revenge, and we others will be his victims.
    Friedrich Nietzsche 1844–1900 German philosopher

'Tis just like a summer birdcage in a garden; the birds
that are without despair to get in, and the birds that are
within despair, and are in a consumption, for fear they
shall never get out.
    John Webster c.1580–c.1625 English dramatist

Discontent

He spoke with a certain what-is-it in his voice, and I could see that, if not actually disgruntled, he was far from being gruntled.
P. G. Wodehouse 1881–1975 English writer

Discovery ⇨Invention and Discovery

✳ Dogs

The great pleasure of a dog is that you may make a fool of yourself with him and not only will he not scold you, but he will make a fool of himself too.
Samuel Butler 1835–1902 English novelist

Near this spot are deposited the remains of one who possessed beauty without vanity, strength without insolence, courage without ferocity, and all the virtues of Man, without his vices.
Lord Byron 1788–1824 English poet, *epitaph on his Newfoundland dog*

Brothers and Sisters, I bid you beware
Of giving your heart to a dog to tear.
Rudyard Kipling 1865–1936 English writer

A door is what a dog is perpetually on the wrong side of.
Ogden Nash 1902-71 American humorist

I am his Highness' dog at Kew;
Pray, tell me sir, whose dog are you?
Alexander Pope 1688–1744 English poet, *engraved on the collar of a dog*

That indefatigable and unsavoury engine of pollution, the dog.
John Sparrow 1906-92 English academic

The more one gets to know of men, the more one values dogs.

A. Toussenel 1803–85 French writer, *attributed to Mme Roland in the form 'The more I see of men, the more I like dogs'*

The dog is a gentleman; I hope to go to his heaven, not man's.

Mark Twain 1835–1910 American writer

Doubt →Certainty

Oh! let us never, never doubt
What nobody is sure about!

Hilaire Belloc 1870–1953 British writer

How long halt ye between two opinions?

Bible

I'm a man of no convictions. At least, I think I am.

Christopher Hampton 1946– English dramatist

I am too much of a sceptic to deny the possibility of anything.

T. H. Huxley 1825–95 English biologist

I respect faith but doubt is what gets you an education.

Wilson Mizner 1876–1933 American dramatist

Ten thousand difficulties do not make one doubt.

John Henry Newman 1801–90 English theologian

Now, the melancholy god protect thee, and the tailor make thy doublet of changeable taffeta, for thy mind is a very opal.

William Shakespeare 1564–1616 English dramatist

I must have a prodigious quantity of mind; it takes me as much as a week, sometimes, to make it up.

Mark Twain 1835–1910 American writer

Doubt

Life is doubt,
And faith without doubt is nothing but death.
   Miguel de Unamuno 1864–1937 Spanish philosopher

Doubt is not a pleasant condition. But certainty is an absurd one.
   Voltaire 1694–1778 French writer

☀ Drawing

Not a day without a line.
   Apelles Greek painter of the 4th century BC, *proverbial summary of his philosophy*

A picture equals a movement in space.
   Emily Carr 1871–1945 Canadian artist

Treat nature in terms of the cylinder, the sphere, the cone, all in perspective.
   Paul Cézanne 1839–1906 French painter

I rarely draw what I see—I draw what I feel in my body.
   Barbara Hepworth 1903–75 English sculptor

Drawing is the true test of art.
   J. A. D. Ingres 1780–1867 French painter

An active line on a walk, moving freely without a goal. A walk for walk's sake.
   Paul Klee 1879–1940 German-Swiss painter

☀ Dreams

Have you noticed…there is never any third act in a nightmare? They bring you to a climax of terror and then leave you there. They are the work of poor dramatists.
   Max Beerbohm 1872–1956 English critic

The armoured cars of dreams, contrived to let us do
so many a dangerous thing.
    Elizabeth Bishop 1911–79 American poet

All the things one has forgotten scream for help in
dreams.
    Elias Canetti 1905–94 Bulgarian-born writer

When we dream that we are dreaming, the moment of
awakening is at hand.
    J. M. Coetzee 1940–   South African novelist

The interpretation of dreams is the royal road to a
knowledge of the unconscious activities of the mind.
    Sigmund Freud 1856–1939 Austrian psychiatrist

The dream of reason produces monsters.
    Goya 1746–1828 Spanish painter

Was it a vision, or a waking dream?
Fled is that music:—do I wake or sleep?
    John Keats 1795–1821 English poet

They who dream by day are cognizant of many things
which escape those who dream only by night.
    Edgar Allan Poe 1809–49 American writer

O God! I could be bounded in a nut-shell, and count
myself a king of infinite space, were it not that I have bad
dreams.
    William Shakespeare 1564–1616 English dramatist

    The quick Dreams,
The passion-wingèd Ministers of thought.
    Percy Bysshe Shelley 1792–1822 English poet

Drink

One reason why I don't drink is because I wish to know when I am having a good time.
Nancy Astor 1879–1964 British politician

When the wine is in, the wit is out.
Thomas Becon 1512–67 English clergyman

Wine is a mocker, strong drink is raging.
Bible

Freedom and Whisky gang thegither!
Robert Burns 1759–96 Scottish poet

I have taken more out of alcohol than alcohol has taken out of me.
Winston Churchill 1874–1965 British statesman

A man shouldn't fool with booze until he's fifty; then he's a damn fool if he doesn't.
William Faulkner 1897–1962 American novelist

I often wonder what the Vintners buy
One half so precious as the Goods they sell.
Edward Fitzgerald 1809–83 English poet

Drink not the third glass.
George Herbert 1593–1633 English poet

And malt does more than Milton can
To justify God's ways to man.
A. E. Housman 1859–1936 English poet

You're not drunk if you can lie on the floor without holding on.
Dean Martin 1917–95 American actor

Candy
Is dandy
But liquor

Is quicker.
> **Ogden Nash** 1902–71 American humorist

Wine is for drinking and enjoying, talking about it is deadly dull.
> **Jancis Robinson** 1950– English journalist

I'm only a beer teetotaller, not a champagne teetotaller.
> **George Bernard Shaw** 1856–1950 Irish dramatist

I'm not so think as you drunk I am.
> **J. C. Squire** 1884–1958 English man of letters

Wine is bottled poetry.
> **Robert Louis Stevenson** 1850–94 Scottish novelist

The lips that touch liquor must never touch mine.
> **George W. Young** 1846–1919

Drugs ✳

I'll die young, but it's like kissing God.
> **Lenny Bruce** 1925–66 American comedian, *on his drug addiction*

Junk is the ideal product…the ultimate merchandise. No sales talk necessary. The client will crawl through a sewer and beg to buy.
> **William S. Burroughs** 1914–97 American novelist

I experimented with marijuana a time or two. And I didn't like it, and I didn't inhale.
> **Bill Clinton** 1946– American statesman

Thou hast the keys of Paradise, oh just, subtle, and mighty opium!
> **Thomas De Quincey** 1785–1859 English essayist

Drugs is like getting up and having a cup of tea in the morning.
> **Noel Gallagher** 1967– English pop singer

Drugs

In this country, don't forget, a habit is no damn private hell. There's no solitary confinement outside of jail. A habit is hell for those you love.
   Billie Holiday 1915–59 American singer

Every form of addiction is bad, no matter whether the narcotic be alcohol or morphine or idealism.
   Carl Gustav Jung 1875–1961 Swiss psychologist

Sure thing, man. I used to be a laboratory myself once.
   Keith Richards 1943– English rock musician, *on being asked to autograph a fan's school chemistry book*

A drug is neither moral or immoral—it's a chemical compound.
   Frank Zappa 1940–93 American rock musician

※ The Earth

The earth is the Lord's, and all that therein is: the compass of the world, and they that dwell therein.
   Bible

Topography displays no favourites; North's as near as West.
More delicate than the historians' are the map-makers' colours.
   Elizabeth Bishop 1911–79 American poet

How inappropriate to call this planet Earth when it is clearly Ocean.
   Arthur C. Clarke 1917–2008 English science fiction writer

Now there is one outstandingly important fact regarding Spaceship Earth, and that is that no instruction book came with it.
   R. Buckminster Fuller 1895–1983 American designer

In my view, climate change is the most severe problem we are facing today—more serious even than the threat of terrorism.
David King 1939- British scientist

To me, it underscores our responsibility to deal more kindly with one another, and to preserve and cherish the pale blue dot, the only home we've ever known.
Carl Sagan 1934-96 American astronomer, *of Earth as photographed by Voyager 1*

We have a beautiful
mother
Her green lap
immense
Her brown embrace
eternal
Her blue body
everything
we know.
Alice Walker 1944- American poet

Need for a knowledge of geography is greater than the need of gardens for water after the stars have failed to fulfil their promise of rain.
Yāqūt d. 1229 Arab geographer

Eating ⇒Cookery, Food

Tell me what you eat and I will tell you what you are.
Anthelme Brillat-Savarin 1755-1826 French gourmet

Some have meat and cannot eat,
Some cannot eat that want it:
But we have meat and we can eat,
Sae let the Lord be thankit.
Robert Burns 1759-96 Scottish poet

Eating

Hunger is the best sauce in the world.
Cervantes 1547–1616 Spanish novelist

It's a very odd thing—
As odd as can be—
That whatever Miss T eats
Turns into Miss T.
Walter de la Mare 1873–1956 English poet

Gluttony is an emotional escape, a sign something is eating us.
Peter De Vries 1910–93 American novelist

ANTHONY HOPKINS: I do wish we could chat longer, but I'm having an old friend for dinner.
Thomas Harris 1940– and **Ted Tally** 1952– American writer and screenwriter, *in the film* The Silence of the Lambs

I don't eat anything with a face.
Linda McCartney 1941–98 American photographer

Time for a little something.
A. A. Milne 1882–1956 English writer

One should eat to live, and not live to eat.
Molière 1622–73 French comic dramatist

The appetite grows by eating.
François Rabelais c.1494–c.1553 French humanist

Now good digestion wait on appetite,
And health on both!
William Shakespeare 1564–1616 English dramatist

We each day dig our graves with our teeth.
Samuel Smiles 1812–1904 English writer

He sows hurry and reaps indigestion.
Robert Louis Stevenson 1850–94 Scottish novelist

I'll fill hup the chinks wi' cheese.
R. S. Surtees 1805–64 English novelist

MICHAEL DOUGLAS: Lunch is for wimps.
   Stanley Weiser and **Oliver Stone** 1946– American
   screenwriters, *in the film* Wall Street

One cannot think well, love well, sleep well, if one has
not dined well.
   Virginia Woolf 1882–1941 English novelist

Economics ✳

It's the economy, stupid.
   Anonymous *slogan of Bill Clinton's first presidential campaign*

There's no such thing as a free lunch.
   Anonymous

There is enough in the world for everyone's need, but not
enough for everyone's greed.
   Frank Buchman 1878–1961 American evangelist

Capitalism is using its money; we socialists throw it away.
   Fidel Castro 1927– Cuban statesman

Inflation is the one form of taxation that can be imposed
without legislation.
   Milton Friedman 1912–2006 American economist

Trickle-down theory—the less than elegant metaphor that
if one feeds the horse enough oats, some will pass
through to the road for the sparrows.
   J. K. Galbraith 1908–2006 American economist

Finance is, as it were, the stomach of the country, from
which all the other organs take their tone.
   W. E. Gladstone 1809–98 British statesman

The safest way to double your money is to fold it over
and put it in your pocket.
   Frank McKinney ('Kin') Hubbard 1868–1930 American
   humorist

Economics

The green shoots of economic spring are appearing once again.

Norman Lamont 1942– British politician, *often quoted as 'the green shoots of recovery'*

If the policy isn't hurting, it isn't working.

John Major 1943– British statesman, *on controlling inflation*

We have always known that heedless self-interest was bad morals; we know now that it is bad economics.

Franklin D. Roosevelt 1882–1945 American statesman

Call a thing immoral or ugly, soul-destroying or a degradation of man, a peril to the peace of the world or to the well-being of future generations: as long as you have not shown it to be 'uneconomic' you have not really questioned its right to exist, grow, and prosper.

E. F. Schumacher 1911–77 German-born economist

It's a recession when your neighbour loses his job; it's a depression when you lose yours.

Harry S. Truman 1884–1972 American statesman

What a country calls its vital economic interests are not the things which enable its citizens to live, but the things which enable it to make war.

Simone Weil 1909–43 French philosopher

MICHAEL DOUGLAS: Greed—for lack of a better word—is good. Greed is right. Greed works.

Stanley Weiser and **Oliver Stone** 1946– American screenwriters, *in the film Wall Street*

It is not that pearls fetch a high price *because* men have dived for them; but on the contrary, men dive for them because they fetch a high price.

Richard Whately 1787–1863 English philosopher

Education ⇒ Examinations, Teaching

What one knows is, in youth, of little moment; they know enough who know how to learn.
Henry Brooks Adams 1838–1918 American historian

Give me a child for the first seven years, and you may do what you like with him afterwards.
Anonymous *attributed as a Jesuit maxim*

I said...how, and why, young children, were sooner allured by love, than driven by beating, to attain good learning.
Roger Ascham 1515–68 English scholar

Studies serve for delight, for ornament, and for ability.
Francis Bacon 1561–1626 English courtier

The dread of beatings! Dread of being late!
And, greatest dread of all, the dread of games!
John Betjeman 1906–84 English poet

Ask me my three main priorities for Government, and I tell you: education, education and education.
Tony Blair 1953– British statesman

That lyf so short, the craft so long to lerne.
Geoffrey Chaucer c.1343–1400 English poet

In education there should be no class distinction.
Confucius 551–479 BC Chinese philosopher

C-l-e-a-n, clean, verb active, to make bright, to scour. W-i-n, win, d-e-r, der, winder, a casement. When the boy knows this out of the book, he goes and does it.
Charles Dickens 1812–70 English novelist

A University should be a place of light, of liberty, and of learning.
Benjamin Disraeli 1804–81 British statesman

Education

Study as if you were to live for ever; live as if you were to die tomorrow.
St Edmund of Abingdon c.1175–1240 English scholar

You send your child to the schoolmaster, but 'tis the schoolboys who educate him.
Ralph Waldo Emerson 1803–82 American writer

The proper study of mankind is books.
Aldous Huxley 1894–1963 English novelist

If you educate a man you educate one person, but if you educate a woman you educate a family.
Ruby Manikan Indian church leader

Universities never reform themselves; everyone knows that.
Lord Melbourne 1779–1848 English statesman

My spelling is Wobbly. It's good spelling but it Wobbles, and the letters get in the wrong places.
A. A. Milne 1882–1956 English writer

Know then thyself, presume not God to scan;
The proper study of mankind is man.
Alexander Pope 1688–1744 English poet

I would I had bestowed that time in the tongues that I have in fencing, dancing, and bear-baiting. O! had I but followed the arts!
William Shakespeare 1564–1616 English dramatist

Education is what survives when what has been learned has been forgotten.
B. F. Skinner 1904–90 American psychologist

What does education often do? It makes a straight-cut ditch of a free, meandering brook.
Henry David Thoreau 1817–62 American writer

The best thing for being sad…is to learn something.
T. H. White 1906–64 English novelist

Effort

We're number two. We try harder.
Anonymous *advertising slogan for Avis car rentals*

Madam, if a thing is possible, consider it done; the
impossible? that will be done.
Charles Alexandre de Calonne 1734–1802 French statesman

Now, *here*, you see, it takes all the running *you* can do, to
keep in the same place. If you want to get somewhere
else, you must run at least twice as fast as that!
Lewis Carroll 1832–98 English writer

Oh, how I am tired of the struggle!
Johann Wolfgang von Goethe 1749–1832 German writer

HOMER SIMPSON: Kids, you tried your best, and you
failed miserably. The lesson is, never try.
Matt Groening 1954– American humorist

If something is worth doing, then it's worth overdoing.
Justin Hawkins 1975– English rock musician

Between us and excellence, the gods have placed the sweat
of our brows.
Hesiod fl. c.700 BC Greek poet

Mountains will go into labour, and a silly little mouse
will be born.
Horace 65–8 BC Roman poet

I had done all that I could; and no man is well pleased to
have his all neglected, be it ever so little.
Samuel Johnson 1709–84 English lexicographer

Our salvation is in striving to achieve what we know we'll
never achieve.
Ryszard Kapuscinski 1932–2007 Polish journalist

Effort

Superhuman effort isn't worth a damn unless it achieves results.

Ernest Shackleton 1874–1922 British explorer

Things won are done; joy's soul lies in the doing.

William Shakespeare 1564–1616 English dramatist

✳ Elections ⇒Democracy

Elections are won by men and women chiefly because most people vote against somebody rather than for somebody.

Franklin P. Adams 1881–1960 American journalist

Vote early and vote often.

Anonymous *US election slogan, already current by 1858*

Vote for the man who promises least; he'll be the least disappointing.

Bernard Baruch 1870–1965 American financier

One man shall have one vote.

John Cartwright 1740–1824 English political reformer

Hell, I never vote *for* anybody. I always vote *against*.

W. C. Fields 1880–1946 American humorist

I always voted at my party's call,
And I never thought of thinking for myself at all.

W. S. Gilbert 1836–1911 English writer

To give victory to the right, not bloody bullets, but peaceful ballots only, are necessary.

Abraham Lincoln 1809–65 American statesman, *usually quoted as 'The ballot is stronger than the bullet'*

If voting changed anything, they'd abolish it.

Ken Livingstone 1945– British politician

One of the nuisances of the ballot is that when the oracle has spoken you never know what it means.
Lord Salisbury 1830–1903 British statesman

It's not the voting that's democracy, it's the counting.
Tom Stoppard 1937– British dramatist

Ending ✳

It ain't over till it's over.
Yogi Berra 1925– American baseball player

Better is the end of a thing than the beginning thereof.
Bible

Now this is not the end. It is not even the beginning of the end. But it is, perhaps, the end of the beginning.
Winston Churchill 1874–1965 British statesman, *on the Battle of Egypt*

The party's over, it's time to call it a day.
Betty Comden 1917–2006 and **Adolph Green** 1915–2002 American songwriters

This is the way the world ends
Not with a bang but a whimper.
T. S. Eliot 1888–1965 American-born British poet

In my end is my beginning.
Mary, Queen of Scots 1542–87

The opera ain't over 'til the fat lady sings.
Proverb

The rest is silence.
William Shakespeare 1564–1616 English dramatist

This is the beginning of the end.
Charles-Maurice de Talleyrand 1754–1838 French statesman, *on the announcement of Napoleon's Pyrrhic victory at Borodino, 1812*

Ending

They think it's all over—it is now.
Kenneth Wolstenholme 1920–2002 English sports commentator

✳ Enemies

He who has a thousand friends has not a friend to spare,
And he who has one enemy will meet him everywhere.
Ali ibn-Abi-Talib c.602–661 Arab ruler

Not while I'm alive 'e ain't!
Ernest Bevin 1881–1951 British politician, *reply to the observation that Nye Bevan was sometimes his own worst enemy*

Love your enemies, do good to them which hate you.
Bible

An injury is much sooner forgotten than an insult.
Lord Chesterfield 1694–1773 English writer

You can calculate the worth of a man by the number of his enemies, and the importance of a work of art by the harm that is spoken of it.
Gustave Flaubert 1821–80 French novelist

Better to have him inside the tent pissing out, than outside pissing in.
Lyndon Baines Johnson 1908–73 American statesman, *of J. Edgar Hoover*

People wish their enemies dead—but I do not; I say give them the gout, give them the stone!
Lady Mary Wortley Montagu 1689–1762 English writer

I have none. I had them all shot.
Ramón María Narváez 1800–68 Spanish statesman, *asked on his deathbed if he forgave his enemies*

The enemies of my enemies are my friends.
Proverb

There is nothing in the whole world so painful as feeling that one is not liked. It always seems to me that people who hate me must be suffering from some strange form of lunacy.

Sei Shōnagon c.966–c.1013 Japanese diarist

I have always made one prayer to God, a very short one. Here it is, 'My God, make our enemies very ridiculous!'

Voltaire 1694–1778 French writer

England ⇒ Britain, London

I will not cease from mental fight,
Nor shall my sword sleep in my hand,
Till we have built Jerusalem,
In England's green and pleasant land.

William Blake 1757–1827 English poet

Oh, to be in England
Now that April's there.

Robert Browning 1812–89 English poet

The Thames is liquid history.

John Burns 1858–1943 British politician, *to an American, who had compared the Thames disparagingly with the Mississippi*

In England there are sixty different religions, and only one sauce.

Francesco Caracciolo 1752–99 Neapolitan diplomat

Mad dogs and Englishmen
Go out in the midday sun.

Noël Coward 1899–1973 English dramatist

What should they know of England who only England know?

Rudyard Kipling 1865–1936 English writer

England is a nation of shopkeepers.

Napoleon I 1769–1821 French emperor

England

England expects that every man will do his duty.
> **Horatio, Lord Nelson** 1758–1805 British admiral, *at the battle of Trafalgar*

There'll always be an England.
> **Ross Parker** 1914–74 and **Hugh Charles** 1907–95 British songwriters

Ask any man what nationality he would prefer to be, and ninety-nine out of a hundred will tell you that they would prefer to be Englishmen.
> **Cecil Rhodes** 1853–1902 South African statesman

This royal throne of kings, this sceptred isle,
This earth of majesty, this seat of Mars…
This blessèd plot, this earth, this realm, this England.
> **William Shakespeare** 1564–1616 English dramatist

You never find an Englishman among the under-dogs—except in England, of course.
> **Evelyn Waugh** 1903–66 English novelist

The English country gentleman galloping after a fox—the unspeakable in full pursuit of the uneatable.
> **Oscar Wilde** 1854–1900 Irish dramatist

We must be free or die, who speak the tongue
That Shakespeare spake; the faith and morals hold
Which Milton held.
> **William Wordsworth** 1770–1850 English poet

✳ The Environment →The Country, Pollution

Think globally, act locally.
> **Anonymous** *Friends of the Earth slogan*

Come, friendly bombs, and fall on Slough!
It isn't fit for humans now,
There isn't grass to graze a cow.

Swarm over, Death!
John Betjeman 1906–84 English poet

Woe unto them that join house to house, that lay field to
field, till there be no place.
Bible

And was Jerusalem builded here
Among these dark Satanic mills?
William Blake 1757–1827 English poet

O all ye Green Things upon the Earth, bless ye the Lord.
Book of Common Prayer 1662

I do not know of any environmental group in any
country that does not view its government as an
adversary.
Gro Harlem Brundtland 1939– Norwegian stateswoman

What would the world be, once bereft
Of wet and wildness? Let them be left,
O let them be left, wildness and wet;
Long live the weeds and the wilderness yet.
Gerard Manley Hopkins 1844–89 English poet

I am I plus my surroundings and if I do not preserve the
latter, I do not preserve myself.
José Ortega y Gasset 1883–1955 Spanish writer

The parks are the lungs of London.
William Pitt 1708–78 British statesman

Consult the genius of the place in all.
Alexander Pope 1688–1744 English poet

It's not that easy being green.
Joe Raposo 1937–89 American songwriter, *sung by the Muppet
Kermit the frog*

Small is beautiful.
E. F. Schumacher 1911–77 German-born economist

The Environment

If I were a Brazilian without land or money or the means
to feed my children, I would be burning the rain forest
too.
Sting 1951– English rock singer

In wildness is the preservation of the world.
Henry David Thoreau 1817–62 American writer

✤ Envy and Jealousy

Thou shalt not covet thy neighbour's house, thou shalt
not covet thy neighbour's wife.
Bible

Jealousy is no more than feeling alone against smiling
enemies.
Elizabeth Bowen 1899–1973 Anglo-Irish novelist

The danger chiefly lies in acting well;
No crime's so great as daring to excel.
Charles Churchill 1731–64 English poet

Thou shalt not covet; but tradition
Approves all forms of competition.
Arthur Hugh Clough 1819–61 English poet

Some folks rail against other folks, because other folks
have what some folks would be glad of.
Henry Fielding 1707–54 English novelist

To jealousy, nothing is more frightful than laughter.
Françoise Sagan 1935–2004 French novelist

 O! beware, my lord, of jealousy;
It is the green-eyed monster which doth mock
The meat it feeds on.
William Shakespeare 1564–1616 English dramatist

Equality →Human Rights

Equality may perhaps be a right, but no power on earth can ever turn it into a fact.
Honoré de Balzac 1799–1850 French novelist

He maketh his sun to rise on the evil and on the good, and sendeth rain on the just and on the unjust.
Bible

A man's a man for a' that.
Robert Burns 1759–96 Scottish poet

When every one is somebodee,
Then no one's anybody.
W. S. Gilbert 1836–1911 English writer

Your levellers wish to level *down* as far as themselves; but they cannot bear levelling *up* to themselves.
Samuel Johnson 1709–84 English lexicographer

I have a dream that one day on the red hills of Georgia the sons of former slaves and the sons of former slave owners will be able to sit down together at the table of brotherhood.
Martin Luther King 1929–68 American civil rights leader

All animals are equal but some animals are more equal than others.
George Orwell 1903–50 English novelist

Hath not a Jew eyes? hath not a Jew hands, organs, dimensions, senses, affections, passions?…If you prick us, do we not bleed? if you tickle us, do we not laugh? if you poison us, do we not die? and if you wrong us, shall we not revenge?
William Shakespeare 1564–1616 English dramatist

Equality

Make all men equal today, and God has so created them that they shall all be unequal tomorrow.
Anthony Trollope 1815–82 English novelist

✳ Europe

Whoever speaks of Europe is wrong, [it is] a geographical concept.
Otto von Bismarck 1815–98 German statesman

Fog in Channel—Continent isolated.
Russell Brockbank 1913–79 British cartoonist, *newspaper placard in cartoon*

You ask if they were happy. This is not a characteristic of a European. To be contented—that's for the cows.
Coco Chanel 1883–1971 French couturière

From Stettin in the Baltic to Trieste in the Adriatic an iron curtain has descended across the Continent.
Winston Churchill 1874–1965 British statesman

Without Britain Europe would remain only a torso.
Ludwig Erhard 1897–1977 German statesman

It means the end of a thousand years of history.
Hugh Gaitskell 1906–63 British politician, *on a European federation*

If I want to talk to Europe who do I call?
Henry Kissinger 1923– American politician

The policy of European integration is in reality a question of war and peace in the 21st century.
Helmut Kohl 1930– German statesman

I want the whole of Europe to have one currency; it will make trading much easier.
Napoleon I 1769–1821 French emperor

You're thinking of Europe as Germany and France. I don't. I think that's old Europe. If you look at the entire Nato Europe today, the centre of gravity is shifting to the east.
Donald Rumsfeld 1932– American politician

Better fifty years of Europe than a cycle of Cathay.
Alfred, Lord Tennyson 1809–92 English poet

In my lifetime all our problems have come from mainland Europe and all the solutions have come from the English-speaking nations of the world.
Margaret Thatcher 1925– British stateswoman

We are not on the outskirts of Europe, we are at the centre of Europe.
Viktor Yushchenko 1954– Ukrainian statesman

Evil ⇒Goodness

The fearsome, word-and-thought-defying *banality of evil*.
Hannah Arendt 1906–75 American philosopher

I and the public know
What all schoolchildren learn,
Those to whom evil is done
Do evil in return.
W. H. Auden 1907–73 English poet

With love for mankind and hatred of sins.
St Augustine of Hippo AD 354–430 Roman theologian, *often quoted as 'Love the sinner but hate the sin'*

There is no peace, saith the Lord, unto the wicked.
Bible

It is necessary only for the good man to do nothing for evil to triumph.
Edmund Burke 1729–97 Irish-born politician

Evil

The face of 'evil' is always the face of total need.
William S. Burroughs 1914–97 American novelist

As soon as men decide that all means are permitted to fight an evil, then their good becomes indistinguishable from the evil that they set out to destroy.
Christopher Dawson 1889–1970 English historian

What we call evil is simply ignorance bumping its head in the dark.
Henry Ford 1863–1947 American car manufacturer

But if he does really think that there is no distinction between virtue and vice, why, Sir, when he leaves our houses, let us count our spoons.
Samuel Johnson 1709–84 English lexicographer

No one ever suddenly became depraved.
Juvenal c.AD 60–c.130 Roman satirist

Farewell remorse! All good to me is lost;
Evil, be thou my good.
John Milton 1608–74 English poet

An orgy looks particularly alluring seen through the mists of righteous indignation.
Malcolm Muggeridge 1903–90 British journalist

By the pricking of my thumbs,
Something wicked this way comes.
William Shakespeare 1564–1616 English dramatist

The line dividing good and evil cuts through the heart of every human being. And who is willing to destroy a piece of his own heart?
Alexander Solzhenitsyn 1918–2008 Russian novelist

Examinations ✳

Truth is no more at issue in an examination than thirst at a wine-tasting or fashion at a striptease.

Alan Bennett 1934– English writer

Examinations are formidable even to the best prepared, for the greatest fool may ask more than the wisest man can answer.

Charles Caleb Colton c.1780–1832 English clergyman

Life isn't like coursework, baby. It's one damn essay crisis after another.

Boris Johnson 1964– British politician

I evidently knew more about economics than my examiners.

John Maynard Keynes 1883–1946 English economist, *explaining why he performed badly in the Civil Service examinations*

These are not statistics, these are people's futures.

Estelle Morris 1952– British politician, *on queries over A-level grades*

If we have to have an exam at 11, let us make it one for humour, sincerity, imagination, character—and where is the examiner who could test such qualities?

A. S. Neill 1883–1973 Scottish teacher

In examinations those who do not wish to know ask questions of those who cannot tell.

Walter Raleigh 1861–1922 English critic

Do not on any account attempt to write on both sides of the paper at once.

W. C. Sellar 1898–1951 and **R. J. Yeatman** 1898–1968 British writers

Examinations

Had silicon been a gas, I would have been a major-general by now.

James McNeill Whistler 1834–1903 American-born painter, *having been found 'deficient in chemistry' in a West Point examination*

✳ Exercise →Health

If you walk hard enough, you probably don't need any other God.

Bruce Chatwin 1940–89 English travel writer

The wise, for cure, on exercise depend;
God never made his work for man to mend.

John Dryden 1631–1700 English poet

Exercise is the yuppie version of bulimia.

Barbara Ehrenreich 1941– American sociologist

Exercise is bunk. If you are healthy, you don't need it: if you are sick you shouldn't take it.

Henry Ford 1863–1947 American car manufacturer

The sovereign invigorator of the body is exercise, and of all the exercises, walking is best.

Thomas Jefferson 1743–1826 American statesman

The only exercise I take is walking behind the coffins of friends who took exercise.

Peter O'Toole 1932– Irish-born British actor

Avoid running at all times.

Leroy ('Satchel') Paige 1906–82 American baseball player

Those who do not find time for exercise will have to find time for illness.

Proverb

All you need to run is good shoes.

Paula Radcliffe 1973– British long-distance runner

There's no easy way out [of exercise]. If there were, I would have bought it. And believe me, it would be one of my favourite things!
Oprah Winfrey 1954– American talk show hostess

Experience ✳

All experience is an arch to build upon.
Henry Brooks Adams 1838–1918 American historian

You should make a point of trying every experience once, excepting incest and folk-dancing.
Anonymous

Experience isn't interesting till it begins to repeat itself—in fact, till it does that, it hardly *is* experience.
Elizabeth Bowen 1899–1973 Anglo-Irish novelist

Experience is the best of schoolmasters, only the school fees are heavy.
Thomas Carlyle 1795–1881 Scottish historian

The courtiers who surround him [Louis XVIII] have forgotten nothing and learnt nothing.
Charles Dumouriez 1739–1823 French general

We had the experience but missed the meaning.
T. S. Eliot 1888–1965 American-born British poet

Experience is not what happens to a man; it is what a man does with what happens to him.
Aldous Huxley 1894–1963 English novelist

We took risks, we knew we took them; things have come out against us, and therefore we have no cause for complaint.
Robert Falcon Scott 1868–1912 English explorer

Experience

Education is when you read the fine print; experience is what you get when you don't.
Pete Seeger 1919– American folk singer

Experience is the name everyone gives to their mistakes.
Oscar Wilde 1854–1900 Irish dramatist

✳ Failure ⇒Success

History to the defeated
May say Alas but cannot help or pardon.
W. H. Auden 1907–73 English poet

Ever tried. Ever failed. No matter. Try again. Fail again. Fail better.
Samuel Beckett 1906–89 Irish writer

She knows there's no success like failure
And that failure's no success at all.
Bob Dylan 1941– American singer

Man is not made for defeat. A man can be destroyed but not defeated.
Ernest Hemingway 1899–1961 American novelist

Failure is not an option.
Gene Kranz 1933– American space flight director, *summarized version of announcement to ground crew in Houston as Apollo 13 approached the critical earth-to-moon decision loop*

Vae victis.
Down with the defeated!
Livy 59 BC–AD 17 Roman historian

Show me a good loser and I'll show you a loser.
Vince Lombardi 1913–70 American football coach

There is only one step from the sublime to the ridiculous.
Napoleon I 1769–1821 French emperor

> We fail!
> But screw your courage to the sticking-place,
> And we'll not fail.
> **William Shakespeare** 1564–1616 English dramatist

Fame ✳

Seven wealthy towns contend for HOMER dead
Through which the living HOMER begged his bread.
Anonymous

There's no such thing as bad publicity except your own
obituary.
Brendan Behan 1923–64 Irish dramatist

Let us now praise famous men, and our fathers that
begat us.
Bible

A prophet is not without honour, save in his own
country, and in his own house.
Bible

I awoke one morning and found myself famous.
Lord Byron 1788–1824 English poet

After a while you learn that privacy is something you can
sell, but you can't buy it back.
Bob Dylan 1941– American singer

The deed is all, the glory nothing.
Johann Wolfgang von Goethe 1749–1832 German writer

Far from the madding crowd's ignoble strife,
Their sober wishes never learned to stray;
Along the cool sequestered vale of life
They kept the noiseless tenor of their way.
Thomas Gray 1716–71 English poet

Fame

Popularity? It is glory's small change.
Victor Hugo 1802–85 French writer

Kids want to be famous. They don't want to be good at anything any more.
Ronan Keating 1977– Irish pop singer

We're more popular than Jesus now; I don't know which will go first—rock 'n' roll or Christianity.
John Lennon 1940–80 English pop singer, *of the Beatles*

Fame is the spur that the clear spirit doth raise
(That last infirmity of noble mind)
To scorn delights, and live laborious days.
John Milton 1608–74 English poet

Famous men have the whole earth as their memorial.
Pericles c.495–429 BC Greek statesman

So long as men can breathe, or eyes can see,
So long lives this, and this gives life to thee.
William Shakespeare 1564–1616 English dramatist

You always hide just in the middle of the limelight.
George Bernard Shaw 1856–1950 Irish dramatist, *to T. E. Lawrence, who had complained of Press attention*

Celebrity is a mask that eats into the face.
John Updike 1932–2009 American writer

In the future everybody will be world famous for fifteen minutes.
Andy Warhol 1927–87 American artist

❋ The Family ⇒Children, Parents

He that hath wife and children hath given hostages to fortune; for they are impediments to great enterprises, either of virtue or mischief.
Francis Bacon 1561–1626 English courtier

Thy wife shall be as the fruitful vine: upon the walls of thine house.
Thy children like the olive-branches: round about thy table.

Bible

We begin our public affections in our families. No cold relation is a zealous citizen.

Edmund Burke 1729–97 Irish-born politician

[It is] time to turn our attention to pressing challenges like…how to make American families more like the Waltons and a little bit less like the Simpsons.

George Bush 1924– American statesman

Believe me, family solidarity is after all the only good thing. I have been deprived of it, so I know.

Marie Curie 1867–1934 Polish-born French physicist

The truth is that it is not the sins of the fathers that descend unto the third generation, but the sorrows of the mothers.

Marilyn French 1929–2009 American writer

One would be in less danger
From the wiles of the stranger
If one's own kin and kith
Were more fun to be with.

Ogden Nash 1902–71 American humorist

A little more than kin, and less than kind.

William Shakespeare 1564–1616 English dramatist

If a man's character is to be abused, say what you will, there's nobody like a relation to do the business.

William Makepeace Thackeray 1811–63 English novelist

All happy families resemble one another, but each unhappy family is unhappy in its own way.

Leo Tolstoy 1828–1910 Russian novelist

The Family

It is no use telling me that there are bad aunts and good aunts. At the core, they are all alike. Sooner or later, out pops the cloven hoof.

P. G. Wodehouse 1881–1975 English writer

✳ Fashion

A little of what you call frippery is very necessary towards looking like the rest of the world.

Abigail Adams 1744–1818 American letter writer

Fashion often starts off beautiful and becomes ugly, whereas art starts off ugly sometimes and becomes beautiful.

David Bailey 1938– English photographer

Fashion isn't made to be canned. Fashion in cans becomes quickly obsolete.

Coco Chanel 1883–1971 French couturière

One had as good be out of the world, as out of the fashion.

Colley Cibber 1671–1757 English dramatist

Sometimes fashion moves from the moment to the moment to the moment. But where is the integrity in design?

Donna Karan 1948– American fashion designer

Haute Couture should be fun, foolish and almost unwearable.

Christian Lacroix 1951– French couturier

Hip is the sophistication of the wise primitive in a giant jungle.

Norman Mailer 1923–2007 American writer

Fashion is more usually a gentle progression of revisited ideas.
   Bruce Oldfield 1950– English fashion designer

Every generation laughs at the old fashions, but follows religiously the new.
   Henry David Thoreau 1817–62 American writer

It is charming to totter into vogue.
   Horace Walpole 1717–97 English connoisseur

Fate ✳

Must it be? It must be.
   Ludwig van Beethoven 1770–1827 German composer

Canst thou bind the sweet influences of Pleiades, or loose the bands of Orion?
   Bible

Fate is not an eagle, it creeps like a rat.
   Elizabeth Bowen 1899–1973 Anglo-Irish novelist

Nothing have I found stronger than Necessity.
   Euripides c.485–c.406 BC Greek dramatist

There once was a man who said, 'Damn!
It is borne in upon me I am
An engine that moves
In predestinate grooves,
I'm not even a bus, I'm a tram.'
   Maurice Evan Hare 1886–1967 English limerick writer

What we call fate does not come into us from the outside, but emerges from us.
   Rainer Maria Rilke 1875–1926 German poet

Fate

If it be now, 'tis not to come; if it be not to come, it will be now; if it be not now, yet it will come: the readiness is all.

William Shakespeare 1564–1616 English dramatist

We are merely the stars' tennis-balls, struck and bandied Which way please them.

John Webster c.1580–c.1625 English dramatist

Every bullet has its billet.

William III 1650–1702 British monarch

✳ Fathers

You can't understand it until you experience the simple joy of the first time your son points at a seagull and says 'duck'.

Russell Crowe 1964– New Zealand actor, *on fatherhood*

There must be many fathers around the country who have experienced the cruellest, most crushing rejection of all: their children have ended up supporting the wrong team.

Nick Hornby 1957– British writer

After God comes my Papa—that was ever the motto, the axiom of my childhood and I cling to it still!

Wolfgang Amadeus Mozart 1756–91 Austrian composer

Being a father
Is quite a bother,
But I like it, rather.

Ogden Nash 1902–71 American humorist

I can do one of two things. I can be president of the United States or I can control Alice. I cannot possibly do both.

Theodore Roosevelt 1858–1919 American statesman, *on his daughter*

The fundamental defect of fathers, in our competitive society, is that they want their children to be a credit to them.

Bertrand Russell 1872–1970 British philosopher

It doesn't matter who my father was; it matters who I remember he was.

Anne Sexton 1928–74 American poet

It is a wise father that knows his own child.

William Shakespeare 1564–1616 English dramatist

Fatherhood is a mirror in which we catch glimpses of ourselves as we really are.

Hugo Williams 1942– British writer

Fear ✳

We must travel in the direction of our fear.

John Berryman 1914–72 American poet

No passion so effectually robs the mind of all its powers of acting and reasoning as fear.

Edmund Burke 1729–97 Irish-born politician

If hopes were dupes, fears may be liars.

Arthur Hugh Clough 1819–61 English poet

Be afraid. Be very afraid.

David Cronenberg 1943– Canadian film director

I will show you fear in a handful of dust.

T. S. Eliot 1888–1965 American-born British poet

There is no terror in a bang, only in the anticipation of it.

Alfred Hitchcock 1899–1980 British-born film director

Terror…often arises from a pervasive sense of disestablishment; that things are in the unmaking.

Stephen King 1947– American writer

Fear

Fear is, of all passions, that which weakens the judgment most.
Cardinal de Retz 1613–79 French cardinal

The only thing we have to fear is fear itself.
Franklin D. Roosevelt 1882–1945 American statesman

Only the unknown frightens men. But once a man has faced the unknown, that terror becomes known.
Antoine de Saint-Exupéry 1900–44 French novelist

> Present fears
Are less than horrible imaginings.
William Shakespeare 1564–1616 English dramatist

In time we hate that which we often fear.
William Shakespeare 1564–1616 English dramatist

Our deepest fear is not that we are inadequate. Our deepest fear is that we are powerful beyond measure. It is our light, not our darkness, that most frightens us.
Marianne Williamson 1953– American writer

✳ Festivals ⇒Christmas

Hogmanay, like all festivals, being but a bank from which we can only draw what we put in.
J. M. Barrie 1860–1937 Scottish writer

Hurrah for the fun!
Is the pudding done?
Hurrah for the pumpkin pie!
Lydia Maria Child 1802–80 American abolitionist

The true essentials of a feast are only fun and feed.
Oliver Wendell Holmes 1809–94 American physician

The holiest of all holidays are those
Kept by ourselves in silence and apart;
The secret anniversaries of the heart.
Henry Wadsworth Longfellow 1807–82 American poet

Time has no divisions to mark its passage, there is never
a thunderstorm or blare of trumpets to announce the
beginning of a new month or year. Even when a new
century begins it is only we mortals who ring bells and
fire off pistols.
Thomas Mann 1875–1955 German novelist

Tonight's December thirty-first,
Something is about to burst…
Hark, it's midnight, children dear.
Duck! Here comes another year!
Ogden Nash 1902–71 American humorist

Ring out the old, ring in the new,
Ring, happy bells, across the snow:
The year is going, let him go;
Ring out the false, ring in the true.
Alfred, Lord Tennyson 1809–92 English poet

April 1. This is the day upon which we are reminded of
what we are on the other three hundred and sixty-four.
Mark Twain 1835–1910 American writer

Fishing ✳

If fishing is a religion, fly fishing is high church.
Tom Brokaw 1940– American journalist

I love fishing. It's like transcendental meditation with a
punch-line.
Billy Connolly 1942– Scottish comedian

Fishing

Fishing is unquestionably a form of madness but, happily, for the once-bitten there is no cure.
Lord Home 1903–95 British statesman

All men are equal before fish.
Herbert Hoover 1874–1964 American statesman

Fly fishing may be a very pleasant amusement; but angling or float fishing I can only compare to a stick and a string, with a worm at one end and a fool at the other.
Samuel Johnson 1709–84 English lexicographer

As no man is born an artist, so no man is born an angler.
Izaak Walton 1593–1683 English writer

✳ Flight

Had I been a man I might have explored the Poles, or climbed Mount Everest, but as it was, my spirit found outlet in the air.
Amy Johnson 1903–41 English aviator

I feel about airplanes the way I feel about diets. It seems to me that they are wonderful things for other people to go on.
Jean Kerr 1923–2003 American writer

I was astonished at the effect my successful landing in France had on the nations of the world. To me, it was like a match lighting a bonfire.
Charles Lindbergh 1902–74 American aviator

Oh! I have slipped the surly bonds of earth
And danced the skies on laughter-silvered wings;...
And, while with silent lifting mind I've trod
The high, untrespassed sanctity of space,
Put out my hand and touched the face of God.
John Gillespie Magee 1922–41 American airman

I did not fully understand the dread term 'terminal illness' until I saw Heathrow for myself.
Dennis Potter 1935–94 English dramatist

There are only two emotions in a plane: boredom and terror.
Orson Welles 1915–85 American film director

Flowers ✳

Unkempt about those hedges blows
An English unofficial rose.
Rupert Brooke 1887–1915 English poet

Flowers…are a proud assertion that a ray of beauty outvalues all the utilities of the world.
Ralph Waldo Emerson 1803–82 American writer

I sometimes think that never blows so red
The rose as where some buried Caesar bled.
Edward Fitzgerald 1809–83 English poet

Hey, buds below, up is where to grow,
Up with which below can't compare with.
Hurry! It's lovely up here! *Hurry*!
Alan Jay Lerner 1918–86 American songwriter

People from a planet without flowers would think we must be mad with joy the whole time to have such things about us.
Iris Murdoch 1919–99 English novelist

Daffodils,
That come before the swallow dares, and take
The winds of March with beauty.
William Shakespeare 1564–1616 English dramatist

Flowers

I wandered lonely as a cloud
That floats on high o'er vales and hills,
When all at once I saw a crowd,
A host, of golden daffodils;
Beside the lake, beneath the trees,
Fluttering and dancing in the breeze.
William Wordsworth 1770–1850 English poet

To me the meanest flower that blows can give
Thoughts that do often lie too deep for tears.
William Wordsworth 1770–1850 English poet

✳ Food ⇒Cookery, Eating

Shake and shake
The catsup bottle.
None will come,
And then a lot'll.
Richard Armour 1906–89 American poet

I'm President of the United States, and I'm not going to
eat any more broccoli!
George Bush 1924- American statesman

Doubtless God could have made a better berry, but
doubtless God never did.
William Butler 1535–1618 English physician, *on the strawberry*

Take away that pudding—it has no theme.
Winston Churchill 1874–1965 British statesman

OLIVER TWIST: Please, sir, I want some more.
Charles Dickens 1812-70 English novelist

Cheese, milk's leap toward immortality.
Clifton Fadiman 1904-99 American critic

A cucumber should be well sliced, and dressed with pepper and vinegar, and then thrown out, as good for nothing.
Samuel Johnson 1709–84 English lexicographer

I am a great eater of beef, and I believe that does harm to my wit.
William Shakespeare 1564–1616 English dramatist

There is no love sincerer than the love of food.
George Bernard Shaw 1856–1950 Irish dramatist

A hen's egg is, quite simply, a work of art, a masterpiece of design and construction with, it has to be said, brilliant packaging.
Delia Smith English cook

Serenely full, the epicure would say,
Fate cannot harm me, I have dined to-day.
Sydney Smith 1771–1845 English essayist

Many's the long night I've dreamed of cheese—toasted, mostly.
Robert Louis Stevenson 1850–94 Scottish novelist

Cauliflower is nothing but cabbage with a college education.
Mark Twain 1835–1910 American writer

What moistens the lip and what brightens the eye?
What calls back the past, like the rich pumpkin pie?
John Greenleaf Whittier 1807–92 American poet

Foolishness

The world is full of fools, and he who would not see it should live alone and smash his mirror.
Anonymous

Foolishness

There's a sucker born every minute.
Phineas T. Barnum 1810–91 American showman

For ye suffer fools gladly, seeing ye yourselves are wise.
Bible

Never give a sucker an even break.
W. C. Fields 1880–1946 American humorist

Mix a little foolishness with your prudence: it's good to be silly at the right moment.
Horace 65–8 BC Roman poet

A knowledgeable fool is a greater fool than an ignorant fool.
Molière 1622–73 French comic dramatist

Fools rush in where angels fear to tread.
Alexander Pope 1688–1744 English poet

The follies which a man regrets most, in his life, are those which he didn't commit when he had the opportunity.
Helen Rowland 1875–1950 American writer

The ultimate result of shielding men from the effects of folly, is to fill the world with fools.
Herbert Spencer 1820–1903 English philosopher

Let us be thankful for the fools. But for them the rest of us could not succeed.
Mark Twain 1835–1910 American writer

Be wise with speed;
A fool at forty is a fool indeed.
Edward Young 1683–1765 English poet

✳ Football

The great fallacy is that the game is first and last about winning. It is nothing of the kind. The game is about glory, it is about doing things in style and with a flourish,

about going out and beating the lot, not waiting for them to die of boredom.
Danny Blanchflower 1926–93 English footballer

Football, wherein is nothing but beastly fury, and extreme violence, whereof proceedeth hurt, and consequently rancour and malice do remain with them that be wounded.
Thomas Elyot 1499–1546 English diplomat

Football is an art more central to our culture than anything the Arts Council deigns to recognize.
Germaine Greer 1939– Australian feminist

What makes a sane and rational person subject himself to such humiliation? Why on earth does anyone want to become a football referee?
Roy Hattersley 1932– British politician

The natural state of the football fan is bitter disappointment, no matter what the score.
Nick Hornby 1957– British writer

Football is a simple game; 22 men chase a ball for 90 minutes and at the end, the Germans win.
Gary Lineker 1960– English footballer

Oh, he's football crazy, he's football mad
And the football it has robbed him o' the wee bit sense he had.
Jimmie McGregor 1932– Scottish singer

The goal was scored a little bit by the hand of God, another bit by head of Maradona.
Diego Maradona 1960– Argentinian footballer, *on his controversial goal against England in the 1986 World Cup*

Football? It's the beautiful game.
Pelé 1940– Brazilian footballer

Football

To say that these men paid their shillings to watch twenty-two hirelings kick a ball is merely to say that a violin is wood and catgut, that *Hamlet* is so much paper and ink. For a shilling the Bruddersford United AFC offered you Conflict and Art.

J. B. Priestley 1894–1984 English writer

Some people think football is a matter of life and death...I can assure them it is much more serious than that.

Bill Shankly 1913–81 Scottish footballer

Football and cookery are the two most important subjects in the country.

Delia Smith English cook

✳ Forgiveness

Her sins, which are many, are forgiven; for she loved much.

Bible

It is easier to forgive an enemy than to forgive a friend.

William Blake 1757–1827 English poet

I shall be an autocrat: that's my trade. And the good Lord will forgive me: that's his.

Catherine the Great 1729–96 Russian empress

After such knowledge, what forgiveness?

T. S. Eliot 1888–1965 American-born British poet

God may pardon you, but I never can.

Elizabeth I 1533–1603 English monarch

Every one says forgiveness is a lovely idea, until they have something to forgive.

C. S. Lewis 1898–1963 English literary scholar

True reconciliation does not consist in merely forgetting the past.
   Nelson Mandela 1918-   South African statesman

We read that we ought to forgive our enemies; but we do not read that we ought to forgive our friends.
   Cosimo de' Medici 1389-1464 Italian statesman

When a deep injury is done to us, we never recover until we forgive.
   Alan Paton 1903-88 South African writer

To err is human; to forgive, divine.
   Alexander Pope 1688-1744 English poet

Youth, which is forgiven everything, forgives itself nothing: age, which forgives itself everything, is forgiven nothing.
   George Bernard Shaw 1856-1950 Irish dramatist

The stupid neither forgive nor forget; the naïve forgive and forget; the wise forgive but do not forget.
   Thomas Szasz 1920-   Hungarian-born psychiatrist

France ✳

Everything ends this way in France. Weddings, christenings, duels, burials, swindlings, affairs of state— everything is a pretext for a good dinner.
   Jean Anouilh 1910-87 French dramatist

France was long a despotism tempered by epigrams.
   Thomas Carlyle 1795-1881 Scottish historian

How can you govern a country which has 246 varieties of cheese?
   Charles de Gaulle 1890-1970 French statesman

France, mother of arts, of warfare, and of laws.
   Joachim Du Bellay 1522-60 French poet

France

Vive la différence, mais vive l'entente cordiale.
Long live the difference, but long live the Entente
Cordiale.
Elizabeth II 1926– British monarch

GROUNDSKEEPER WILLIE AS FRENCH TEACHER: Bonjourr,
you cheese-eating surrender monkeys.
Matt Groening 1954– American humorist

The French soul is stronger than the French mind, and
Voltaire shatters against Joan of Arc.
Victor Hugo 1802–85 French writer

What is not clear is not French.
Antoine de Rivarol 1753–1801 French man of letters

They order, said I, this matter better in France.
Laurence Sterne 1713–68 English novelist

If the French noblesse had been capable of playing cricket
with their peasants, their chateaux would never have been
burnt.
G. M. Trevelyan 1876–1962 English historian

✳ Friendship

Oh, the comfort—the inexpressible comfort of feeling safe
with a person, having neither to weigh thoughts, nor
measure words, but pouring them all out, just as they are,
chaff and grain together; knowing that a faithful hand
will take and sift them—keep what is worth keeping—
and with the breath of kindness blow the rest away.
Anonymous *often attributed to George Eliot or Dinah Mulock
Craik*

Champagne for my real friends, real pain for my sham
friends.
Francis Bacon 1909–92 Irish painter

We must take our friends as they are.
James Boswell 1740–95 Scottish lawyer

There is no man so friendless but what he can find a friend sincere enough to tell him disagreeable truths.
Edward Bulwer-Lytton 1803–73 British novelist

Should auld acquaintance be forgot
And never brought to mind?
Robert Burns 1759–96 Scottish poet

Friendship is like money, easier made than kept.
Samuel Butler 1835–1902 English novelist

Give me the avowed, erect and manly foe;
Firm I can meet, perhaps return the blow;
But of all plagues, good Heaven, thy wrath can send,
Save me, oh, save me, from the candid friend.
George Canning 1770–1827 British statesman

A woman can become a man's friend only in the following stages—first an acquaintance, next a mistress, and only then a friend.
Anton Chekhov 1860–1904 Russian writer

The only reward of virtue is virtue; the only way to have a friend is to be one.
Ralph Waldo Emerson 1803–82 American writer

HUMPHREY BOGART: Louis, I think this is the beginning of a beautiful friendship.
Julius J. Epstein 1909–2001 et al., American screenwriters, *in the film* Casablanca

My father always used to say that when you die, if you've got five real friends, you've had a great life.
Lee Iacocca 1924– American businessman

If a man does not make new acquaintance as he advances through life, he will soon find himself left alone. A man, Sir, should keep his friendship in constant repair.
Samuel Johnson 1709–84 English lexicographer

Friendship

However rare true love may be, true friendship is rarer.

Duc de la Rochefoucauld 1613–80 French moralist

Oh I get by with a little help from my friends,
Mm, I get high with a little help from my friends.

John Lennon 1940–80 and **Paul McCartney** 1942– English pop singers

To like and dislike the same things, that is indeed true friendship.

Sallust 86–35 BC Roman historian

Friendship is constant in all other things
Save in the office and affairs of love.

William Shakespeare 1564–1616 English dramatist

I do not believe that friends are necessarily the people you like best, they are merely the people who got there first.

Peter Ustinov 1921–2004 British actor

✳ The Future

'We are always doing', says he, 'something for Posterity, but I would fain see Posterity do something for us.'

Joseph Addison 1672–1719 English writer

Some of the jam we thought was for tomorrow, we've already eaten.

Tony Benn 1925– British politician

The future ain't what it used to be.

Yogi Berra 1925– American baseball player

Predictions can be very difficult—especially about the future.

Niels Bohr 1885–1962 Danish physicist

You can never plan the future by the past.

Edmund Burke 1729–97 Irish-born politician

The empires of the future are the empires of the mind.
Winston Churchill 1874–1965 British statesman

I never think of the future. It comes soon enough.
Albert Einstein 1879–1955 German-born theoretical physicist

You cannot fight against the future. Time is on our side.
W. E. Gladstone 1809–98 British statesman

The best way to predict the future is to invent it.
Alan Kay 1940– American computer scientist

We have trained them [men] to think of the Future as a promised land which favoured heroes attain—not as something which everyone reaches at the rate of sixty minutes an hour, whatever he does, whoever he is.
C. S. Lewis 1898–1963 English literary scholar

If you want a picture of the future, imagine a boot stamping on a human face—for ever.
George Orwell 1903–50 English novelist

Lord! we know what we are, but know not what we may be.
William Shakespeare 1564–1616 English dramatist

Gardens ✳

I value my garden more for being full of blackbirds than of cherries, and very frankly give them fruit for their songs.
Joseph Addison 1672–1719 English writer

Nothing is more pleasant to the eye than green grass kept finely shorn.
Francis Bacon 1561–1626 English courtier

A garden is a lovesome thing, God wot!
T. E. Brown 1830–97 Manx schoolmaster

Gardens

As long as one has a garden, one has a future; and as long as one has a future one is alive.

Frances Hodgson Burnett 1849–1924 British-born American novelist

What is a weed? A plant whose virtues have not been discovered.

Ralph Waldo Emerson 1803–82 American writer

He that plants trees loves others beside himself.

Thomas Fuller 1654–1734 English physician

Sowe Carrets in your Gardens, and humbly praise God for them, as for a singular and great blessing.

Richard Gardiner b. c.1533– English writer

The kiss of the sun for pardon,
The song of the birds for mirth,
One is nearer God's Heart in a garden
Than anywhere else on earth.

Dorothy Frances Gurney 1858–1932 English poet

But though an old man, I am but a young gardener.

Thomas Jefferson 1743–1826 American statesman

Our England is a garden, and such gardens are not made
By singing:—'Oh, how beautiful!' and sitting in the shade,
While better men than we go out and start their working lives
At grubbing weeds from gravel paths with broken dinner-knives.

Rudyard Kipling 1865–1936 English writer

A garden was the primitive prison till man with Promethean felicity and boldness luckily sinned himself out of it.

Charles Lamb 1775–1834 English writer

Annihilating all that's made
To a green thought in a green shade.

Andrew Marvell 1621–78 English poet

Come into the garden, Maud,
I am here at the gate alone.
   Alfred, Lord Tennyson 1809–92 English poet

The Generation Gap ⇒Youth ✳

What's the point in growing old if you can't hound and
persecute the young?
   Kenneth Clarke 1940– British politician

Come mothers and fathers,
Throughout the land
And don't criticize
What you can't understand.
   Bob Dylan 1941– American singer

Si jeunesse savait; si vieillesse pouvait.
If youth knew; if age could.
   Henri Estienne 1531–98 French printer

Every generation revolts against its fathers and makes
friends with its grandfathers.
   Lewis Mumford 1895–1982 American sociologist

Crabbed age and youth cannot live together:
Youth is full of pleasance, age is full of care.
   William Shakespeare 1564–1616 English dramatist

It's all that the young can do for the old, to shock them
and keep them up to date.
   George Bernard Shaw 1856–1950 Irish dramatist

Nothing so dates a man as to decry the younger
generation.
   Adlai Stevenson 1900–65 American politician

Hope I die before I get old.
   Pete Townshend 1945– British rock musician

The Generation Gap

When I was a boy of 14, my father was so ignorant I could hardly stand to have the old man around. But when I got to be 21, I was astonished at how much the old man had learned in seven years.
> **Mark Twain** 1835–1910 American writer

✳ Genius

Genius is only a greater aptitude for patience.
> **Comte de Buffon** 1707–88 French naturalist

Everybody has talent at twenty-five. The difficult thing is to have it at fifty.
> **Edgar Degas** 1834–1917 French artist

Mediocrity knows nothing higher than itself, but talent instantly recognizes genius.
> **Arthur Conan Doyle** 1859–1930 Scottish-born writer

Great wits are sure to madness near allied,
And thin partitions do their bounds divide.
> **John Dryden** 1631–1700 English poet

Genius is one per cent inspiration, ninety-nine per cent perspiration.
> **Thomas Alva Edison** 1847–1931 American inventor

Little minds are interested in the extraordinary; great minds in the commonplace.
> **Elbert Hubbard** 1859–1915 American writer

The true genius is a mind of large general powers, accidentally determined to some particular direction.
> **Samuel Johnson** 1709–84 English lexicographer

It's not fun being a genius. It's torture.
> **John Lennon** 1940–80 English pop singer

Genius does what it must, and Talent does what it can.
> **Owen Meredith** 1831–91 English statesman

Every positive value has its price in negative terms…The genius of Einstein leads to Hiroshima.

Pablo Picasso 1881–1973 Spanish painter

Genius is always allowed some leeway, once the hammer has been pried from its hands and the blood has been cleaned up.

Terry Pratchett 1948– English novelist

It takes a lot of time to be a genius, you have to sit around so much doing nothing, really doing nothing.

Gertrude Stein 1874–1946 American writer

When a true genius appears in the world, you may know him by this sign, that the dunces are all in confederacy against him.

Jonathan Swift 1667–1745 Irish poet and satirist

I have nothing to declare except my genius.

Oscar Wilde 1854–1900 Irish dramatist, *at the New York Custom House*

Gifts ⇒Charity

Surprises are foolish things. The pleasure is not enhanced, and the inconvenience is often considerable.

Jane Austen 1775–1817 English novelist

It is more blessed to give than to receive.

Bible

They gave it me,—for an un-birthday present.

Lewis Carroll 1832–98 English writer

One must be poor to know the luxury of giving.

George Eliot 1819–80 English novelist

A gift though small is welcome.

Homer 8th century BC Greek poet

Gifts

I know it's not much, but it's the best I can do,
My gift is my song and this one's for you.
> **Elton John** 1947– and **Bernie Taupin** 1950– English pop
> singer and English songwriter

Presents, I often say, endear Absents.
> **Charles Lamb** 1775–1834 English writer

Why is it no one ever sent me yet
One perfect limousine, do you suppose?
Ah no, it's always just my luck to get
One perfect rose.
> **Dorothy Parker** 1893–1967 American critic

SEAN CONNERY: The key to a woman's heart is an
unexpected gift at an unexpected time.
> **Mike Rich** 1959– American screenwriter, *in the film* Finding
> Forrester

I am not in the giving vein to-day.
> **William Shakespeare** 1564–1616 English dramatist

✳ God ⇒Religion

The nature of God is a circle of which the centre is
everywhere and the circumference is nowhere.
> **Anonymous**

In the beginning was the Word, and the Word was with
God, and the Word was God.
> **Bible**

He that loveth not knoweth not God; for God is love.
> **Bible**

When men stop believing in God they don't believe in
nothing; they believe in anything.
> **G. K. Chesterton** 1874–1936 English writer

God moves in a mysterious way
His wonders to perform.
    William Cowper 1731–1800 English poet

God is subtle but he is not malicious.
    Albert Einstein 1879–1955 German-born theoretical physicist

Operationally, God is beginning to resemble not a ruler
but the last fading smile of a cosmic Cheshire cat.
    Julian Huxley 1887–1975 English biologist

An honest God is the noblest work of man.
    Robert G. Ingersoll 1833–99 American agnostic

God seems to have left the receiver off the hook, and
time is running out.
    Arthur Koestler 1905–83 Hungarian-born writer

Praise belongs to God, the Lord of all Being,
the All-merciful, the All-compassionate.
    The Koran

Though the mills of God grind slowly, yet they grind
   exceeding small;
Though with patience He stands waiting, with exactness
   grinds He all.
    Henry Wadsworth Longfellow 1807–82 American poet

Whatever your heart clings to and confides in, that is
really your God.
    Martin Luther 1483–1546 German theologian

If the triangles were to make a God they would give him
three sides.
    Montesquieu 1689–1755 French political philosopher

The Buddha, the Godhead, resides quite as comfortably in
the circuits of a digital computer or the gears of a cycle
transmission as he does at the top of a mountain or in
the petals of a flower.
    Robert M. Pirsig 1928– American writer

God

Hear, O Israel: the Lord our God, the Lord is One.
The Siddur

O Lord, to what a state dost Thou bring those who love
Thee!
St Teresa of Ávila 1512–82 Spanish mystic

For man proposes, but God disposes.
Thomas à Kempis c.1380–1471 German writer

If God did not exist, it would be necessary to invent him.
Voltaire 1694–1778 French writer

Our God, our help in ages past
Our hope for years to come,
Our shelter from the stormy blast,
And our eternal home.
Isaac Watts 1674–1748 English hymn-writer

☀ Golf

If you watch a game, it's fun. If you play it, it's
recreation. If you work at it, it's golf.
Bob Hope 1903–2003 American comedian

Golf is a good walk spoiled.
Mark Twain 1835–1910 American writer

The least thing upset him on the links. He missed short
putts because of the uproar of the butterflies in the
adjoining meadows.
P. G. Wodehouse 1881–1975 English writer

Golf…is the infallible test. The man who can go into a
patch of rough alone, with the knowledge that only God
is watching him, and play his ball where it lies, is the
man who will serve you faithfully and well.
P. G. Wodehouse 1881–1975 English writer

Good Looks ✳

A pretty girl is like a melody
That haunts you night and day.
Irving Berlin 1888–1989 American songwriter

And she was fayr as is the rose in May.
Geoffrey Chaucer c.1343–1400 English poet

When a woman isn't beautiful, people always say, 'You
have lovely eyes, you have lovely hair.'
Anton Chekhov 1860–1904 Russian writer

Beauty is the lover's gift.
William Congreve 1670–1729 English dramatist

Is it too much to ask that women be spared the daily
struggle for superhuman beauty in order to offer it to the
caresses of a subhumanly ugly mate?
Germaine Greer 1939– Australian feminist

I'm tired of all this nonsense about beauty being only
skin-deep. That's deep enough. What do you want—an
adorable pancreas?
Jean Kerr 1923–2003 American writer

The Lord prefers common-looking people. That is why he
makes so many of them.
Abraham Lincoln 1809–65 American statesman

A beautiful face is a mute recommendation.
Publilius Syrus 1st century BC Roman writer

Shall I compare thee to a summer's day?
Thou art more lovely and more temperate.
William Shakespeare 1564–1616 English dramatist

✳ Goodness →Evil

Every art and every investigation, and likewise every practical pursuit or undertaking, seems to aim at some good: hence it has been well said that the Good is That at which all things aim.
Aristotle 384–322 BC Greek philosopher

He who would do good to another, must do it in minute particulars.
William Blake 1757–1827 English poet

Terrible is the temptation to be good.
Bertolt Brecht 1898–1956 German dramatist

No one can be good for long if goodness is not in demand.
Bertolt Brecht 1898–1956 German dramatist

Integrity has no need of rules.
Albert Camus 1913–60 French writer

No people do so much harm as those who go about doing good.
Mandell Creighton 1843–1901 English prelate

What after all
Is a halo? It's only one more thing to keep clean.
Christopher Fry 1907–2005 English dramatist

I expect to pass through this world but once; any good thing therefore that I can do, or any kindness that I can show to any fellow-creature, let me do it now; let me not defer or neglect it, for I shall not pass this way again.
Stephen Grellet 1773–1855 French missionary

Be good, sweet maid, and let who will be clever.
Charles Kingsley 1819–75 English writer

Good and evil shall not be held equal. Turn away evil with that which is better; and behold the man between whom and thyself there was enmity, shall become, as it were, thy warmest friend.
The Koran

A man who wants to act virtuously in every way necessarily comes to grief among so many who are not virtuous.
Niccolò Machiavelli 1469–1527 Italian political philosopher

Virtue she finds too painful an endeavour,
Content to dwell in decencies for ever.
Alexander Pope 1688–1744 English poet

Dost thou think, because thou art virtuous, there shall be no more cakes and ale?
William Shakespeare 1564–1616 English dramatist

How far that little candle throws his beams!
So shines a good deed in a naughty world.
William Shakespeare 1564–1616 English dramatist

Our goodness derives not from our capacity to think but to love.
St Teresa of Ávila 1512–82 Spanish mystic

Would that we had spent one whole day well in this world!
Thomas à Kempis c.1380–1471 German writer

Virtue knows to a farthing what it has lost by not having been vice.
Horace Walpole 1717–97 English connoisseur

'Goodness, what beautiful diamonds!'
'Goodness had nothing to do with it.'
Mae West 1892–1980 American film actress

Goodness

That best portion of a good man's life,
His little, nameless, unremembered, acts
Of kindness and of love.
William Wordsworth 1770–1850 English poet

Gossip

There is so much good in the worst of us,
And so much bad in the best of us,
That it hardly becomes any of us
To talk about the rest of us.
Anonymous

Careless talk costs lives.
Anonymous *Second World War security slogan*

Every man is surrounded by a neighbourhood of
voluntary spies.
Jane Austen 1775–1817 English novelist

They come together like the Coroner's Inquest, to sit
upon the murdered reputations of the week.
William Congreve 1670–1729 English dramatist

Gossip is a sort of smoke that comes from the dirty
tobacco-pipes of those who diffuse it: it proves nothing
but the bad taste of the smoker.
George Eliot 1819–80 English novelist

Love and scandal are the best sweeteners of tea.
Henry Fielding 1707–54 English novelist

Like all gossip—it's merely one of those half-alive things
that try to crowd out real life.
E. M. Forster 1879–1970 English novelist

No one gossips about other people's secret virtues.
Bertrand Russell 1872–1970 British philosopher

It takes your enemy and your friend, working together, to hurt you to the heart: the one to slander you and the other to get the news to you.
Mark Twain 1835–1910 American writer

There is only one thing in the world worse than being talked about, and that is not being talked about.
Oscar Wilde 1854–1900 Irish dramatist

Government →Politics

Let them hate, so long as they fear.
Accius 170–c.86 BC Roman poet

The happiness of society is the end of government.
John Adams 1735–1826 American statesman

Dullness in matters of government is a good sign, and not a bad one.
Walter Bagehot 1826–77 English economist

The object of government in peace and in war is not the glory of rulers or of races, but the happiness of the common man.
William Henry Beveridge 1879–1963 British economist

England is the mother of Parliaments.
John Bright 1811–89 English politician

The poor have sometimes objected to being governed badly; the rich have always objected to being governed at all.
G. K. Chesterton 1874–1936 English writer

It is a 'beautiful maxim' that it is necessary to save five *sous* on unessential things, and to pour out millions when it is a question of your glory.
Jean-Baptiste Colbert 1619–83 French statesman

Government

No Government can be long secure without a formidable Opposition.
Benjamin Disraeli 1804–81 British statesman

Though God hath raised me high, yet this I count the glory of my crown: that I have reigned with your loves.
Elizabeth I 1533–1603 English monarch

If the Government is big enough to give you everything you want, it is big enough to take away everything you have.
Gerald Ford 1909–2006 American statesman

The state is like the human body. Not all of its functions are dignified.
Anatole France 1844–1924 French man of letters

My people and I have come to an agreement which satisfies us both. They are to say what they please, and I am to do what I please.
Frederick the Great 1712–86 Prussian monarch

Your business is not to govern the country but it is, if you think fit, to call to account those who do govern it.
W. E. Gladstone 1809–98 British statesman, *to the House of Commons*

Many journalists have fallen for the conspiracy theory of government. I do assure you that they would produce more accurate work if they adhered to the cock-up theory.
Bernard Ingham 1932– British journalist

The important thing for Government is not to do things which individuals are doing already, and to do them a little better or a little worse; but to do those things which at present are not done at all.
John Maynard Keynes 1883–1946 English economist

To govern is to choose.
Duc de Lévis 1764–1830 French soldier

It is much safer for a prince to be feared than loved, if he is to fail in one of the two.
Niccolò Machiavelli 1469–1527 Italian political philosopher

BIG BROTHER IS WATCHING YOU.
George Orwell 1903–50 English novelist

The best government is that which governs least.
John L. O'Sullivan 1813–95 American journalist

For forms of government let fools contest;
Whate'er is best administered is best.
Alexander Pope 1688–1744 English poet

Wherever you have an efficient government you have a dictatorship.
Harry S. Truman 1884–1972 American statesman

Governments need both shepherds and butchers.
Voltaire 1694–1778 French writer

Greatness ✻

The beauty of Israel is slain upon thy high places: how are the mighty fallen!
Bible

JOHN CUSACK: I'm looking for a dare-to-be-great situation.
Cameron Crowe 1957– American film director, *in the film* Say Anything

To be great is to be misunderstood.
Ralph Waldo Emerson 1803–82 American writer

A man does not attain the status of Galileo merely because he is persecuted; he must also be right.
Stephen Jay Gould 1941–2002 American palaeontologist

Greatness

But be not afraid of greatness: some men are born great, some achieve greatness, and some have greatness thrust upon them.
William Shakespeare 1564–1616 English dramatist

All the world's great have been little boys who wanted the moon.
John Steinbeck 1902–68 American novelist

✳ Habit

The less of routine, the more of life.
Amos Bronson Alcott 1799–1888 American reformer

Routine, in an intelligent man, is a sign of ambition.
W. H. Auden 1907–73 English poet

Habit is a great deadener.
Samuel Beckett 1906–89 Irish writer

Habit with him was all the test of truth,
'It must be right: I've done it from my youth.'
George Crabbe 1754–1832 English poet

Sow an act, and you reap a habit. Sow a habit and you reap a character. Sow a character, and you reap a destiny.
Charles Reade 1814–84 English writer

Good habits: they are never good, because they are habits.
Jean-Paul Sartre 1905–80 French philosopher

✳ Happiness

Mirth is like a flash of lightning that breaks through a gloom of clouds, and glitters for a moment: cheerfulness keeps up a kind of day-light in the mind.
Joseph Addison 1672–1719 English writer

Happiness

A large income is the best recipe for happiness I ever heard of. It certainly may secure all the myrtle and turkey part of it.
Jane Austen 1775–1817 English novelist

Happiness washes away many things, just as suffering washes away many things.
Heinrich Böll 1917–85 German writer

There may be Peace without Joy, and Joy without Peace, but the two combined make Happiness.
John Buchan 1875–1940 Scottish novelist

Happiness is…finding two olives in your martini when you're hungry.
Johnny Carson 1925–2005 American comedian

If you want others to be happy, practise compassion. If you want to be happy, practise compassion.
Dalai Lama 1935– Tibetan monk

For all the happiness mankind can gain
Is not in pleasure, but in rest from pain.
John Dryden 1631–1700 English poet

Happiness makes up in height for what it lacks in length.
Robert Frost 1874–1963 American poet

Point me out the happy man and I will point you out either egotism, selfishness, evil—or else an absolute ignorance.
Graham Greene 1904–91 English novelist

I can sympathize with people's pains, but not with their pleasures. There is something curiously boring about somebody else's happiness.
Aldous Huxley 1894–1963 English novelist

Happiness is not an ideal of reason but of imagination.
Immanuel Kant 1724–1804 German philosopher

Happiness

A man enjoys the happiness he feels, a woman the happiness she gives.
> **Pierre Choderlos de Laclos** 1741–1803 French soldier

Happiness writes white.
> **Philip Larkin** 1922–85 English poet

Happiness is a warm gun.
> **John Lennon** 1940–80 English pop singer

Ask yourself whether you are happy, and you cease to be so.
> **John Stuart Mill** 1806–73 English philosopher

Not to admire, is all the art I know,
To make men happy, and to keep them so.
> **Alexander Pope** 1688–1744 English poet

I always say I don't think everyone has the right to happiness or to be loved. Even the Americans have written into their constitution that you have the right to the 'pursuit of happiness'. You have the right to try but that is all.
> **Claire Rayner** 1931– English journalist

To be without some of the things you want is an indispensable part of happiness.
> **Bertrand Russell** 1872–1970 British philosopher

Freude, schöner Götterfunken,
Tochter aus Elysium.

Joy, beautiful radiance of the gods, daughter of Elysium.
> **Friedrich von Schiller** 1759–1805 German poet

But a lifetime of happiness! No man alive could bear it: it would be hell on earth.
> **George Bernard Shaw** 1856–1950 Irish dramatist

Call no man happy before he dies, he is at best but fortunate.
> **Solon** c.640–after 556 BC Greek statesman

Hatred ✳

Better is a dinner of herbs where love is, than a stalled ox and hatred therewith.
Bible

I do not love thee, Dr Fell.
The reason why I cannot tell;
But this I know, and know full well,
I do not love thee, Dr Fell.
Thomas Brown 1663–1704 English satirist

Now hatred is by far the longest pleasure;
Men love in haste, but they detest at leisure.
Lord Byron 1788–1824 English poet

Love, friendship, respect do not unite people as much as common hatred for something.
Anton Chekhov 1860–1904 Russian writer

I never hated a man enough to give him diamonds back.
Zsa Zsa Gabor 1919– Hungarian-born film actress

We can scarcely hate any one that we know.
William Hazlitt 1778–1830 English essayist

If you hate a person, you hate something in him that is part of yourself. What isn't part of ourselves doesn't disturb us.
Hermann Hesse 1877–1962 German writer

No one is born hating another person because of the colour of his skin, or his background, or his religion. People must learn to hate, and if they can learn to hate, they can be taught to love, for love comes more naturally to the human heart than its opposite.
Nelson Mandela 1918– South African statesman

Hatred

Always remember, others may hate you. Those who hate you don't win unless you hate them. And then you destroy yourself.

Richard Nixon 1913-94 American statesman

For hate is not conquered by hate: hate is conquered by love. This is a law eternal.

Pali Tripitaka c.2nd century BC Buddhist sacred texts

✳ Health →Exercise, Sickness

The first law of dietetics seems to be: if it tastes good, it's bad for you.

Isaac Asimov 1920-92 Russian-born science fiction writer

The first wealth is health.

Ralph Waldo Emerson 1803-82 American writer

It was brilliant. You die of a heart attack but so what? You die thin.

Bob Geldof 1954- Irish rock musician, *on the Atkins diet*

Health is worth more than learning.

Thomas Jefferson 1743-1826 American statesman

Mens sana in corpore sano.

A sound mind in a sound body.

Juvenal c.AD 60-c.130 Roman satirist

Diets are like boyfriends—it never really works to go back to them.

Nigella Lawson 1960- British writer

Life's not just being alive, but being well.

Martial c.AD 40-c.104 Roman epigrammatist

The best doctors are Dr Diet, Dr Quiet, and Dr Merryman.

Proverb

Look to your health; and if you have it, praise God, and value it next to a good conscience; for health is the second blessing that we mortals are capable of; a blessing that money cannot buy.

    Izaak Walton 1593–1683 English writer

The Heart ✻

The desires of the heart are as crooked as corkscrews
Not to be born is the best for man.

    W. H. Auden 1907–73 English poet

There is a road from the eye to the heart that does not go through the intellect.

    G. K. Chesterton 1874–1936 English writer

The human heart likes a little disorder in its geometry.

    Louis de Bernières 1954– British novelist

A man who has not passed through the inferno of his passions has never overcome them.

    Carl Gustav Jung 1875–1961 Swiss psychologist

Calm of mind, all passion spent.

    John Milton 1608–74 English poet

The heart is an organ of fire.

    Michael Ondaatje 1943– Canadian writer

The heart has its reasons which reason knows nothing of.

    Blaise Pascal 1623–62 French scientist and philosopher

Unlearn'd, he knew no schoolman's subtle art,
No language, but the language of the heart.

    Alexander Pope 1688–1744 English poet

        A man whose blood
Is very snow-broth; one who never feels
The wanton stings and motions of the sense.

    William Shakespeare 1564–1616 English dramatist

The Heart

The heart of another is a dark forest.
Ivan Turgenev 1818–83 Russian novelist

Now that my ladder's gone
I must lie down where all ladders start
In the foul rag and bone shop of the heart.
W. B. Yeats 1865–1939 Irish poet

✳ Heaven

And I saw a new heaven and a new earth: for the first heaven and the first earth were passed away; and there was no more sea.
Bible

The true paradises are the paradises that we have lost.
Marcel Proust 1871–1922 French novelist

My idea of heaven is, eating *pâté de foie gras* to the sound of trumpets.
Sydney Smith 1771–1845 English essayist

I will spend my heaven doing good on earth.
St Teresa of Lisieux 1873–97 French nun

Heaven for climate, and hell for society.
Mark Twain 1835–1910 American writer

✳ Hell

Hell, madam, is to love no more.
Georges Bernanos 1888–1948 French writer

Abandon all hope, you who enter!
Dante Alighieri 1265–1321 Italian poet, *inscription at the entrance to Hell*

What is hell?
Hell is oneself,
Hell is alone, the other figures in it
Merely projections.
>   **T. S. Eliot** 1888–1965 American-born British poet

Better to reign in hell, than serve in heaven.
>   **John Milton** 1608–74 English poet

Hell is other people.
>   **Jean-Paul Sartre** 1905–80 French philosopher

A perpetual holiday is a good working definition of hell.
>   **George Bernard Shaw** 1856–1950 Irish dramatist

Hell is a city much like London.
>   **Percy Bysshe Shelley** 1792–1822 English poet

Heroes ✳

We can be heroes
Just for one day.
>   **David Bowie** 1947– English rock musician

ANDREA: Unhappy the land that has no heroes!...
GALILEO: No. Unhappy the land that needs heroes.
>   **Bertolt Brecht** 1898–1956 German dramatist

No man is a hero to his valet.
>   **Mme Cornuel** 1605–94 French society hostess

Every hero becomes a bore at last.
>   **Ralph Waldo Emerson** 1803–82 American writer

Ultimately a hero is a man who would argue with the
Gods, and so awakens devils to contest his vision.
>   **Norman Mailer** 1923–2007 American writer

Heroing is one of the shortest-lived professions there is.
>   **Will Rogers** 1879–1935 American actor

Heroes

A hero is the one who does what he can. The others don't.
Romain Rolland 1866–1944 French writer

In this world I would rather live two days like a tiger, than two hundred years like a sheep.
Tipu Sultan c.1750–99

✳ History

If history records good things of good men, the thoughtful hearer is encouraged to imitate what is good.
The Venerable Bede AD 673–735 English historian

History repeats itself; historians repeat one another.
Rupert Brooke 1887–1915 English poet

History is the essence of innumerable biographies.
Thomas Carlyle 1795–1881 Scottish historian

History is philosophy from examples.
Dionysius of Halicarnassus fl. 30–7 BC Greek historian

History is more or less bunk.
Henry Ford 1863–1947 American car manufacturer

History is past politics, and politics is present history.
E. A. Freeman 1823–92 English historian

History…is, indeed, little more than the register of the crimes, follies, and misfortunes of mankind.
Edward Gibbon 1737–94 English historian

War makes rattling good history; but Peace is poor reading.
Thomas Hardy 1840–1928 English novelist

Hegel says somewhere that all great events and personalities in world history reappear in one fashion or another. He forgot to add: the first time as tragedy, the second as farce.

Karl Marx 1818–83 German philosopher

Happy the people whose annals are blank in history-books!

Montesquieu 1689–1755 French political philosopher

History is not what you thought. *It is what you can remember.*

W. C. Sellar 1898–1951 and **R. J. Yeatman** 1898–1968 British writers

Human history becomes more and more a race between education and catastrophe.

H. G. Wells 1866–1946 English novelist

Home →Houses, Housework

Home is home, though it be never so homely.

John Clarke d. 1658 English schoolmaster

'Home is the place where, when you have to go there,
They have to take you in.'
'I should have called it
Something you somehow haven't to deserve.'

Robert Frost 1874–1963 American poet

What's the good of a home if you are never in it?

George Grossmith 1847–1912 and **Weedon Grossmith** 1854–1919 English writers

One never reaches home. But wherever friendly paths intersect the whole world looks like home for a time.

Hermann Hesse 1877–1962 German writer

Home

Any old place I can hang my hat is home sweet home to me.

William Jerome 1865–1932 American songwriter

The accent of one's birthplace lingers in the mind and in the heart as it does in one's speech.

Duc de la Rochefoucauld 1613–80 French moralist

E.T. phone home.

Melissa Mathison 1950– American screenwriter, *in the film* E.T.

Mid pleasures and palaces though we may roam,
Be it ever so humble, there's no place like home.

J. H. Payne 1791–1852 American actor

Home is where you come to when you have nothing better to do.

Margaret Thatcher 1925– British stateswoman

※ Honour

The louder he talked of his honour, the faster we counted our spoons.

Ralph Waldo Emerson 1803–82 American writer

GROUCHO MARX: Remember, you're fighting for this woman's honour…which is probably more than she ever did.

Bert Kalmar 1884–1947 et al., American screenwriters, *in the film* Duck Soup

I could not love thee, Dear, so much,
Loved I not honour more.

Richard Lovelace 1618–58 English poet

But he that filches from me my good name
Robs me of that which not enriches him,
And makes me poor indeed.

William Shakespeare 1564–1616 English dramatist

O! I have lost my reputation. I have lost the immortal
part of myself, and what remains is bestial.
William Shakespeare 1564–1616 English dramatist

His honour rooted in dishonour stood,
And faith unfaithful kept him falsely true.
Alfred, Lord Tennyson 1809–92 English poet

Honours ✳

Gongs and medals and ribbons really belong on a
Christmas tree.
J. G. Ballard 1930–2009 British writer

The rank is but the guinea's stamp,
The man's the gowd for a' that!
Robert Burns 1759–96 Scottish poet

A medal glitters, but it also casts a shadow.
Winston Churchill 1874–1965 British statesman, *on the envy
caused by the award of honours*

What I like about the Order of the Garter is that there is
no damned merit about it.
Lord Melbourne 1779–1848 English statesman

When I want a peerage, I shall buy it like an honest man.
Lord Northcliffe 1865–1922 British newspaper proprietor

There is no stronger craving in the world than that of the
rich for titles, except perhaps that of the titled for riches.
Hesketh Pearson 1887–1964 English biographer

Titles distinguish the mediocre, embarrass the superior,
and are disgraced by the inferior.
George Bernard Shaw 1856–1950 Irish dramatist

What harm have I ever done to the Labour Party?
R. H. Tawney 1880–1962 British economic historian, *on
declining the offer of a peerage*

Honours

Kind hearts are more than coronets,
And simple faith than Norman blood.
  Alfred, Lord Tennyson 1809–92 English poet

People fail you, children disappoint you, thieves break in,
moths corrupt, but an OBE goes on for ever.
  Fay Weldon 1931– British novelist

✳ Hope ⇒Despair, Optimism

Hope is a good breakfast, but it is a bad supper.
  Francis Bacon 1561–1626 English courtier

Hope deferred maketh the heart sick: but when the desire
cometh, it is a tree of life.
  Bible

He that lives upon hope will die fasting.
  Benjamin Franklin 1706–90 American statesman and
  scientist

Walk on, walk on, with hope in your heart,
And you'll never walk alone.
  Oscar Hammerstein II 1895–1960 American songwriter

Hope is definitely not the same thing as optimism. It is
not the conviction that something will turn out well, but
the certainty that something makes sense, regardless of
how it turns out.
  Václav Havel 1936– Czech statesman

He that lives in hope danceth without music.
  George Herbert 1593–1633 English poet

Nil desperandum.
Never despair.
  Horace 65–8 BC Roman poet

After all, tomorrow is another day.
  Margaret Mitchell 1900–49 American novelist

Hope springs eternal in the human breast:
Man never Is, but always To be blest.
> **Alexander Pope** 1688–1744 English poet

Hospitality ✳

Be not forgetful to entertain strangers: for thereby some
have entertained angels unawares.
> **Bible**

Come in the evening, or come in the morning,
Come when you're looked for, or come without warning.
> **Thomas Davis** 1814–45 Irish poet

Hospitality consists in a little fire, a little food, and an
immense quiet.
> **Ralph Waldo Emerson** 1803–82 American writer

It's life's losers who really want to please—and wanting to
please is a prerequisite of hospitality.
> **A. A. Gill** 1954– British food critic

A host is like a general: misfortunes often reveal his
genius.
> **Horace** 65–8 BC Roman poet

Some people can stay longer in an hour than others can
in a week.
> **William Dean Howells** 1837–1920 American writer

For I, who hold sage Homer's rule the best,
Welcome the coming, speed the going guest.
> **Alexander Pope** 1688–1744 English poet

Unbidden guests
Are often welcomest when they are gone.
> **William Shakespeare** 1564–1616 English dramatist

This door will open at a touch to welcome every friend.
> **Henry Van Dyke** 1852–1933 American minister

✳ Houses ⇒Home

Houses are built to live in and not to look on; therefore let use be preferred before uniformity, except where both may be had.

Francis Bacon 1561–1626 English courtier

For a man's house is his castle, *et domus sua cuique est tutissimum refugium* [and each man's home is his safest refuge].

Edward Coke 1552–1634 English jurist

It takes a heap o' livin' in a house t' make it home.

Edgar A. Guest 1881–1959 American writer

A house is a machine for living in.

Le Corbusier 1887–1965 French architect

There is no such thing as a perfect house. (What one thinks of as perfection is merely what other people are living in.)

Phyllis McGinley 1905–78 American poet

Have nothing in your houses that you do not know to be useful, or believe to be beautiful.

William Morris 1834–96 English artist

Does anybody mind if I don't live in a house that is quaint?
Because, for one thing, quaint houses are generally houses where plumbing ain't.

Ogden Nash 1902–71 American humorist

A comfortable house is a great source of happiness. It ranks immediately after health and a good conscience.

Sydney Smith 1771–1845 English essayist

But every house where Love abides
And Friendship is a guest,
Is surely home, and home, sweet home,

For there the heart can rest.
Henry Van Dyke 1852–1933 American minister

Housework →Home

Conran's Law of Housework—it expands to fill the time available plus half an hour.
Shirley Conran 1932– English writer

There was no need to do any housework at all. After the first four years the dirt doesn't get any worse.
Quentin Crisp 1908–99 English writer

'I hate discussions of feminism that end up with who does the dishes,' she said. So do I. But at the end, there are always the damned dishes.
Marilyn French 1929–2009 American writer

Dirt is only matter out of place.
John Chipman Gray 1839–1915 American lawyer

At the worst, a house unkempt cannot be so distressing as a life unlived.
Rose Macaulay 1881–1958 English novelist

The dust comes secretly day after day,
Lies on my ledge and dulls my shining things.
But O this dust that I shall drive away
Is flowers and Kings,
Is Solomon's temple, poets, Nineveh.
Viola Meynell 1886–1956 English writer

There is scarcely any less bother in the running of a family than in that of an entire state. And domestic business is no less importunate for being less important.
Montaigne 1533–92 French moralist

God walks among the pots and pans.
St Teresa of Ávila 1512–82 Spanish mystic

Housework

MR PRITCHARD: I must dust the blinds and then I must
raise them.
MRS OGMORE-PRITCHARD: And before you let the sun in,
mind it wipes its shoes.
  Dylan Thomas 1914–53 Welsh poet

Hatred of domestic work is a natural and admirable
result of civilization.
  Rebecca West 1892–1983 English writer

✳ The Human Race

We are born of risen apes, not fallen angels, and the apes
were armed killers beside.
  Robert Ardrey 1908–80 American dramatist

Drinking when we are not thirsty and making love all
year round, madam; that is all there is to distinguish us
from other animals.
  Pierre-Augustin Caron de Beaumarchais 1732–99 French
  dramatist

There's a man all over for you, blaming on his boots the
faults of his feet.
  Samuel Beckett 1906–89 Irish writer

We carry within us the wonders we seek without us: there
is all Africa and her prodigies in us.
  Sir Thomas Browne 1605–82 English writer

I hate 'Humanity' and all such abstracts: but I love *people*.
Lovers of 'Humanity' generally hate *people and children*,
and keep parrots or puppy dogs.
  Roy Campbell 1901–57 South African poet

By nature men are alike. Through practice they have
become far apart.
  Confucius 551–479 BC Chinese philosopher

We have Africa in our blood and Africa has our bones.
We are all Africans.
Richard Dawkins 1941– English biologist

What is man, when you come to think upon him, but a
minutely set, ingenious machine for turning, with infinite
artfulness, the red wine of Shiraz into urine?
Isak Dinesen 1885–1962 Danish writer

Is man an ape or an angel? Now I am on the side of the
angels.
Benjamin Disraeli 1804–81 British statesman

Man is a tool-making animal.
Benjamin Franklin 1706–90 American statesman and
scientist

Out of the crooked timber of humanity no straight thing
can ever be made.
Immanuel Kant 1724–1804 German philosopher

To say, for example, that a man is made up of certain
chemical elements is a satisfactory description only for
those who intend to use him as a fertilizer.
H. J. Muller 1890–1967 American geneticist

I teach you the superman. Man is something to be
surpassed.
Friedrich Nietzsche 1844–1900 German philosopher

Man is only a reed, the weakest thing in nature; but he is
a thinking reed.
Blaise Pascal 1623–62 French scientist and philosopher

An honest man's the noblest work of God.
Alexander Pope 1688–1744 English poet

The Human Race

Man is the measure of all things.
Protagoras b. c.485– Greek sophist

How beauteous mankind is! O brave new world,
That has such people in't.
William Shakespeare 1564–1616 English dramatist

What a piece of work is a man! How noble in reason!
how infinite in faculty! in form, in moving, how express
and admirable! in action how like an angel! in
apprehension how like a god! the beauty of the world!
the paragon of animals!
William Shakespeare 1564–1616 English dramatist

There are many wonderful things, and nothing is more
wonderful than man.
Sophocles c.496–406 BC Greek dramatist

I am a man, I count nothing human foreign to me.
Terence c.190–159 BC Roman comic dramatist

Man is the Only Animal that Blushes. Or needs to.
Mark Twain 1835–1910 American writer

We're all of us guinea pigs in the laboratory of God.
Humanity is just a work in progress.
Tennessee Williams 1911–83 American dramatist

✳ Human Rights

We hold these truths to be self-evident, that all men are
created equal, that they are endowed by their Creator
with certain unalienable rights, that among these are life,
liberty and the pursuit of happiness.
American Declaration of Independence 1776

Human Rights

Liberté! Égalité! Fraternité!
Freedom! Equality! Brotherhood!
Anonymous *motto of the French Revolution*

Natural rights is simple nonsense: natural and imprescriptible rights, rhetorical nonsense—nonsense upon stilts.
Jeremy Bentham 1748–1832 English philosopher

Whatever each man can separately do, without trespassing upon others, he has a right to do for himself; and he has a right to a fair portion of all which society, with all its combinations of skill and force, can do in his favour.
Edmund Burke 1729–97 Irish-born politician

No man can put a chain about the ankle of his fellow man without at last finding the other end fastened about his own neck.
Frederick Douglass c.1818–95 American former slave

To no man will we sell, or deny, or delay, right or justice.
Magna Carta 1215

The poorest he that is in England hath a life to live as the greatest he.
Thomas Rainborowe d. 1648 English soldier

Any law which violates the inalienable rights of man is essentially unjust and tyrannical; it is not a law at all.
Maximilien Robespierre 1758–94 French revolutionary

We look forward to a world founded upon four essential human freedoms. The first is freedom of speech and expression—everywhere in the world. The second is freedom of every person to worship God in his own way—everywhere in the world. The third is freedom from want…The fourth is freedom from fear.
Franklin D. Roosevelt 1882–1945 American statesman

Human Rights

That little man...he says women can't have as much rights as men, cause Christ wasn't a woman. Where did your Christ come from? From God and a woman. Man had nothing to do with Him.

Sojourner Truth c.1797–1883 American evangelist

All human beings are born free and equal in dignity and rights.

Universal Declaration of Human Rights 1948

✳ Humour

Among those whom I like or admire, I can find no common denominator, but among those whom I love, I can: all of them make me laugh.

W. H. Auden 1907–73 English poet

For what do we live, but to make sport for our neighbours, and laugh at them in our turn?

Jane Austen 1775–1817 English novelist

I make myself laugh at everything, for fear of having to weep at it.

Pierre-Augustin Caron de Beaumarchais 1732–99 French dramatist

Of all days, the one most surely wasted is the one on which one has not laughed.

Nicolas-Sébastien Chamfort 1741–94 French writer

A difference of taste in jokes is a great strain on the affections.

George Eliot 1819–80 English novelist

The funniest thing about comedy is that you never know why people laugh. I know *what* makes them laugh but trying to get your hands on the *why* of it is like trying to pick an eel out of a tub of water.

W. C. Fields 1880–1946 American humorist

What do you mean, funny? Funny-peculiar or funny ha-ha?

Ian Hay 1876–1952 Scottish writer

[A pun] is a pistol let off at the ear; not a feather to tickle the intellect.

Charles Lamb 1775–1834 English writer

Wit is the epitaph of an emotion.

Friedrich Nietzsche 1844–1900 German philosopher

Laughter is pleasant, but the exertion is too much for me.

Thomas Love Peacock 1785–1866 English writer

Everything is funny as long as it is happening to Somebody Else.

Will Rogers 1879–1935 American actor

I am not only witty in myself, but the cause that wit is in other men.

William Shakespeare 1564–1616 English dramatist

Brevity is the soul of wit.

William Shakespeare 1564–1616 English dramatist

Delight hath a joy in it either permanent or present. Laughter hath only a scornful tickling.

Philip Sidney 1554–86 English writer

Humour is emotional chaos remembered in tranquillity.

James Thurber 1894–1961 American humorist

We are not amused.

Queen Victoria 1819–1901 British monarch

It's hard to be funny when you have to be clean.

Mae West 1892–1980 American film actress

✳ Hypocrisy

Ye are like unto whited sepulchres, which indeed appear beautiful outward, but are within full of dead men's bones, and of all uncleanness.
Bible

Compound for sins, they are inclined to,
By damning those they have no mind to.
Samuel Butler 1612–80 English poet

The smylere with the knyf under the cloke.
Geoffrey Chaucer c.1343–1400 English poet

Keep up appearances; there lies the test;
The world will give thee credit for the rest.
Outward be fair, however foul within;
Sin if thou wilt, but then in secret sin.
Charles Churchill 1731–64 English poet

Hypocrisy is a tribute which vice pays to virtue.
Duc de la Rochefoucauld 1613–80 French moralist

Hypocrisy, the only evil that walks
Invisible, except to God alone.
John Milton 1608–74 English poet

       I want that glib and oily art
To speak and purpose not.
William Shakespeare 1564–1616 English dramatist

All Reformers, however strict their social conscience, live in houses just as big as they can pay for.
Logan Pearsall Smith 1865–1946 American writer

I sit on a man's back, choking him and making him carry me, and yet assure myself and others that I am very sorry for him and wish to ease his lot by all possible means—except by getting off his back.
Leo Tolstoy 1828–1910 Russian novelist

Idealism ✳

A cause may be inconvenient, but it's magnificent. It's like champagne or high heels, and one must be prepared to suffer for it.
Arnold Bennett 1867–1931 English novelist

Where there is no vision, the people perish.
Bible

Oh, the vision thing.
George Bush 1924– American statesman, *responding to the suggestion that he turn his attention from short-term campaign objectives and look to the longer term*

There's only one corner of the universe you can be certain of improving, and that's your own self.
Aldous Huxley 1894–1963 English novelist

Each time a man stands up for an ideal...he sends forth a tiny ripple of hope, and...those ripples build a current which can sweep down the mightiest walls of oppression and resistance.
Robert Kennedy 1925–68 American politician

If a man hasn't discovered something he will die for, he isn't fit to live.
Martin Luther King 1929–68 American civil rights leader

We are all in the gutter, but some of us are looking at the stars.
Oscar Wilde 1854–1900 Irish dramatist

I have spread my dreams under your feet;
Tread softly because you tread on my dreams.
W. B. Yeats 1865–1939 Irish poet

✳ Ideas →Thinking

Nothing is more dangerous than an idea, when you have only one idea.

Alain 1868–1951 French poet

There is one thing stronger than all the armies in the world; and that is an idea whose time has come.

Anonymous

Probable impossibilities are to be preferred to improbable possibilities.

Aristotle 384–322 BC Greek philosopher

It isn't that they can't see the solution. It is that they can't see the problem.

G. K. Chesterton 1874–1936 English writer

Every now and then a man's mind is stretched by a new idea or sensation, and never shrinks back to its former dimensions.

Oliver Wendell Holmes 1809–94 American physician

A stand can be made against invasion by an army; no stand can be made against invasion by an idea.

Victor Hugo 1802–85 French writer

When you are a Bear of Very Little Brain, and you Think of Things, you find sometimes that a Thing which seemed very Thingish inside you is quite different when it gets out into the open and has other people looking at it.

A. A. Milne 1882–1956 English writer

You see things; and you say 'Why?' But I dream things that never were; and I say 'Why not?'

George Bernard Shaw 1856–1950 Irish dramatist

How seldom is it that theories stand the wear and tear of practice!

Anthony Trollope 1815–82 English novelist

Ideas won't keep. Something must be done about them.
Alfred North Whitehead 1861–1947 English philosopher

Idleness ✷

A man who has nothing to do with his own time has no conscience in his intrusion on that of others.
Jane Austen 1775–1817 English novelist

Go to the ant thou sluggard; consider her ways, and be wise.
Bible

The foul sluggard's comfort: 'It will last my time.'
Thomas Carlyle 1795–1881 Scottish historian

Idleness is only the refuge of weak minds.
Lord Chesterfield 1694–1773 English writer

It is better to wear out than to rust out.
Richard Cumberland 1631–1718 English divine

It is impossible to enjoy idling thoroughly unless one has plenty of work to do.
Jerome K. Jerome 1859–1927 English writer

I was raised to feel that doing nothing was a sin. I had to learn to do nothing.
Jenny Joseph 1932– English poet

Far from idleness being the root of evil, rather it is the true good.
Sören Kierkegaard 1813–55 Danish philosopher

The time you enjoy wasting is not wasted time.
Laurence Peter 1919–90 Canadian writer, *commenting on a remark by Bertrand Russell*

For Satan finds some mischief still
For idle hands to do.
Isaac Watts 1674–1748 English hymn-writer

Idleness

Procrastination is the thief of time.
Edward Young 1683–1765 English poet

✳ Ignorance

Ignorance is not innocence but sin.
Robert Browning 1812–89 English poet

Whatever Nature has in store for mankind, unpleasant as
it may be, men must accept, for ignorance is never better
than knowledge.
Enrico Fermi 1901–54 Italian-born American physicist

> Where ignorance is bliss,
'Tis folly to be wise.
Thomas Gray 1716–71 English poet

Ignorance, madam, pure ignorance.
Samuel Johnson 1709–84 English lexicographer, *on being
asked why he had defined* pastern *as the 'knee' of a horse*

You know everybody is ignorant, only on different
subjects.
Will Rogers 1879–1935 American actor

Learn to say, 'I don't know'. If used when appropriate, it
will be often.
Donald Rumsfeld 1932– American politician

For most men, an ignorant enjoyment is better than an
informed one; it is better to conceive the sky as a blue
dome than a dark cavity; and the cloud as a golden
throne than a sleety mist.
John Ruskin 1819–1900 English critic

If one does not know to which port one is sailing, no
wind is favourable.
Seneca ('the Younger') c.4 BC–AD 65 Roman philosopher

As any fule kno.
>   **Geoffrey Willans** 1911–58 and **Ronald Searle** 1920– English
>   writers

Imagination ✳

All fantasy should have a solid base in reality.
>   **Max Beerbohm** 1872–1956 English critic

To see a world in a grain of sand
And a heaven in a wild flower
Hold infinity in the palm of your hand
And eternity in an hour.
>   **William Blake** 1757–1827 English poet

Fantasy is like jam; you have to spread it on a solid slice
of bread.
>   **Italo Calvino** 1923–85 Italian writer

When the imagination sleeps, words are emptied of their
meaning.
>   **Albert Camus** 1913–60 French writer

Go, and catch a falling star,
Get with child a mandrake root,
Tell me, where all past years are,
Or who cleft the Devil's foot.
Teach me to hear mermaids singing.
>   **John Donne** 1572–1631 English poet

Where there is no imagination there is no horror.
>   **Arthur Conan Doyle** 1859–1930 Scottish-born writer

Imagination is more important than knowledge.
>   **Albert Einstein** 1879–1955 German-born theoretical physicist

Imagination

Were it not for imagination, Sir, a man would be as
happy in the arms of a chambermaid as of a Duchess.
   Samuel Johnson 1709–84 English lexicographer

Heard melodies are sweet, but those unheard
Are sweeter.
   John Keats 1795–1821 English poet

Imagine there's no heaven
It's easy if you try.
   John Lennon 1940–80 English pop singer

His imagination resembled the wings of an ostrich. It
enabled him to run, though not to soar.
   Lord Macaulay 1800–59 English historian

The lunatic, the lover, and the poet,
Are of imagination all compact.
   William Shakespeare 1564–1616 English dramatist

Must then a Christ perish in torment in every age to save
those that have no imagination?
   George Bernard Shaw 1856–1950 Irish dramatist

Whither is fled the visionary gleam?
Where is it now, the glory and the dream?
   William Wordsworth 1770–1850 English poet

✳ Indifference

All colours will agree in the dark.
   Francis Bacon 1561–1626 English courtier

Because thou art lukewarm, and neither cold nor hot, I
will spew thee out of my mouth.
   Bible

Catholics and Communists have committed great crimes,
but at least they have not stood aside, like an established
society, and been indifferent. I would rather have blood
on my hands than water like Pilate.
Graham Greene 1904–91 English novelist

Let them eat cake.
Marie-Antoinette 1755–93 French queen, *on being told that
her people had no bread*

I wish I could care what you do or where you go but I
can't...My dear, I don't give a damn.
Margaret Mitchell 1900–49 American novelist, *'Frankly, my
dear, I don't give a damn!' in Sidney Howard's screenplay for*
Gone With the Wind

Vacant heart and hand, and eye,—
Easy live and quiet die.
Sir Walter Scott 1771–1832 Scottish novelist

It is the disease of not listening, the malady of not
marking, that I am troubled withal.
William Shakespeare 1564–1616 English dramatist

The worst sin towards our fellow creatures is not to hate
them, but to be indifferent to them: that's the essence of
inhumanity.
George Bernard Shaw 1856–1950 Irish dramatist

I was much further out than you thought
And not waving but drowning.
Stevie Smith 1902–71 English poet

The opposite of love is not hate, it's indifference. The
opposite of art is not ugliness, it's indifference. The
opposite of faith is not heresy, it's indifference. And the
opposite of life is not death, it's indifference.
Elie Wiesel 1928– Romanian-born American writer

Indifference

Cast a cold eye
On life, on death.
Horseman pass by!
W. B. Yeats 1865–1939 Irish poet

✳ Individuality

It is easier to live through someone else than to become complete yourself.
Betty Friedan 1921–2006 American feminist

In friendship or in love, the two side by side raise hands together to find what one cannot reach alone.
Kahlil Gibran 1883–1931 Lebanese-born American writer

To be like everyone else. Isn't that what we all want in the end?
Carol Shields 1935–2003 Canadian writer

Most people are other people. Their thoughts are someone else's opinions, their lives a mimicry, their passions a quotation.
Oscar Wilde 1854–1900 Irish dramatist

✳ Intelligence

See the happy moron,
He doesn't give a damn,
I wish I were a moron,
My God! perhaps I am!
Anonymous

To the man-in-the-street, who, I'm sorry to say,
Is a keen observer of life,
The word 'Intellectual' suggests straight away
A man who's untrue to his wife.
W. H. Auden 1907–73 English poet

A man is not necessarily intelligent because he has plenty of ideas, any more than he is a good general because he has plenty of soldiers.

Nicolas-Sébastien Chamfort 1741–94 French writer

'Excellent,' I cried. 'Elementary,' said he.

Arthur Conan Doyle 1859–1930 Scottish-born writer, *commonly quoted as 'Elementary, my dear Watson'*

As a human being, one has been endowed with just enough intelligence to be able to see clearly how utterly inadequate that intelligence is when confronted with what exists.

Albert Einstein 1879–1955 German-born theoretical physicist

The test of a first-rate intelligence is the ability to hold two opposed ideas in the mind at the same time, and still retain the ability to function.

F. Scott Fitzgerald 1896–1940 American novelist

So dumb he can't fart and chew gum at the same time.

Lyndon Baines Johnson 1908–73 American statesman, *of Gerald Ford*

Sir, I have found you an argument; but I am not obliged to find you an understanding.

Samuel Johnson 1709–84 English lexicographer

I think, therefore I am is the statement of an intellectual who underrates toothaches.

Milan Kundera 1929– Czech novelist

No one in this world, so far as I know—and I have searched the records for years, and employed agents to help me—has ever lost money by underestimating the intelligence of the great masses of the plain people.

H. L. Mencken 1880–1956 American journalist

You beat your pate, and fancy wit will come:
Knock as you please, there's nobody at home.

Alexander Pope 1688–1744 English poet

Intelligence

With stupidity the gods themselves struggle in vain.
Friedrich von Schiller 1759–1805 German poet

✳ Invention and Discovery

When man wanted to make a machine that would walk
he created the wheel, which does not resemble a leg.
Guillaume Apollinaire 1880–1918 French poet

Eureka!
I've got it!
Archimedes c.287–212 BC Greek mathematician

Printing, gunpowder, and the mariner's needle
[compass]…these three have changed the whole face and
state of things throughout the world.
Francis Bacon 1561–1626 English courtier

Through the unknown, we'll find the new.
Charles Baudelaire 1821–67 French poet

The discovery of a new dish does more for human
happiness than the discovery of a star.
Anthelme Brillat-Savarin 1755–1826 French gourmet

LORD CARNARVON: Can you see anything?
CARTER: Yes, wonderful things.
Howard Carter 1874–1939 English archaeologist, *on first looking into the tomb of Tutankhamun*

Why sir, there is every possibility that you will soon be
able to tax it!
Michael Faraday 1791–1867 English scientist, *to Gladstone, when asked about the usefulness of electricity*

What is the use of a new-born child?
Benjamin Franklin 1706–90 American statesman and scientist, *when asked what was the use of a new invention*

Invention and Discovery

Then felt I like some watcher of the skies
When a new planet swims into his ken.
John Keats 1795–1821 English poet

Praise without end the go-ahead zeal
of whoever it was invented the wheel;
but never a word for the poor soul's sake
that thought ahead, and invented the brake.
Howard Nemerov 1920–91 American writer

I don't know what I may seem to the world, but as to
myself, I seem to have been only like a boy playing on the
sea-shore and diverting myself in now and then finding a
smoother pebble or a prettier shell than ordinary, whilst
the great ocean of truth lay all undiscovered before me.
Isaac Newton 1642–1727 English mathematician

I remembered the line from the Hindu scripture, the
Bhagavad Gita…'I am become death, the destroyer of
worlds.'
J. Robert Oppenheimer 1904–67 American physicist, *on the
explosion of the first atomic bomb near Alamogordo, New
Mexico*

Semper aliquid novi Africam adferre.
Africa always brings [us] something new.
Pliny the Elder AD 23–79 Roman senator

If you wish to make an apple pie from scratch, you must
first invent the universe.
Carl Sagan 1934–96 American astronomer

Discovery consists of seeing what everybody has seen and
thinking what nobody has thought.
Albert von Szent-Györgyi 1893–1986 Hungarian-born
biochemist

Name the greatest of all the inventors. Accident.
Mark Twain 1835–1910 American writer

✳ Ireland

We've never been cool, we're hot. Irish people are Italians who can't dress, Jamaicans who can't dance.

Bono 1960– Irish rock musician

For the great Gaels of Ireland
Are the men that God made mad,
For all their wars are merry,
And all their songs are sad.

G. K. Chesterton 1874–1936 English writer

Ulster will fight; Ulster will be right.

Lord Randolph Churchill 1849–94 British politician

The famous
Northern reticence, the tight gag of place
And times.

Seamus Heaney 1939– Irish poet

Ireland is the old sow that eats her farrow.

James Joyce 1882–1941 Irish novelist

Ireland is a small but insuppressible island half an hour nearer the sunset than Great Britain.

Thomas Kettle 1880–1916 Irish economist

In Ireland the inevitable never happens and the unexpected constantly occurs.

John Pentland Mahaffy 1839–1919 Irish writer

Spenser's Ireland
has not altered;—
a place as kind as it is green,
the greenest place I've never seen.

Marianne Moore 1887–1972 American poet

Romantic Ireland's dead and gone,
It's with O'Leary in the grave.

W. B. Yeats 1865–1939 Irish poet

Jealousy ⇒Envy and Jealousy

Journalism ⇒News ❋

The Times has made many ministries.
Walter Bagehot 1826-77 English economist

I read the newspapers avidly. It is my one form of continuous fiction.
Aneurin Bevan 1897-1960 British politician

When seagulls follow a trawler, it is because they think sardines will be thrown into the sea.
Eric Cantona 1966– French footballer, *at a press conference*

When the legend becomes fact, print the legend.
Willis Goldbeck and **James Warner Bellah** American screenwriters, *in the film* The Man Who Shot Liberty Valance

You furnish the pictures and I'll furnish the war.
William Randolph Hearst 1863-1951 American newspaper publisher, *message to the artist Frederic Remington in Havana, Cuba, during the Spanish-American War of 1898*

Power without responsibility: the prerogative of the harlot throughout the ages.
Rudyard Kipling 1865-1936 English writer, *summing up Lord Beaverbrook's political standpoint* vis-à-vis *the* Daily Express

A good newspaper, I suppose, is a nation talking to itself.
Arthur Miller 1915-2005 American dramatist

All the news that's fit to print.
Adolph S. Ochs 1858-1935 American publisher, *motto of the* New York Times

A cynical, mercenary, demagogic, corrupt press will produce in time a people as base as itself.
Joseph Pulitzer 1847-1911 Hungarian-born American editor

Journalism

The men with the muck-rakes are often indispensable to the well-being of society; but only if they know when to stop raking the muck.
Theodore Roosevelt 1858–1919 American statesman

Comment is free, but facts are sacred.
C. P. Scott 1846–1932 British journalist

Ever noticed that no matter what happens in one day, it exactly fits in the newspaper?
Jerry Seinfeld 1954– American comedian

Comment is free but facts are on expenses.
Tom Stoppard 1937– British dramatist

We must try to find ways to starve the terrorist and the hijacker of the oxygen of publicity on which they depend.
Margaret Thatcher 1925– British stateswoman

The report of my death was an exaggeration.
Mark Twain 1835–1910 American writer, *usually quoted as 'Reports of my death have been greatly exaggerated'*

Journalism—an ability to meet the challenge of filling the space.
Rebecca West 1892–1983 English writer

Rock journalism is people who can't write interviewing people who can't talk for people who can't read.
Frank Zappa 1940–93 American rock musician

 Justice →The Law

Jedem das Seine.
To each his own.
Anonymous *inscription on the gate of Buchenwald concentration camp; often quoted as 'Everyone gets what he deserves'*

Audi partem alteram.

Hear the other side.

St Augustine of Hippo AD 354–430 Roman theologian

Life for life,
Eye for eye, tooth for tooth.

Bible

It is better that ten guilty persons escape than one innocent suffer.

William Blackstone 1723–80 English jurist

When I hear of an 'equity' in a case like this, I am reminded of a blind man in a dark room—looking for a black hat—which isn't there.

Lord Bowen 1835–94 English judge

No! No! Sentence first—verdict afterwards.

Lewis Carroll 1832–98 English writer

Justice is truth in action.

Benjamin Disraeli 1804–81 British statesman

All sensible people are selfish, and nature is tugging at every contract to make the terms of it fair.

Ralph Waldo Emerson 1803–82 American writer

Fiat justitia et pereat mundus.

Let justice be done, though the world perish.

Ferdinand I 1503–64 Holy Roman emperor

Justice should not only be done, but should manifestly and undoubtedly be seen to be done.

Lord Hewart 1870–1943 British lawyer

Injustice anywhere is a threat to justice everywhere.

Martin Luther King 1929–68 American civil rights leader

I have always found that mercy bears richer fruits than strict justice.

Abraham Lincoln 1809–65 American statesman

Justice

In England, justice is open to all—like the Ritz Hotel.
    James Mathew 1830–1908 Irish judge

Here [Paris] they hang a man first, and try him
afterwards.
    Molière 1622–73 French comic dramatist

The quality of mercy is not strained,
It droppeth as the gentle rain from heaven
Upon the place beneath: it is twice blessed;
It blesseth him that gives and him that takes.
    William Shakespeare 1564–1616 English dramatist

Thrice is he armed that hath his quarrel just.
    William Shakespeare 1564–1616 English dramatist

Two wrongs don't make a right, but they make a good
excuse.
    Thomas Szasz 1920– Hungarian-born psychiatrist

✳ Knowledge

Everyman, I will go with thee, and be thy guide,
In thy most need to go by thy side.
    Anonymous Everyman (c.1509–19) *spoken by Knowledge*

The fox knows many things—the hedgehog one *big* one.
    Archilochus Greek poet of the 7th century BC

All men by nature desire knowledge.
    Aristotle 384–322 BC Greek philosopher

For also knowledge itself is power.
    Francis Bacon 1561–1626 English courtier

The price of wisdom is above rubies.
    Bible

For now we see through a glass, darkly; but then face to face: now I know in part; but then shall I know even as also I am known.
> **Bible**

It is better to know nothing than to know what ain't so.
> **Josh Billings** 1818–85 American humorist

If the doors of perception were cleansed everything would appear to man as it is, infinite.
> **William Blake** 1757–1827 English poet

An expert is one who knows more and more about less and less.
> **Nicholas Murray Butler** 1862–1947 American philosopher

Knowledge may give weight, but accomplishments give lustre, and many more people see than weigh.
> **Lord Chesterfield** 1694–1773 English writer

There is no such thing on earth as an uninteresting subject; the only thing that can exist is an uninterested person.
> **G. K. Chesterton** 1874–1936 English writer

In fact the *a priori* reasoning is so entirely satisfactory to me that if the facts won't fit in, why so much the worse for the facts is my feeling.
> **Erasmus Darwin** 1804–81 English physician, *to his brother Charles, after reading his book,* The Origin of Species

MR GRADGRIND: Now, what I want is, Facts...Facts alone are wanted in life.
> **Charles Dickens** 1812–70 English novelist

Where is the wisdom we have lost in knowledge?
Where is the knowledge we have lost in information?
> **T. S. Eliot** 1888–1965 American-born British poet

Mere cleverness is not wisdom.
> **Euripides** c.485–c.406 BC Greek dramatist

Knowledge

Knowledge is of two kinds. We know a subject ourselves, or we know where we can find information upon it.
Samuel Johnson 1709–84 English lexicographer

Dare to know! Have the courage to use your own reason! This is the motto of the Enlightenment.
Immanuel Kant 1724–1804 German philosopher

The motto of all the mongoose family is, 'Run and find out.'
Rudyard Kipling 1865–1936 English writer

We have learned the answers, all the answers:
It is the question that we do not know.
Archibald MacLeish 1892–1982 American poet

Que sais-je?
What do I know?
Montaigne 1533–92 French moralist

A little learning is a dangerous thing;
Drink deep, or taste not the Pierian spring.
Alexander Pope 1688–1744 English poet

Knowledge without conscience is but the ruin of the soul.
François Rabelais c.1494–c.1553 French humanist

There are known knowns; there are things we know we know. We also know there are known unknowns; that is to say we know there are some things we do not know. But there are also unknown unknowns—the ones we don't know we don't know.
Donald Rumsfeld 1932– American politician

I know nothing except the fact of my ignorance.
Socrates 469–399 BC Greek philosopher

Everybody gets so much information all day long that they lose their common sense.
Gertrude Stein 1874–1946 American writer

Knowledge is good. It does not have to look good or sound good or even do good. It is good just by being knowledge. And the only thing that makes it knowledge is that it is true. You can't have too much of it and there is no little too little to be worth having.

Tom Stoppard 1937– British dramatist

UMA THURMAN: That was a little bit more information than I needed to know.

Quentin Tarantino 1963– American film director, *in the film* Pulp Fiction

Get your facts first, and then you can distort 'em as much as you please.

Mark Twain 1835–1910 American writer

All the business of war, and indeed all the business of life, is to endeavour to find out what you don't know by what you do; that's what I called 'guessing what was at the other side of the hill'.

Duke of Wellington 1769–1852 British general

Language ⇒Meaning, Words

One picture is worth ten thousand words.

Frederick R. Barnard

A word fitly spoken is like apples of gold in pictures of silver.

Bible

A definition is the enclosing a wilderness of idea within a wall of words.

Samuel Butler 1835–1902 English novelist

Take care of the sense, and the sounds will take care of themselves.

Lewis Carroll 1832–98 English writer

Language

Colourless green ideas sleep furiously.

Noam Chomsky 1928– American linguist, *illustrating that grammatical structure is independent of meaning*

This is the sort of English up with which I will not put.

Winston Churchill 1874–1965 British statesman, *on prepositions*

The man who first abused his fellows with swear-words instead of bashing their brains out with a club should be counted among those who laid the foundations of civilization.

John Cohen 1911– British psychologist

He who understands baboon would do more towards metaphysics than Locke.

Charles Darwin 1809–82 English naturalist

Language is fossil poetry.

Ralph Waldo Emerson 1803–82 American writer

Merely corroborative detail, intended to give artistic verisimilitude to an otherwise bald and unconvincing narrative.

W. S. Gilbert 1836–1911 English writer

The only person entitled to use the imperial 'we' in speaking of himself is a king, an editor, and a man with a tapeworm.

Robert G. Ingersoll 1833–99 American agnostic

Language is the dress of thought.

Samuel Johnson 1709–84 English lexicographer

The mystery of language was revealed to me. I knew then that 'w-a-t-e-r' meant the wonderful cool something that was flowing over my hand. That living word awakened my soul, gave it light, joy, set it free!

Helen Keller 1880–1968 American writer

All that is not prose is verse; and all that is not verse is prose.
> **Molière** 1622–73 French comic dramatist

Good heavens! For more than forty years I have been speaking prose without knowing it.
> **Molière** 1622–73 French comic dramatist

It's very hard to talk quantum using a language originally designed to tell other monkeys where the ripe fruit is.
> **Terry Pratchett** 1948– English novelist

Slang is a language that rolls up its sleeves, spits on its hands and goes to work.
> **Carl Sandburg** 1878–1967 American poet

You taught me language; and my profit on't
Is, I know how to curse.
> **William Shakespeare** 1564–1616 English dramatist

A language is a dialect with an army and a navy.
> **Max Weinreich** 1894–1969 American Yiddish scholar

The limits of my language mean the limits of my world.
> **Ludwig Wittgenstein** 1889–1951 Austrian-born philosopher

Languages ✳

The great breeding people had gone out and multiplied; colonies in every clime attest our success; French is the *patois* of Europe; English is the language of the world.
> **Walter Bagehot** 1826–77 English economist

To God I speak Spanish, to women Italian, to men French, and to my horse—German.
> **Charles V** 1500–58 Holy Roman emperor

Languages

I like to be beholden to the great metropolitan English speech, the sea which receives tributaries from every region under heaven.
Ralph Waldo Emerson 1803–82 American writer

My English text is chaste, and all licentious passages are left in the obscurity of a learned language.
Edward Gibbon 1737–94 English historian, *parodied as 'decent obscurity' in the* Anti-Jacobin

He who does not know foreign languages knows nothing of his own.
Johann Wolfgang von Goethe 1749–1832 German writer

I am always sorry when any language is lost, because languages are the pedigree of nations.
Samuel Johnson 1709–84 English lexicographer

We are walking lexicons. In a single sentence of idle chatter we preserve Latin, Anglo-Saxon, Norse; we carry a museum inside our heads, each day we commemorate peoples of whom we have never heard.
Penelope Lively 1933– English novelist

It is impossible for an Englishman to open his mouth without making some other Englishman hate or despise him.
George Bernard Shaw 1856–1950 Irish dramatist

England and America are two countries divided by a common language.
George Bernard Shaw 1856–1950 Irish dramatist

The English language is nobody's special property. It is the property of the imagination: it is the property of the language itself.
Derek Walcott 1930– West Indian writer

The Law ⇒Crime, Justice

Written laws are like spider's webs; they will catch, it is true, the weak and poor, but would be torn in pieces by the rich and powerful.
Anacharsis Scythian prince of the 6th century BC

Law is a bottomless pit.
Dr Arbuthnot 1667–1735 Scottish physician

Bad laws are the worst sort of tyranny.
Edmund Burke 1729–97 Irish-born politician

Salus populi suprema est lex.
The good of the people is the chief law.
Cicero 106–43 BC Roman statesman

Cui bono?
To whose profit?
Cicero 106–43 BC Roman statesman

If the law supposes that…the law is a ass—a idiot.
Charles Dickens 1812–70 English novelist

'You must not tell us what the soldier, or any other man, said, sir,' interposed the judge; 'it's not evidence.'
Charles Dickens 1812–70 English novelist

No poet ever interpreted nature as freely as a lawyer interprets the truth.
Jean Giraudoux 1882–1944 French dramatist

Laws grind the poor, and rich men rule the law.
Oliver Goldsmith 1728–74 Irish writer

A verbal contract isn't worth the paper it is written on.
Sam Goldwyn 1882–1974 American film producer

I know no method to secure the repeal of bad or obnoxious laws so effective as their stringent execution.
Ulysses S. Grant 1822–85 American statesman

The Law

English law does not permit good persons, as such, to strangle bad persons, as such.
  T. H. Huxley 1825–95 English biologist

The more laws and orders are made prominent,
The more thieves and bandits there will be.
  Lao Tzu c.604–c.531 BC Chinese philosopher

I don't know as I want a lawyer to tell me what I cannot do. I hire him to tell me how to do what I want to do.
  John Pierpont Morgan 1837–1913 American financier

Laws were made to be broken.
  Christopher North 1785–1854 Scottish critic

A lawyer with his briefcase can steal more than a hundred men with guns.
  Mario Puzo 1920–99 American novelist

Ignorance of the law excuses no man; not that all men know the law, but because 'tis an excuse every man will plead, and no man can tell how to confute him.
  John Selden 1584–1654 English historian

The first thing we do, let's kill all the lawyers.
  William Shakespeare 1564–1616 English dramatist

The big print giveth, and the fine print taketh away.
  Fulton J. Sheen 1895–1979 American bishop

Everything not forbidden is compulsory.
  T. H. White 1906–64 English novelist

Asking the ignorant to use the incomprehensible to decide the unknowable.
  Hiller B. Zobel 1932– American judge, *on the jury system*

Leadership ✳

Be neither saint nor sophist-led, but be a man.
Matthew Arnold 1822–88 English poet

By the structure of the world we often want, at the sudden occurrence of a grave tempest, to change the helmsman—to replace the pilot of the calm by the pilot of the storm.
Walter Bagehot 1826–77 English economist

If the blind lead the blind, both shall fall into the ditch.
Bible

The art of leadership is saying no, not yes. It is very easy to say yes.
Tony Blair 1953– British statesman

The art of leadership…consists in consolidating the attention of the people against a single adversary and taking care that nothing will split up that attention.
Adolf Hitler 1889–1945 German dictator

A leader is best when people barely know he exists…He acts without unnecessary speech, and when the work is done the people say 'We did it ourselves'.
Lao Tzu c.604–c.531 BC Chinese philosopher

The final test of a leader is that he leaves behind him in other men the conviction and the will to carry on.
Walter Lippmann 1889–1974 American journalist

To grasp and hold a vision, that is the very essence of successful leadership—not only on the movie set where I learned it, but everywhere.
Ronald Reagan 1911–2004 American statesman

Never be a pioneer. It's the Early Christian that gets the fattest lion.
Saki 1870–1916 Scottish writer

Leadership

I don't mind how much my Ministers talk, so long as they do what I say.
    Margaret Thatcher 1925– British stateswoman

The buck stops here.
    Harry S. Truman 1884–1972 American statesman

✳ Leisure

We are closer to the ants than to the butterflies. Very few people can endure much leisure.
    Gerald Brenan 1894–1987 British writer

There's sand in the porridge and sand in the bed,
And if this is pleasure we'd rather be dead.
    Noël Coward 1899–1973 English dramatist

What is this life if, full of care,
We have no time to stand and stare.
    W. H. Davies 1871–1940 Welsh poet

Cannot avoid contrasting deliriously rapid flight of time when on a holiday with very much slower passage of days, and even hours, in other and more familiar surroundings.
    E. M. Delafield 1890–1943 English writer

Man is so made that he can only find relaxation from one kind of labour by taking up another.
    Anatole France 1844–1924 French man of letters

How pleasant to sit on the beach,
On the beach, on the sand, in the sun,
With ocean galore within reach,
And nothing at all to be done!
    Ogden Nash 1902–71 American humorist

To be able to fill leisure intelligently is the last product of
civilization.

    Bertrand Russell 1872–1970 British philosopher

If all the year were playing holidays,
To sport would be as tedious as to work;
But when they seldom come, they wished for come.

    William Shakespeare 1564–1616 English dramatist

We're all going on a summer holiday,
No more worries for a week or two.

    Bruce Welch 1941– and **Brian Bennett** 1940– English
    musicians

The world is too much with us; late and soon,
Getting and spending, we lay waste our powers.

    William Wordsworth 1770–1850 English poet

Letters ✳

Letters of thanks, letters from banks,
Letters of joy from girl and boy.

    W. H. Auden 1907–73 English poet

She'll vish there wos more, and that's the great art o'
letter writin'.

    Charles Dickens 1812–70 English novelist

Sir, more than kisses, letters mingle souls.

    John Donne 1572–1631 English poet

It is wonderful how much news there is when people
write every other day; if they wait for a month, there is
nothing that seems worth telling.

    O. Douglas 1877–1948 Scottish writer

All letters, methinks, should be free and easy as one's
discourse, not studied as an oration, nor made up of hard
words like a charm.

    Dorothy Osborne 1627–95 English letter writer

Letters

Don't think that this is a letter. It is only a small eruption of a disease called friendship.
Jean Renoir 1894–1979 French film director

A woman seldom writes her mind but in her postscript.
Richard Steele 1672–1729 Irish-born essayist

✳ Liberty

Liberty is always unfinished business.
Anonymous

Liberty is liberty, not equality or fairness or justice or human happiness or a quiet conscience.
Isaiah Berlin 1909–97 British philosopher

The people never give up their liberties except under some delusion.
Edmund Burke 1729–97 Irish-born politician

The condition upon which God hath given liberty to man is eternal vigilance.
John Philpot Curran 1750–1817 Irish judge

I know not what course others may take; but as for me, give me liberty, or give me death!
Patrick Henry 1736–99 American statesman

It is better to die on your feet than to live on your knees.
Dolores Ibarruri 1895–1989 Spanish communist leader

The enemies of Freedom do not argue; they shout and they shoot.
Dean Inge 1860–1954 English writer

We shall pay any price, bear any burden, meet any hardship, support any friend, oppose any foe to assure the survival and the success of liberty.
John F. Kennedy 1917–63 American statesman

Liberty is precious—so precious that it must be rationed.
Lenin 1870–1924 Russian revolutionary

Stone walls do not a prison make,
Nor iron bars a cage.
Richard Lovelace 1618–58 English poet

Freedom is always and exclusively freedom for the one who thinks differently.
Rosa Luxemburg 1871–1919 German revolutionary

If men are to wait for liberty till they become wise and good in slavery, they may indeed wait for ever.
Lord Macaulay 1800–59 English historian

The liberty of the individual must be thus far limited; he must not make himself a nuisance to other people.
John Stuart Mill 1806–73 English philosopher

Freedom is the freedom to say that two plus two make four. If that is granted, all else follows.
George Orwell 1903–50 English novelist

O liberty! what crimes are committed in thy name!
Mme Roland 1754–93 French revolutionary

Man was born free, and everywhere he is in chains.
Jean-Jacques Rousseau 1712–78 French philosopher

What is freedom of expression? Without the freedom to offend, it ceases to exist.
Salman Rushdie 1947– Indian-born British novelist

Liberty means responsibility. That is why most men dread it.
George Bernard Shaw 1856–1950 Irish dramatist

A free society is a society where it is safe to be unpopular.
Adlai Stevenson 1900–65 American politician

✳ Libraries ⇒Books, Reading

I have always imagined Paradise as a kind of library.
Jorge Luis Borges 1899–1986 Argentinian writer

The true University of these days is a collection of books.
Thomas Carlyle 1795–1881 Scottish historian

A man should keep his little brain attic stocked with all
the furniture that he is likely to use, and the rest he can
put away in the lumber room of his library, where he can
get it if he wants it.
Arthur Conan Doyle 1859–1930 Scottish-born writer

No place affords a more striking conviction of the vanity
of human hopes, than a public library.
Samuel Johnson 1709–84 English lexicographer

Your *borrowers of books*—those mutilators of collections,
spoilers of the symmetry of shelves, and creators of odd
volumes.
Charles Lamb 1775–1834 English writer

A library is thought in cold storage.
Lord Samuel 1870–1963 British politician

Come, and take choice of all my library,
And so beguile thy sorrow.
William Shakespeare 1564–1616 English dramatist

✳ Lies ⇒Deceit, Truth

An abomination unto the Lord, but a very present help in
time of trouble.
Anonymous *definition of a lie, an amalgamation of two biblical
verses*

One sometimes sees more clearly in the man who lies than in the man who tells the truth. Truth, like the light, blinds. Lying, on the other hand, is a beautiful twilight, which gives to each object its value.
  Albert Camus 1913–60 French writer

That branch of the art of lying which consists in very nearly deceiving your friends without quite deceiving your enemies.
  Francis M. Cornford 1874–1943 English academic, *on propaganda*

There are three kinds of lies: lies, damned lies and statistics.
  Benjamin Disraeli 1804–81 British statesman

Without lies humanity would perish of despair and boredom.
  Anatole France 1844–1924 French man of letters

In human relations kindness and lies are worth a thousand truths.
  Graham Greene 1904–91 English novelist

Whoever would lie usefully should lie seldom.
  Lord Hervey 1696–1743 English politician

The broad mass of a nation…will more easily fall victim to a big lie than to a small one.
  Adolf Hitler 1889–1945 German dictator

There is no worse lie than a truth misunderstood by those who hear it.
  William James 1842–1910 American philosopher

The lie in the soul is a true lie.
  Benjamin Jowett 1817–93 English classicist

He would, wouldn't he?
  Mandy Rice-Davies 1944– English model, *on hearing that Lord Astor denied her allegations*

Lies

For my part, if a lie may do thee grace,
I'll gild it with the happiest terms I have.
William Shakespeare 1564–1616 English dramatist

It is well said in the old proverb, 'a lie will go round the
world while truth is pulling its boots on'.
C. H. Spurgeon 1834–92 English preacher

The cruellest lies are often told in silence.
Robert Louis Stevenson 1850–94 Scottish novelist

One of the most striking differences between a cat and a
lie is that a cat has only nine lives.
Mark Twain 1835–1910 American writer

He will lie even when it is inconvenient: the sign of the
true artist.
Gore Vidal 1925– American writer

✳ Life →Life Sciences, Lifestyles

The Answer to the Great Question Of...Life, the Universe
and Everything...[is] Forty-two.
Douglas Adams 1952–2001 English writer

It is in life as it is in ways, the shortest way is commonly
the foulest, and surely the fairer way is not much about.
Francis Bacon 1561–1626 English courtier

'Such,' he said, 'O King, seems to me the present life of
men on earth, in comparison with that time which to us
is uncertain, as if when on a winter's night you sit
feasting with your ealdormen and thegns,—a single
sparrow should fly swiftly into the hall, and coming in at
one door, instantly fly out through another'.
The Venerable Bede AD 673–735 English historian

Man that is born of a woman is of few days, and full of trouble.

Bible

All that a man hath will he give for his life.

Bible

Life is just a bowl of cherries.

Lew Brown 1893–1958 American songwriter

W. C. FIELDS: It's a funny old world—a man's lucky if he gets out of it alive.

Walter de Leon and **Paul M. Jones** American screenwriters, *in the film* You're Telling Me

All that matters is love and work.

Sigmund Freud 1856–1939 Austrian psychiatrist

Man wants but little here below,
Nor wants that little long.

Oliver Goldsmith 1728–74 Irish writer

No arts; no letters; no society; and which is worst of all, continual fear and danger of violent death; and the life of man, solitary, poor, nasty, brutish, and short.

Thomas Hobbes 1588–1679 English philosopher

The crown of life is neither happiness nor annihilation; it is understanding.

Winifred Holtby 1898–1935 British novelist

Life is just one damned thing after another.

Elbert Hubbard 1859–1915 American writer

As far as we can discern, the sole purpose of human existence is to kindle a light in the darkness of mere being.

Carl Gustav Jung 1875–1961 Swiss psychologist

Life must be understood backwards; but…it must be lived forwards.

Sören Kierkegaard 1813–55 Danish philosopher

Life

Life is first boredom, then fear.
Philip Larkin 1922–85 English poet

Life is like a sewer. What you get out of it depends on what you put into it.
Tom Lehrer 1928– American humorist

Life is just what happens to you,
while you're busy making other plans.
John Lennon 1940–80 English pop singer

Life well spent is long.
Leonardo da Vinci 1452–1519 Italian painter

Life is real! Life is earnest!
And the grave is not its goal;
Dust thou art, to dust returnest,
Was not spoken of the soul.
Henry Wadsworth Longfellow 1807–82 American poet

What, knocked a tooth out? Never mind, dear, laugh it off, laugh it off; it's all part of life's rich pageant.
Arthur Marshall 1910–89 British journalist

We live, not as we wish to, but as we can.
Menander 342–c.292 BC Greek comic dramatist

I've looked at life from both sides now,
From win and lose and still somehow
It's life's illusions I recall;
I really don't know life at all.
Joni Mitchell 1945– Canadian singer

Man is born to live, not to prepare for life.
Boris Pasternak 1890–1960 Russian novelist

I have had everything in life, truly everything. So if it were all taken away, then God and I would be even.
Luciano Pavarotti 1935–2007 Italian operatic tenor

TOM HANKS: My momma always said life was like a box of chocolates…you never know what you're gonna get.
Eric Roth 1945- American screenwriter, *in the film* Forrest Gump

All the world's a stage,
And all the men and women merely players:
They have their exits and their entrances;
And one man in his time plays many parts,
His acts being seven ages.
William Shakespeare 1564–1616 English dramatist

Life is not meant to be easy, my child; but take courage:
it can be delightful.
George Bernard Shaw 1856–1950 Irish dramatist

Not to be born is, past all prizing, best.
Sophocles c.496–406 BC Greek dramatist

Our life is frittered away by detail…Simplify, simplify.
Henry David Thoreau 1817–62 American writer

Expect nothing. Live frugally
on surprise.
Alice Walker 1944- American poet

This world is a comedy to those that think, a tragedy to
those that feel.
Horace Walpole 1717–97 English connoisseur

There seems to be a general overall pattern in most lives,
that nothing happens, and nothing happens, and then all
of a sudden everything happens.
Fay Weldon 1931- British novelist

Never to have lived is best, ancient writers say;
Never to have drawn the breath of life, never to have
  looked into the eye of day;
The second best's a gay goodnight and quickly turn away.
W. B. Yeats 1865–1939 Irish poet

Life

Life is a rainbow which also includes black.
Yevgeny Yevtushenko 1933– Russian poet

✳ Life Sciences →Science

The Microbe is so very small
You cannot make him out at all.
Hilaire Belloc 1870–1953 British writer

Men will not be content to manufacture life: they will
want to improve on it.
J. D. Bernal 1901–71 Irish-born physicist

It has, I believe, been often remarked that a hen is only
an egg's way of making another egg.
Samuel Butler 1835–1902 English novelist

We have discovered the secret of life!
Francis Crick 1916–2004 English biophysicist, *on the discovery
of the structure of DNA*

Almost all aspects of life are engineered at the molecular
level, and without understanding molecules we can only
have a very sketchy understanding of life itself.
Francis Crick 1916–2004 English biophysicist

I have called this principle, by which each slight variation,
if useful, is preserved, by the term of Natural Selection.
Charles Darwin 1809–82 English naturalist

I'd lay down my life for two brothers or eight cousins.
J. B. S. Haldane 1892–1964 Scottish mathematical biologist

Life exists in the universe only because the carbon atom
possesses certain exceptional properties.
James Jeans 1877–1946 Scottish astronomer

The biologist passes, the frog remains.
Jean Rostand 1894–1977 French biologist, *sometimes quoted
as 'Theories pass. The frog remains'*

Genes are not like engineering blueprints; they are more like recipes in a cookbook. They tell us what ingredients to use, in what quantities, and in what order—but they do not provide a complete, accurate plan of the final result.

> **Ian Stewart** 1945-   British mathematician

So, naturalists observe, a flea
Hath smaller fleas that on him prey;
And these have smaller fleas to bite 'em,
And so proceed *ad infinitum.*

> **Jonathan Swift** 1667–1745 Irish poet and satirist

Water is life's *mater* and *matrix*, mother and medium. There is no life without water.

> **Albert von Szent-Györgyi** 1893–1986 Hungarian-born biochemist

Biology is the search for the chemistry that works.

> **R. J. P. Williams** 1926-   British chemist

Lifestyles ⇒Life

What is the secret of my long life? I really don't know— cigarettes, whisky and wild, wild women!

> **Henry Allingham** 1896–2009, *the oldest British survivor of the First World War*

I've lived a life that's full, I've travelled each and ev'ry highway
And more, much more than this. I did it my way.

> **Paul Anka** 1941-   Canadian singer

Love and do what you will.

> **St Augustine of Hippo** AD 354–430 Roman theologian

A man hath no better thing under the sun, than to eat, and to drink, and to be merry.

> **Bible**

Lifestyles

Thou shalt love thy neighbour as thyself.
Bible

The hippies wanted peace and love. We wanted Ferraris,
blondes and switchblades.
Alice Cooper 1948– American rock singer

Do what thou wilt shall be the whole of the Law.
Aleister Crowley 1875–1947 English diabolist

Dream as if you'll live forever. Live as if you'll die today.
James Dean 1931–55 American actor

Live in the sunshine, swim the sea,
Drink the wild air's salubrity.
Ralph Waldo Emerson 1803–82 American writer

RUSSELL CROWE: What we do in life echoes in eternity.
David Franzoni 1947– et al., American screenwriters, *in the
film* Gladiator

Just trust yourself and you'll learn the art of living.
Johann Wolfgang von Goethe 1749–1832 German writer

If I had but two loaves of bread I would sell one of them,
and buy White Hyacinths to feed my soul.
Elbert Hubbard 1859–1915 American writer

Live all you can; it's a mistake not to. It doesn't so much
matter what you do in particular, so long as you have
your life. If you haven't had that, what *have* you had?
Henry James 1843–1916 American novelist

Turn on, tune in and drop out.
Timothy Leary 1920–96 American psychologist

Believe me! The secret of reaping the greatest fruitfulness
and the greatest enjoyment from life is *to live dangerously*!
Friedrich Nietzsche 1844–1900 German philosopher

To live at all is miracle enough.
Mervyn Peake 1911–68 British novelist

Fais ce que voudras.
Do what you like.
> **François Rabelais** c.1494–c.1553 French humanist

You only live once, and the way I live, once is enough.
> **Frank Sinatra** 1915–98 American singer and actor

Take short views, hope for the best, and trust in God.
> **Sydney Smith** 1771–1845 English essayist

Keep your eyes open and your mouth shut.
> **John Steinbeck** 1902–68 American novelist

It's better to burn out
Than to fade away.
> **Neil Young** 1945– Canadian singer

Literature ⇒Writing

A losing trade, I assure you, sir: literature is a drug.
> **George Borrow** 1803–81 English writer

All tragedies are finished by a death,
All comedies are ended by a marriage;
The future states of both are left to faith.
> **Lord Byron** 1788–1824 English poet

Literature is a luxury; fiction is a necessity.
> **G. K. Chesterton** 1874–1936 English writer

The central function of imaginative literature is to make
you realize that other people act on moral convictions
different from your own.
> **William Empson** 1906–84 English critic

Yes—oh dear yes—the novel tells a story.
> **E. M. Forster** 1879–1970 English novelist

Works of serious purpose and grand promises often have
a purple patch or two stitched on, to shine far and wide.
> **Horace** 65–8 BC Roman poet

Literature

It takes a great deal of history to produce a little literature.
> **Henry James** 1843–1916 American novelist

Never trust the artist. Trust the tale.
> **D. H. Lawrence** 1885–1930 English writer

Literature is news that STAYS news.
> **Ezra Pound** 1885–1972 American poet

Remarks are not literature.
> **Gertrude Stein** 1874–1946 American writer

A novel is a mirror which passes over a highway. Sometimes it reflects to your eyes the blue of the skies, at others the churned-up mud of the road.
> **Stendhal** 1783–1842 French novelist

The good ended happily, and the bad unhappily. That is what fiction means.
> **Oscar Wilde** 1854–1900 Irish dramatist

✳ London

Was für Plunder!
What rubbish!
> **Gebhard Lebrecht Blücher** 1742–1819 Prussian field marshal, *often misquoted as* 'Was für plündern [*What a place to plunder*]!'

The great wen of all.
> **William Cobbett** 1762–1835 English political reformer

Crowds without company, and dissipation without pleasure.
> **Edward Gibbon** 1737–94 English historian

Maybe it's because I'm a Londoner
That I love London so.
> **Hubert Gregg** 1914–2004 English songwriter

When a man is tired of London, he is tired of life.
Samuel Johnson 1709–84 English lexicographer

I thought of London spread out in the sun,
Its postal districts packed like squares of wheat.
Philip Larkin 1922–85 English poet

Earth has not anything to show more fair:
Dull would he be of soul who could pass by
A sight so touching in its majesty.
William Wordsworth 1770–1850 English poet

Love ➡ Lovers, Marriage, Sex

Love is, above all, the gift of oneself!
Jean Anouilh 1910–87 French dramatist

With love, you see, even too much is not enough.
Pierre-Augustin Caron de Beaumarchais 1732–99 French dramatist

Love is free; it is not practised as a way of achieving other ends.
Pope Benedict XVI 1927– German cleric

Many waters cannot quench love, neither can the floods drown it.
Bible

Greater love hath no man than this, that a man lay down his life for his friends.
Bible

Though I speak with the tongues of men and of angels, and have not charity, I am become as sounding brass, or a tinkling cymbal…
And though I have all faith; so that I could remove mountains; and have not charity, I am nothing.
Bible

Love

And now abideth faith, hope, charity, these three; but the greatest of these is charity.
Bible

There is no fear in love; but perfect love casteth out fear.
Bible

Love seeketh not itself to please,
Nor for itself hath any care;
But for another gives its ease,
And builds a Heaven in Hell's despair.
William Blake 1757–1827 English poet

Say what you will, 'tis better to be left than never to have been loved.
William Congreve 1670–1729 English dramatist

The love that moves the sun and the other stars.
Dante Alighieri 1265–1321 Italian poet

Much love much trial, but what an utter desert is life without love.
Charles Darwin 1809–82 English naturalist

Selfhood begins with a walking away,
And love is proved in the letting go.
C. Day-Lewis 1904–72 English poet

Love itself is what is left over when being in love has burned away.
Louis de Bernières 1954– British novelist

If you could see my legs when I take my boots off, you'd form some idea of what unrequited affection is.
Charles Dickens 1812–70 English novelist

Love built on beauty, soon as beauty, dies.
John Donne 1572–1631 English poet

I am the Love that dare not speak its name.
Lord Alfred Douglas 1870–1945 English poet

Oh, if only we could lean over the soul we love and see as in a mirror the image we cast there!

André Gide 1869–1951 French novelist

If I love you, what does that matter to you!

Johann Wolfgang von Goethe 1749–1832 German writer

There is no disguise which can hide love for long where it exists, or feign it where it does not.

Duc de la Rochefoucauld 1613–80 French moralist

Only the flow matters; live and let live, love and let love. There is no point to love.

D. H. Lawrence 1885–1930 English writer

Where both deliberate, the love is slight;
Who ever loved that loved not at first sight?

Christopher Marlowe 1564–93 English dramatist

Had we but world enough, and time,
This coyness, lady, were no crime.

Andrew Marvell 1621–78 English poet

The love that lasts longest is the love that is never returned.

W. Somerset Maugham 1874–1965 English novelist

If I am pressed to say why I loved him, I feel it can only be explained by replying: 'Because it was he; because it was me.'

Montaigne 1533–92 French moralist

No, there's nothing half so sweet in life
As love's young dream.

Thomas Moore 1779–1852 Irish musician

Love is so short, forgetting is so long.

Pablo Neruda 1904–73 Chilean poet

I find no peace, and I am not at war,
I fear and hope, and burn and I am ice.

Petrarch 1304–74 Italian poet

Love

Birds do it, bees do it,
Even educated fleas do it.
Let's do it, let's fall in love.
>   **Cole Porter** 1891–1964 American songwriter

Love consists in this, that two solitudes protect and touch
and greet each other.
>   **Rainer Maria Rilke** 1875–1926 German poet

Life has taught us that love does not consist in gazing at
each other but in looking together in the same direction.
>   **Antoine de Saint-Exupéry** 1900–44 French novelist

Love means not ever having to say you're sorry.
>   **Erich Segal** 1937–   American writer

The course of true love never did run smooth.
>   **William Shakespeare** 1564–1616 English dramatist

>   Then, must you speak
Of one that loved not wisely but too well.
>   **William Shakespeare** 1564–1616 English dramatist

For stony limits cannot hold love out,
And what love can do that dares love attempt.
>   **William Shakespeare** 1564–1616 English dramatist

>   To be wise, and love,
Exceeds man's might.
>   **William Shakespeare** 1564–1616 English dramatist

Let me not to the marriage of true minds
Admit impediments. Love is not love
Which alters when it alteration finds.
>   **William Shakespeare** 1564–1616 English dramatist

'Tis better to have loved and lost
Than never to have loved at all.
>   **Alfred, Lord Tennyson** 1809–92 English poet

Love conquers all things: let us too give in to Love.
>   **Virgil** 70–19 BC Roman poet

Yet each man kills the thing he loves,
By each let this be heard,
Some do it with a bitter look,
Some with a flattering word.
The coward does it with a kiss,
The brave man with a sword!
   Oscar Wilde 1854–1900 Irish dramatist

A pity beyond all telling,
Is hid in the heart of love.
   W. B. Yeats 1865–1939 Irish poet

Lovers ✳

One is never too old for romance.
   Ingrid Bergman 1915–82 Swedish actress

A man chases a girl (until she catches him).
   Irving Berlin 1888–1989 American songwriter

Right worshipful and well-beloved Valentine, I commend
myself to you with all my heart, wishing to hear that all
is well with you: I beseech Almighty God to keep you
well according to his pleasure and your heart's desire.
   Margery Brews *letter to John Paston, 1477*

He's more myself than I am. Whatever our souls are
made of his and mine are the same.
   Emily Brontë 1818–48 English writer

If thou must love me, let it be for nought
Except for love's sake only.
   Elizabeth Barrett Browning 1806–61 English poet

How do I love thee? Let me count the ways.
   Elizabeth Barrett Browning 1806–61 English poet

Lovers

O, my Luve's like a red, red rose
That's newly sprung in June;
O my Luve's like the melodie
That's sweetly play'd in tune.
Robert Burns 1759–96 Scottish poet

My heart has made its mind up
And I'm afraid it's you.
Wendy Cope 1945– English poet

My soul is so knit to yours that it is but a divided life I
live without you.
George Eliot 1819–80 English novelist

Stay, little Valentine, stay,
Each day is Valentine's day.
Lorenz Hart 1895–1943 American songwriter

I was more pleased with possessing your heart than with
any other happiness.
Héloise c.1098–1164 French abbess

All you need is love.
John Lennon 1940–80 and **Paul McCartney** 1942– English
pop singers

So many contradictions, so many contrary movements are
true, and can be explained in three words: *I love you.*
Julie de Lespinasse 1732–76 French literary hostess

The life that I have
Is all that I have
And the life that I have
Is yours.
The love that I have
Of the life that I have
Is yours and yours and yours.
Leo Marks 1920–2001 English cryptographer, *given to the
British secret agent Violette Szabo (1921–45), for use with the
Special Operations Executive*

Difficult or easy, pleasant or bitter, you are the same you:
I cannot live with you—or without you.
Martial c.AD 40–c.104 Roman epigrammatist

I want to do with you
what spring does with the cherry trees.
Pablo Neruda 1904–73 Chilean poet

       It were all one
That I should love a bright particular star
And think to wed it, he is so above me.
William Shakespeare 1564–1616 English dramatist

The fickleness of the women I love is only equalled by the
infernal constancy of the women who love me.
George Bernard Shaw 1856–1950 Irish dramatist

Why so pale and wan, fond lover?
Prithee, why so pale?
Will, when looking well can't move her,
Looking ill prevail?
John Suckling 1609–42 English poet

Why is it that the most unoriginal thing we can say to
one another is still the thing we long to hear? 'I love you'
is always a quotation.
Jeanette Winterson 1959– English novelist

Luck ✳

What we call luck is the inner man externalized. We make
things happen to us.
Robertson Davies 1913–95 Canadian novelist

The best mascot is a good mechanic.
Amelia Earhart 1898–1937 American aviator

Luck

There is much good luck in the world, but it is luck. We are none of us safe. We are children, playing or quarrelling on the line.

E. M. Forster 1879–1970 English novelist

Care and diligence bring luck.

Thomas Fuller 1654–1734 English physician

Some folk want their luck buttered.

Thomas Hardy 1840–1928 English novelist

Watch out w'en you'er gittin all you want. Fattenin' hogs ain't in luck.

Joel Chandler Harris 1848–1908 American writer

All you know about it [luck] for certain is that it's bound to change.

Bret Harte 1836–1902 American poet

Miracles do happen, but one has to work very hard for them.

Chaim Weizmann 1874–1952 Russian-born Israeli statesman

Luck is preparation meeting opportunity.

Oprah Winfrey 1954– American talk show hostess

✳ Madness

Babylon in all its desolation is a sight not so awful as that of the human mind in ruins.

Scrope Davies c.1783–1852 English conversationalist

Whom God would destroy He first sends mad.

James Duport 1606–79 English scholar, *summarizing a Greek original*

Mad, is he? Then I hope he will *bite* some of my other generals.

George II 1683–1760 British monarch, *replying to the Duke of Newcastle, who had complained that General Wolfe was a madman*

There was only one catch and that was Catch-22...Orr would be crazy to fly more missions and sane if he didn't, but if he was sane he had to fly them. If he flew them he was crazy and didn't have to; but if he didn't want to he was sane and had to.
Joseph Heller 1923–99 American novelist

Every one is more or less mad on one point.
Rudyard Kipling 1865–1936 English writer

Madness need not be all breakdown. It may also be break-through.
R. D. Laing 1927–89 Scottish psychiatrist

They called me mad, and I called them mad, and damn them, they outvoted me.
Nathaniel Lee c.1653–92 English dramatist

Is there no way out of the mind?
Sylvia Plath 1932–63 American poet

The psychopath is the furnace that gives no heat.
Derek Raymond 1931–94 English writer

Though this be madness, yet there is method in't.
William Shakespeare 1564–1616 English dramatist

O! let me not be mad, not mad, sweet heaven;
Keep me in temper; I would not be mad!
William Shakespeare 1564–1616 English dramatist

Management ⇒Careers, Planning

Committee—a group of men who individually can do nothing but as a group decide that nothing can be done.
Fred Allen 1894–1956 American humorist

A place for everything and everything in its place.
Mrs Beeton 1836–65 English cookery writer

Management

You're either part of the solution or you're part of the problem.
Eldridge Cleaver 1935-98 American political activist

Meetings are a great trap...However, they are indispensable when you don't want to do anything.
J. K. Galbraith 1908-2006 American economist

If you want people motivated to do a good job, give them a good job to do.
Frederick Herzberg 1923-2000 American management researcher

A camel is a horse designed by a committee.
Alec Issigonis 1906-88 British engineer

There cannot be a crisis next week. My schedule is already full.
Henry Kissinger 1923- American politician

If it ain't broke, don't fix it.
Bert Lance 1931- American government official

Every time I create an appointment, I create a hundred malcontents and one ingrate.
Louis XIV 1638-1715 French monarch

There is always a well-known solution to every human problem—neat, plausible, and wrong.
H. L. Mencken 1880-1956 American journalist

Time spent on any item of the agenda will be in inverse proportion to the sum involved.
C. Northcote Parkinson 1909-93 English writer

In a hierarchy every employee tends to rise to his level of incompetence.
Laurence Peter 1919-90 Canadian writer

Surround yourself with the best people you can find, delegate authority, and don't interfere.
Ronald Reagan 1911-2004 American statesman

There is nothing in the world which does not have its decisive moment, and the masterpiece of good management is to recognize and grasp this moment.
Cardinal de Retz 1613–79 French cardinal

A problem left to itself dries up or goes rotten. But fertilize a problem with a solution—you'll hatch out dozens.
N. F. Simpson 1919– English dramatist

The shortest way to do many things is to do only one thing at once.
Samuel Smiles 1812–1904 English writer

You're fired!
Donald Trump 1946– American businessman, *in the UK associated with the English businessman Alan Sugar (1947–)*

Dans ce pays-ci il est bon de tuer de temps en temps un amiral pour encourager les autres.
In this country [England] it is thought well to kill an admiral from time to time to encourage the others.
Voltaire 1694–1778 French writer

Manners ⇒Behaviour, Punctuality

Evil communications corrupt good manners.
Bible

The tribute which intelligence pays to humbug.
St John Brodrick 1856–1942 British politician, *definition of tact*

Curtsey while you're thinking what to say. It saves time.
Lewis Carroll 1832–98 English writer

Take the tone of the company that you are in.
Lord Chesterfield 1694–1773 English writer

Manners

Very notable was his distinction between coarseness and vulgarity (coarseness, revealing something; vulgarity, concealing something).
E. M. Forster 1879-1970 English novelist

The art of pleasing consists in being pleased.
William Hazlitt 1778-1830 English essayist

An insolent reply from a polite person is a bad sign.
Hippocrates c.460-357 BC Greek physician

To Americans, English manners are far more frightening than none at all.
Randall Jarrell 1914-65 American poet

THUMPER: If you can't say something nice...don't say nothing at all.
Larry Morey 1905-71, *in the film* Bambi

Manners maketh man.
Proverb *motto of William of Wykeham (1324-1404)*

Stand not upon the order of your going.
William Shakespeare 1564-1616 English dramatist

He is the very pineapple of politeness!
Richard Brinsley Sheridan 1751-1816 Irish dramatist

Manners are especially the need of the plain. The pretty can get away with anything.
Evelyn Waugh 1903-66 English novelist

✳ Marriage ⇒Love, Weddings

It is a truth universally acknowledged, that a single man in possession of a good fortune, must be in want of a wife.
Jane Austen 1775-1817 English novelist

Wives are young men's mistresses, companions for middle age, and old men's nurses.
Francis Bacon 1561–1626 English courtier

Being a husband is a whole-time job. That is why so many husbands fail. They cannot give their entire attention to it.
Arnold Bennett 1867–1931 English novelist

What therefore God hath joined together, let not man put asunder.
Bible

To have and to hold from this day forward, for better for worse, for richer for poorer, in sickness and in health, to love, cherish, and to obey, till death us do part.
Book of Common Prayer 1662

Still I can't contradict, what so oft has been said,
'Though women are angels, yet wedlock's the devil.'
Lord Byron 1788–1824 English poet

The deep, deep peace of the double-bed after the hurly-burly of the chaise-longue.
Mrs Patrick Campbell 1865–1940 English actress, *on her recent marriage*

Oh! how many torments lie in the small circle of a wedding-ring!
Colley Cibber 1671–1757 English dramatist

I learnt a long time ago that the only people who count in any marriage are the two that are in it.
Hillary Rodham Clinton 1947– American lawyer

Marriage is a wonderful invention; but, then again, so is a bicycle repair kit.
Billy Connolly 1942– Scottish comedian

The heart of marriage is memories.
Bill Cosby 1937– American actor

Marriage

I would be married, but I'd have no wife,
I would be married to a single life.
> **Richard Crashaw** c.1612–49 English poet

The chains of marriage are so heavy that it takes two to
bear them, and sometimes three.
> **Alexandre Dumas** 1824–95 French writer

Man's best possession is a sympathetic wife.
> **Euripides** c.485–c.406 BC Greek dramatist

Keep your eyes wide open before marriage, half shut
afterwards.
> **Benjamin Franklin** 1706–90 American statesman and
scientist

Do you think your mother and I should have lived
comfortably so long together, if ever we had been
married?
> **John Gay** 1685–1732 English writer

You shall be together when the white wings of death
scatter your days.
Ay, you shall be together even in the silent memory of
God.
But let there be spaces in your togetherness,
And let the winds of the heavens dance between you.
> **Kahlil Gibran** 1883–1931 Lebanese-born American writer

I…chose my wife, as she did her wedding gown, not for a
fine glossy surface, but such qualities as would wear well.
> **Oliver Goldsmith** 1728–74 Irish writer

Then be not coy, but use your time;
And while ye may, go marry:
For having lost but once your prime,
You may for ever tarry.
> **Robert Herrick** 1591–1674 English poet

The triumph of hope over experience.
> **Samuel Johnson** 1709–84 English lexicographer, *of a man who remarried immediately after the death of a wife with whom he had been unhappy*

The best thing about being married is having someone who puts out the rubbish.
> **Ulrika Jonsson** 1967– Swedish-born television presenter

Marriage is one long fit of compromise, deep and wide.
> **Barbara Kingsolver** 1955– American writer

I am your clay.
You are my clay.
In life we share a single quilt.
In death we will share one coffin.
> **Kuan Tao-sheng** 1262–1319 Chinese poet

One doesn't have to get anywhere in a marriage. It's not a public conveyance.
> **Iris Murdoch** 1919–99 English novelist

The great secret of a successful marriage is to treat all disasters as incidents and none of the incidents as disasters.
> **Harold Nicolson** 1886–1968 English diplomat

Tolerance is the one essential ingredient.
> **Philip, Duke of Edinburgh** 1921– Greek-born husband of Elizabeth II, *his recipe for a successful marriage*

It doesn't much signify whom one marries, for one is sure to find next morning that it was someone else.
> **Samuel Rogers** 1763–1855 English poet

A young man married is a man that's marred.
> **William Shakespeare** 1564–1616 English dramatist

Marriage is popular because it combines the maximum of temptation with the maximum of opportunity.
> **George Bernard Shaw** 1856–1950 Irish dramatist

Marriage

Chains do not hold a marriage together. It is threads, hundreds of tiny threads which sew people together through the years. That is what makes a marriage last—more than passion or even sex!
Simone Signoret 1921–85 French actress

Marriage is like life in this—that it is a field of battle, and not a bed of roses.
Robert Louis Stevenson 1850–94 Scottish novelist

Marriage isn't a word…it's a *sentence*!
King Vidor 1895–1982 American film director

In married life three is company and two none.
Oscar Wilde 1854–1900 Irish dramatist

✳ Mathematics

Let no one enter who does not know geometry [mathematics].
Anonymous *inscription on Plato's door, probably at the Academy at Athens*

If in other sciences we should arrive at certainty without doubt and truth without error, it behoves us to place the foundations of knowledge in mathematics.
Roger Bacon *c.*1220–*c.*92 English philosopher and friar

They are neither finite quantities, or quantities infinitely small, nor yet nothing. May we not call them the ghosts of departed quantities?
Bishop George Berkeley 1685–1753 Irish philosopher, *on Newton's infinitesimals*

I never could make out what those damned dots meant.
Lord Randolph Churchill 1849–94 British politician, *on decimal points*

Mathematics

Equations are more important to me, because politics is for the present, but an equation is something for eternity.
Albert Einstein 1879–1955 German-born theoretical physicist

There is no 'royal road' to geometry.
Euclid fl. c.300 BC Greek mathematician

This book is written in mathematical language and its characters are triangles, circles and other geometrical figures, without whose help…one wanders in vain through a dark labyrinth.
Galileo Galilei 1564–1642 Italian astronomer, *often quoted as 'The book of nature is written…'*

Prime numbers are what is left when you have taken all the patterns away. I think prime numbers are like life.
Mark Haddon 1962– British novelist

Beauty is the first test: there is no permanent place in the world for ugly mathematics.
Godfrey Harold Hardy 1877–1947 English mathematician

Someone told me that each equation I included in the book would halve the sales.
Stephen Hawking 1942– English theoretical physicist

God made the integers, all the rest is the work of man.
Leopold Kronecker 1823–91 German mathematician

In mathematics you don't understand things. You just get used to them.
John von Neumann 1903–57 American mathematician

There are 10 types of people in the country: those who understand binary and those who don't.
Jeremy Paxman 1950– British journalist

God is always doing geometry.
Plato 429–347 BC Greek philosopher

Mathematics

What would life be like without arithmetic, but a scene of horrors?

Sydney Smith 1771–1845 English essayist

✳ Meaning ⇒Words

No one means all he says, and yet very few say all they mean, for words are slippery and thought is viscous.

Henry Brooks Adams 1838–1918 American historian

'Then you should say what you mean,' the March Hare went on. 'I do,' Alice hastily replied; 'at least—at least I mean what I say—that's the same thing, you know.' 'Not the same thing a bit!' said the Hatter. 'Why, you might just as well say that "I see what I eat" is the same thing as "I eat what I see!" '

Lewis Carroll 1832–98 English writer

It depends on what the meaning of 'is' is.

Bill Clinton 1946– American statesman

The meaning doesn't matter if it's only idle chatter of a transcendental kind.

W. S. Gilbert 1836–1911 English writer

It all depends what you mean by...

C. E. M. Joad 1891–1953 English philosopher, *characteristic response to questions*

God and I both knew what it meant once; now God alone knows.

Friedrich Klopstock 1724–1803 German poet

I pray thee, understand a plain man in his plain meaning.

William Shakespeare 1564–1616 English dramatist

The little girl had the making of a poet in her who, being told to be sure of her meaning before she spoke, said, 'How can I know what I think till I see what I say?'

Graham Wallas 1858–1932 British political scientist

Medicine →Health, Sickness

Medicinal discovery,
It moves in mighty leaps,
It leapt straight past the common cold
And gave it us for keeps.
Pam Ayres 1947- English writer

Cure the disease and kill the patient.
Francis Bacon 1561–1626 English courtier

The remedy is worse than the disease.
Francis Bacon 1561–1626 English courtier

Physician, heal thyself.
Bible

He that sinneth before his Maker, let him fall into the
hand of the physician.
Bible (Apocrypha)

We all labour against our own cure, for death is the cure
of all diseases.
Sir Thomas Browne 1605–82 English writer

Every day, in every way, I am getting better and better.
Émile Coué 1857–1926 French psychologist, *to be said 15 to 20
times, morning and evening*

Life is short, the art long.
Hippocrates c.460–357 BC Greek physician, *often quoted as
'Ars longa, vita brevis'*

As to diseases, make a habit of two things—to help, or at
least to do no harm.
Hippocrates c.460–357 BC Greek physician

It may seem a strange principle to enunciate as the very
first requirement in a Hospital that it should do the sick
no harm.
Florence Nightingale 1820–1910 English nurse

253

Medicine

One finger in the throat and one in the rectum makes a good diagnostician.

William Osler 1849–1919 Canadian-born physician

Throw physic to the dogs; I'll none of it.

William Shakespeare 1564–1616 English dramatist

Formerly, when religion was strong and science weak, men mistook magic for medicine; now, when science is strong and religion weak, men mistake medicine for magic.

Thomas Szasz 1920– Hungarian-born psychiatrist

✳ Meeting ⇒Parting

Gin a body meet a body
Comin thro' the rye,
Gin a body kiss a body
Need a body cry?

Robert Burns 1759–96 Scottish poet

'Is there anybody there?' said the Traveller,
Knocking on the moonlit door.

Walter de la Mare 1873–1956 English poet

HUMPHREY BOGART: Of all the gin joints in all the towns in all the world, she walks into mine.

Julius J. Epstein 1909–2001 et al., American screenwriters, *in the film* Casablanca

Some enchanted evening,
You may see a stranger,
You may see a stranger,
Across a crowded room.

Oscar Hammerstein II 1895–1960 American songwriter

Not many sounds in life, and I include all urban and all rural sounds, exceed in interest a knock at the door.

Charles Lamb 1775–1834 English writer

Memory

How d'ye do, and how is the old complaint?
> **Lord Palmerston** 1784–1865 British statesman, *reputed to be his greeting to all those he did not know*

We'll meet again, don't know where,
Don't know when,
But I know we'll meet again some sunny day.
> **Ross Parker** 1914–74 and **Hugh Charles** 1907–95 British songwriters

When shall we three meet again
In thunder, lightning, or in rain?
> **William Shakespeare** 1564–1616 English dramatist

Ill met by moonlight, proud Titania.
> **William Shakespeare** 1564–1616 English dramatist

Dr Livingstone, I presume?
> **Henry Morton Stanley** 1841–1904 British explorer

Why don't you come up sometime, and see me?
> **Mae West** 1892–1980 American film actress

Memory ✳

And we forget because we must
And not because we will.
> **Matthew Arnold** 1822–88 English poet

Someone said that God gave us memory so that we might have roses in December.
> **J. M. Barrie** 1860–1937 Scottish writer

Nobody can remember more than seven of anything.
> **St Robert Bellarmine** 1542–1621 Italian cardinal, *reason for omitting the eight beatitudes from his catechism*

Memories are not shackles, Franklin, they are garlands.
> **Alan Bennett** 1934– English writer

Memory

We'll tak a cup o' kindness yet,
For auld lang syne.
> **Robert Burns** 1759–96 Scottish poet

Our memories are card-indexes consulted, and then put back in disorder by authorities whom we do not control.
> **Cyril Connolly** 1903–74 English writer

Everyone seems to remember with great clarity what they were doing on November 22nd, 1963, at the precise moment they heard President Kennedy was dead.
> **Frederick Forsyth** 1938– English novelist

What are those blue remembered hills,
What spires, what farms are those?
> **A. E. Housman** 1859–1936 English poet

The true art of memory is the art of attention.
> **Samuel Johnson** 1709–84 English lexicographer

A cigarette that bears a lipstick's traces,
An airline ticket to romantic places;
And still my heart has wings
These foolish things
Remind me of you.
> **Holt Marvell** 1901–69 English songwriter

You may break, you may shatter the vase, if you will,
But the scent of the roses will hang round it still.
> **Thomas Moore** 1779–1852 Irish musician

Better by far you should forget and smile
Than that you should remember and be sad.
> **Christina Rossetti** 1830–94 English poet

There's rosemary, that's for remembrance; pray, love, remember.
> **William Shakespeare** 1564–1616 English dramatist

Men

Are all men in disguise except those crying?
Dannie Abse 1923– Welsh-born poet

ANTHONY QUINN: Am I not a man? And is not a man
stupid? I'm a man, so I married. Wife, children, house,
everything, the full catastrophe.
Michael Cacoyannis 1922– Cypriot-born film director, *in the film* Zorba the Greek

Older men treat women like possessions, which is why I
like younger men.
Joan Collins 1933– British actress

A man…is *so* in the way in the house!
Elizabeth Gaskell 1810–65 English novelist

Man is Nature's sole mistake!
W. S. Gilbert 1836–1911 English writer

Years ago, manhood was an opportunity for achievement,
and now it is a problem to be overcome.
Garrison Keillor 1942– American writer

Why can't a woman be more like a man?
Men are so honest, so thoroughly square;
Eternally noble, historically fair.
Alan Jay Lerner 1918–86 American songwriter

Give me macho, or give me death.
Madonna 1958– American pop singer

Somehow a bachelor never quite gets over the idea that
he is a thing of beauty and a boy forever.
Helen Rowland 1875–1950 American writer

Sigh no more, ladies, sigh no more,
Men were deceivers ever.
William Shakespeare 1564–1616 English dramatist

Men

It's not the men in my life that counts—it's the life in my men.

Mae West 1892–1980 American film actress

✳ Men and Women ⇒Woman's Role

Women are really much nicer than men:
No wonder we like them.

Kingsley Amis 1922–95 English novelist

In societies where men are truly confident of their own worth, women are not merely tolerated but valued.

Aung San Suu Kyi 1945– Burmese political leader

Men look at women. Women watch themselves being looked at.

John Berger 1926– British writer

Man's love is of man's life a thing apart,
'Tis woman's whole existence.

Lord Byron 1788–1824 English poet

The man's desire is for the woman; but the woman's desire is rarely other than for the desire of the man.

Samuel Taylor Coleridge 1772–1834 English poet

Any woman who is sure of her own wits is a match at any time for a man who is not sure of his own temper.

Wilkie Collins 1824–89 English novelist

There is more difference within the sexes than between them.

Ivy Compton-Burnett 1884–1969 English novelist

In the sex-war thoughtlessness is the weapon of the male, vindictiveness of the female.

Cyril Connolly 1903–74 English writer

A woman needs a man like a fish needs a bicycle.

Irina Dunn Australian writer and politician

Men and Women

Men are from Mars, women are from Venus.
>**John Gray** 1951– American writer

Women have very little idea of how much men hate them.
>**Germaine Greer** 1939– Australian feminist

The female of the species is more deadly than the male.
>**Rudyard Kipling** 1865–1936 English writer

A woman can forgive a man for the harm he does her, but she can never forgive him for the sacrifices he makes on her account.
>**W. Somerset Maugham** 1874–1965 English novelist

He for God only, she for God in him.
>**John Milton** 1608–74 English poet

I admit it is better fun to punt than to be punted, and that a desire to have all the fun is nine-tenths of the law of chivalry.
>**Dorothy L. Sayers** 1893–1957 English writer

Whereas nature turns girls into women, society has to make boys into men.
>**Anthony Stevens** British psychiatrist

'Tis strange what a man may do, and a woman yet think him an angel.
>**William Makepeace Thackeray** 1811–63 English novelist

After all these years, I see that I was mistaken about Eve in the beginning; it is better to live outside the Garden with her than inside it without her.
>**Mark Twain** 1835–1910 American writer

Me Tarzan, you Jane.
>**Johnny Weissmuller** 1904–84 American film actor

Whatever women do they must do twice as well as men to be thought half as good.
>**Charlotte Whitton** 1896–1975 Canadian writer

Men and Women

All women become like their mothers. That is their
tragedy. No man does. That's his.
Oscar Wilde 1854–1900 Irish dramatist

✳ Middle Age

Years ago we discovered the exact point, the dead centre
of middle age. It occurs when you are too young to take
up golf and too old to rush up to the net.
Franklin P. Adams 1881–1960 American journalist

You are living in a land you no longer recognize. You
don't know the language.
Martin Amis 1949– English novelist

I am past thirty, and three parts iced over.
Matthew Arnold 1822–88 English poet

Nel mezzo del cammin di nostra vita.
Midway along the path of our life.
Dante Alighieri 1265–1321 Italian poet

At eighteen our convictions are hills from which we look;
at forty-five they are caves in which we hide.
F. Scott Fitzgerald 1896–1940 American novelist

The afternoon of human life must also have a significance
of its own and cannot be merely a pitiful appendage to
life's morning.
Carl Gustav Jung 1875–1961 Swiss psychologist

Men at forty
Learn to close softly
The doors to rooms they will not be
Coming back to.
Donald Justice 1925–2004 American poet

At forty-five,
What next, what next?
At every corner,
I meet my Father,
my age, still alive.
> **Robert Lowell** 1917–77 American poet

The lovely thing about being forty is that you can
appreciate twenty-five-year-old men more.
> **Colleen McCullough** 1937– Australian writer

Do you think my mind is maturing late,
Or simply rotted early?
> **Ogden Nash** 1902–71 American humorist, *on facing forty*

One of the pleasures of middle age is to *find out* that one
was right, and that one was much righter than one knew
at say 17 or 23.
> **Ezra Pound** 1885–1972 American poet

One's prime is elusive. You little girls, when you grow up,
must be on the alert to recognise your prime at whatever
time of your life it may occur.
> **Muriel Spark** 1918–2006 British novelist

By the time you hit 50, I reckon you've earned your
wrinkles, so why not be proud of them?
> **Twiggy** 1949– English model

The Mind ✳

It is not enough to have a good mind; the main thing is
to use it well.
> **René Descartes** 1596–1650 French philosopher

On earth there is nothing great but man; in man there is
nothing great but mind.
> **William Hamilton** 1788–1856 Scottish metaphysician

The Mind

O the mind, mind has mountains; cliffs of fall
Frightful, sheer, no-man-fathomed.
Gerard Manley Hopkins 1844–89 English poet

Everyone complains of his memory, and no one
complains of his judgement.
Duc de la Rochefoucauld 1613–80 French moralist

The mind loves the unknown. It loves images whose
meaning is unknown, since the meaning of the mind
itself is unknown.
René Magritte 1898–1967 Belgian surrealist painter

The mind is its own place, and in itself
Can make a heaven of hell, a hell of heaven.
John Milton 1608–74 English poet

Those who are caught in mental cages can often picture
freedom, it just has no attractive power.
Iris Murdoch 1919–99 English novelist

That's the classical mind at work, runs fine inside but
looks dingy on the surface.
Robert M. Pirsig 1928– American writer

Noble deeds and hot baths are the best cures for
depression.
Dodie Smith 1896–1990 English writer

Why waste money on psychotherapy when you can listen
to the B Minor Mass?
Michael Torke 1961– American composer

✳ Misfortune

Prosperity doth best discover vice, but adversity doth best
discover virtue.
Francis Bacon 1561–1626 English courtier

And always keep a-hold of Nurse
For fear of finding something worse.
    Hilaire Belloc 1870–1953 British writer

Man is born unto trouble, as the sparks fly upward.
    Bible

There is no greater pain than to remember a happy time
when one is in misery.
    Dante Alighieri 1265–1321 Italian poet

In the words of one of my more sympathetic
correspondents, it has turned out to be an 'annus
horribilis'.
    Elizabeth II 1926– British monarch

I left the room with silent dignity, but caught my foot in
the mat.
    George Grossmith 1847–1912 and **Weedon Grossmith**
1854–1919 English writers

In the misfortune of our best friends, we always find
something which is not displeasing to us.
    Duc de la Rochefoucauld 1613–80 French moralist

When fortune empties her chamberpot on your head,
smile—and say 'we are going to have a summer shower'.
    John A. Macdonald 1815–91 Canadian statesman

now and then
there is a person born
who is so unlucky
that he runs into accidents
which started to happen
to somebody else.
    Don Marquis 1878–1937 American poet

All the misfortunes of men derive from one single thing,
which is their inability to be at ease in a room.
    Blaise Pascal 1623–62 French scientist and philosopher

Misfortune

I had never had a piece of toast
Particularly long and wide,
But fell upon the sanded floor,
And always on the buttered side.
James Payn 1830–98 English writer

Sweet are the uses of adversity,
Which like the toad, ugly and venomous,
Wears yet a precious jewel in his head.
William Shakespeare 1564–1616 English dramatist

The fatal law of gravity: when you are down everything
falls on you.
Sylvia Townsend Warner 1893–1978 English writer

One likes people much better when they're battered down
by a prodigious siege of misfortune than when they
triumph.
Virginia Woolf 1882–1941 English novelist

❊ Mistakes

Truth lies within a little and certain compass, but error is
immense.
Henry St John, 1st Viscount Bolingbroke 1678–1751 English
politician

It is worse than a crime, it is a blunder.
Antoine Boulay de la Meurthe 1761–1840 French statesman,
on hearing of the execution of the Duc d'Enghien

I would rather be wrong, by God, with Plato…than be
correct with those men.
Cicero 106–43 BC Roman statesman, *of Pythagoreans*

I beseech you, in the bowels of Christ, think it possible
you may be mistaken.
Oliver Cromwell 1599–1658 English statesman

Errors, like straws, upon the surface flow;
He who would search for pearls must dive below.
John Dryden 1631–1700 English poet

If all else fails, immortality can always be assured by a spectacular error.
J. K. Galbraith 1908–2006 American economist

Mistakes are a fact of life
It is the response to error that counts.
Nikki Giovanni 1943– American poet

An expert is someone who knows some of the worst mistakes that can be made in his subject and who manages to avoid them.
Werner Heisenberg 1901–76 German mathematical physicist

Sometimes even excellent Homer nods.
Horace 65–8 BC Roman poet

Crooked things may be as stiff and unflexible as straight: and men may be as positive in error as in truth.
John Locke 1632–1704 English philosopher

To err is human, but it feels divine.
Dolly Parton 1946– American singer

The man who makes no mistakes does not usually make anything.
Edward John Phelps 1822–1900 American lawyer

One Galileo in two thousand years is enough.
Pope Pius XII 1876–1958 Italian cleric, *on being asked to proscribe the works of Teilhard de Chardin*

A man should never be ashamed to own he has been in the wrong, which is but saying, in other words, that he is wiser to-day than he was yesterday.
Alexander Pope 1688–1744 English poet

Mistakes

'Forward, the Light Brigade!'
Was there a man dismayed?
Not though the soldier knew
Some one had blundered.
  Alfred, Lord Tennyson 1809–92 English poet

To lose one parent, Mr Worthing, may be regarded as a misfortune; to lose both looks like carelessness.
  Oscar Wilde 1854–1900 Irish dramatist

✹ Moderation

Nothing in excess.
  Anonymous *inscribed on the temple of Apollo at Delphi*

To many, total abstinence is easier than perfect moderation.
  St Augustine of Hippo AD 354–430 Roman theologian

We know what happens to people who stay in the middle of the road. They get run down.
  Aneurin Bevan 1897–1960 British politician

I would remind you that extremism in the defence of liberty is no vice! And let me remind you also that moderation in the pursuit of justice is no virtue!
  Barry Goldwater 1909–98 American politician

There's nothing in the middle of the road but yellow stripes and dead armadillos.
  Jim Hightower 1943– American politician

There is moderation in everything.
  Horace 65–8 BC Roman poet

You will go most safely by the middle way.
  Ovid 43 BC–c.AD 17 Roman poet

To gild refinèd gold, to paint the lily…
Is wasteful and ridiculous excess.
  William Shakespeare 1564–1616 English dramatist

Above all, gentlemen, not the slightest zeal.
  Charles-Maurice de Talleyrand 1754–1838 French statesman

Use, do not abuse…Neither abstinence nor excess ever
renders man happy.
  Voltaire 1694–1778 French writer

Money ⇒Poverty, Wealth

Nothing that costs only a dollar is worth having.
  Elizabeth Arden 1876–1966 American businesswoman

Money is like muck, not good except it be spread.
  Francis Bacon 1561–1626 English courtier

Money, it turned out, was exactly like sex, you thought of
nothing else if you didn't have it and thought of other
things if you did.
  James Baldwin 1924–87 American writer

Money speaks sense in a language all nations understand.
  Aphra Behn 1640–89 English writer

The love of money is the root of all evil.
  Bible

The sinews of war, unlimited money.
  Cicero 106–43 BC Roman statesman

MR MICAWBER: Annual income twenty pounds, annual
expenditure nineteen nineteen six, result happiness.
Annual income twenty pounds, annual expenditure
twenty pounds ought and six, result misery.
  Charles Dickens 1812–70 English novelist

Money doesn't talk, it swears.
  Bob Dylan 1941– American singer

Money

Money makes the world go around.
Fred Ebb 1932–2004 American songwriter

Money without brains is always dangerous.
Napoleon Hill 1883–1970 American writer

A bank is a place that will lend you money if you can prove that you don't need it.
Bob Hope 1903–2003 American comedian

If possible honestly, if not, somehow, make money.
Horace 65–8 BC Roman poet

When a feller says, 'It hain't the money, but th' principle o' th' thing,', it's the money.
Frank McKinney ('Kin') Hubbard 1868–1930 American humorist

For I don't care too much for money,
For money can't buy me love.
John Lennon 1940–80 and **Paul McCartney** 1942– English pop singers

Take care of the pence, and the pounds will take care of themselves.
William Lowndes 1652–1724 English politician

Money is like a sixth sense without which you cannot make a complete use of the other five.
W. Somerset Maugham 1874–1965 English novelist

Money couldn't buy friends but you got a better class of enemy.
Spike Milligan 1918–2002 Irish comedian

I want to spend, and spend, and spend.
Vivian Nicholson 1936– British pools winner, *said to reporters on arriving to collect her winnings of £152,000*

Expenditure rises to meet income.
C. Northcote Parkinson 1909–93 English writer

'My boy,' he says, 'always try to rub up against money, for if you rub up against money long enough, some of it may rub off on you.'
Damon Runyon 1884–1946 American writer

I can get no remedy against this consumption of the purse: borrowing only lingers and lingers it out, but the disease is incurable.
William Shakespeare 1564–1616 English dramatist

Pennies don't fall from heaven. They have to be earned on earth.
Margaret Thatcher 1925– British stateswoman

You can be young without money but you can't be old without it.
Tennessee Williams 1911–83 American dramatist

Morality ✳

Morality is a private and costly luxury.
Henry Brooks Adams 1838–1918 American historian

Waste no more time arguing what a good man should be. Be one.
Marcus Aurelius AD 121–180 Roman emperor

Standards are always out of date. That is what makes them standards.
Alan Bennett 1934– English writer

Food comes first, then morals.
Bertolt Brecht 1898–1956 German dramatist

The end justifies the means.
Hermann Busenbaum 1600–68 German theologian

Morality

What I know most surely about morality and the duty of man I owe to sport.

Albert Camus 1913–60 French writer, *often quoted as '...I owe to football'*

The last temptation is the greatest treason:
To do the right deed for the wrong reason.

T. S. Eliot 1888–1965 American-born British poet

State a moral case to a ploughman and a professor. The former will decide it as well, and often better than the latter, because he has not been led astray by artificial rules.

Thomas Jefferson 1743–1826 American statesman

Two things fill the mind with ever new and increasing wonder and awe, the more often and the more seriously reflection concentrates upon them: the starry heaven above me and the moral law within me.

Immanuel Kant 1724–1804 German philosopher

We know no spectacle so ridiculous as the British public in one of its periodical fits of morality.

Lord Macaulay 1800–59 English historian

If people want a sense of purpose, they should get it from their archbishops. They should not hope to receive it from their politicians.

Harold Macmillan 1894–1986 British statesman

The most useful thing about a principle is that it can always be sacrificed to expediency.

W. Somerset Maugham 1874–1965 English novelist

Morality is the herd-instinct in the individual.

Friedrich Nietzsche 1844–1900 German philosopher

There is no good or evil, there is only power, and those too weak to seek it.

J. K. Rowling 1965– English novelist

There is nothing either good or bad, but thinking makes it so.
William Shakespeare 1564–1616 English dramatist

We know that a man can read Goethe or Rilke in the evening, that he can play Bach and Schubert, and go to his day's work at Auschwitz in the morning.
George Steiner 1929– American critic

If your morals make you dreary, depend upon it they are wrong.
Robert Louis Stevenson 1850–94 Scottish novelist

The more things are forbidden, the more popular they become.
Mark Twain 1835–1910 American writer

Moral indignation is jealousy with a halo.
H. G. Wells 1866–1946 English novelist

Mothers ✳

What *do* girls do who haven't any mothers to help them through their troubles?
Louisa May Alcott 1832–88 American novelist

I have reached the age when a woman begins to perceive that she is growing into the person she least plans to resemble: her mother.
Anita Brookner 1928– British novelist

The mother's yearning, that completest type of the life in another life which is the essence of real human love, feels the presence of the cherished child even in the debased, degraded man.
George Eliot 1819–80 English novelist

Mothers

If I were damned of body and soul,
I know whose prayers would make me whole,
Mother o' mine, O mother o' mine.
> **Rudyard Kipling** 1865–1936 English writer

Here's to the happiest years of our lives
Spent in the arms of other men's wives.
Gentlemen!—Our mothers!
> **Edwin Lutyens** 1869–1944 English architect, *proposing a toast*

It is a dead-end job. You've no sooner learned the skills
than you are redundant.
> **Claire Rayner** 1931– English journalist, *on motherhood*

My mother had a good deal of trouble with me, but I
think she enjoyed it.
> **Mark Twain** 1835–1910 American writer

The hand that rocks the cradle
Is the hand that rules the world.
> **William Ross Wallace** 1819–1881 American poet

Mothers go on getting blamed until they're eighty, but
shouldn't take it personally.
> **Katharine Whitehorn** 1928– English journalist

✖ Mountains

The Alps, the Rockies and all other mountains are related
to the earth, the Himalayas to the heavens.
> **J. K. Galbraith** 1908–2006 American economist

There are other Annapurnas in the lives of men.
> **Maurice Herzog** 1919– French mountaineer

Well, we knocked the bastard off!
> **Edmund Hillary** 1919–2008 New Zealand mountaineer, *on
> conquering Mount Everest, 1953*

It is a fine thing to be out on the hills alone. A man can hardly be a beast or a fool alone on a great mountain.
Francis Kilvert 1840–79 English clergyman

Because it's there.
George Leigh Mallory 1886–1924 British mountaineer, *on being asked why he wanted to climb Mount Everest*

Climb the mountains and get their good tidings.
John Muir 1838–1914 Scottish-born American naturalist

My mountain did not seem to me a lifeless thing of rock and ice, but warm and friendly and living. She was a mother hen, and the other mountains were chicks under her wings.
Tenzing Norgay 1914–86 Sherpa mountaineer, *on Everest*

Mountains are the beginning and the end of all natural scenery.
John Ruskin 1819–1900 English critic

Do nothing in haste, look well to each step, and from the beginning think what may be the end.
Edward Whymper 1840–1911 English mountaineer

Murder ✳

Thou shalt not kill.
Bible

Mordre wol out; that se we day by day.
Geoffrey Chaucer c.1343–1400 English poet

Thou shalt not kill; but need'st not strive
Officiously to keep alive.
Arthur Hugh Clough 1819–61 English poet

Murder considered as one of the fine arts.
Thomas De Quincey 1785–1859 English essayist

Murder

Kill a man, and you are an assassin. Kill millions of men,
and you are a conqueror. Kill everyone, and you are a
god.

Jean Rostand 1894–1977 French biologist

Murder most foul, as in the best it is;
But this most foul, strange, and unnatural.

William Shakespeare 1564–1616 English dramatist

I don't think a man who has watched the sun going
down could walk away and commit a murder.

Laurens van der Post 1906–96 South African explorer

 Music →Singing

Beethoven tells you what it's like to be Beethoven and
Mozart tells you what it's like to be human. Bach tells
you what it's like be the universe.

Douglas Adams 1952–2001 English writer

Please do not shoot the pianist. He is doing his best.

Anonymous *printed notice in a dancing saloon, c.1882*

If you still have to ask…shame on you.

Louis Armstrong 1901–71 American jazz musician, *when asked
what jazz is; sometimes quoted as 'Man, if you gotta ask you'll
never know'*

All music is folk music, I ain't never heard no horse sing
a song.

Louis Armstrong 1901–71 American jazz musician

There are two golden rules for an orchestra: start together
and finish together. The public doesn't give a damn what
goes on in between.

Thomas Beecham 1879–1961 English conductor

Music…can name the unnameable, and communicate the
unknowable.

Leonard Bernstein 1918–90 American composer

Music has charms to sooth a savage breast.
William Congreve 1670–1729 English dramatist

Extraordinary how potent cheap music is.
Noël Coward 1899–1973 English dramatist

It is only that which cannot be expressed otherwise that is worth expressing in music.
Frederick Delius 1862–1934 English composer

There is music in the air.
Edward Elgar 1857–1934 English composer

The hills are alive with the sound of music,
With songs they have sung for a thousand years.
Oscar Hammerstein II 1895–1960 American songwriter

Down the road someone is practising scales,
The notes like little fishes vanish with a wink of tails.
Louis MacNeice 1907–63 British poet

Fortissimo at last!
Gustav Mahler 1860–1911 Austrian composer, *on seeing Niagara Falls*

The symphony must be like the world. It must embrace everything.
Gustav Mahler 1860–1911 Austrian composer

Art is not national. It is international. Music is not written in red, white and blue; it is written with the heart's blood of the composer.
Nellie Melba 1861–1931 Australian operatic soprano

Music is spiritual. The music business is not.
Van Morrison 1945– Irish musician

Melody is the essence of music. I compare a good melodist to a fine racer, and counterpoints to hack post-horses.
Wolfgang Amadeus Mozart 1756–91 Austrian composer

Music

If I don't practise for one day, I know it; if I don't practise for two days, the critics know it; if I don't practise for three days, the audience knows it.

Ignacy Jan Paderewski 1860–1941 Polish pianist and statesman

Music is your own experience, your thoughts, your wisdom. If you don't live it, it won't come out of your horn.

Charlie Parker 1920–55 American jazz saxophonist

Music begins to atrophy when it departs too far from the dance…poetry begins to atrophy when it gets too far from music.

Ezra Pound 1885–1972 American poet

Applause is a receipt, not a note of demand.

Artur Schnabel 1882–1951 Austrian-born pianist

If music be the food of love, play on.

William Shakespeare 1564–1616 English dramatist

Hell is full of musical amateurs: music is the brandy of the damned.

George Bernard Shaw 1856–1950 Irish dramatist

Music is feeling, then, not sound.

Wallace Stevens 1879–1955 American poet

A good composer does not imitate; he steals.

Igor Stravinsky 1882–1971 Russian composer

You just pick a chord, go twang, and you've got music.

Sid Vicious 1957–79 British rock musician

✳ Names

Proper names are poetry in the raw. Like all poetry they are untranslatable.

W. H. Auden 1907–73 English poet

With a name like yours, you might be any shape, almost.
Lewis Carroll 1832–98 English writer, *Humpty Dumpty to Alice*

Colin is the sort of name you give your goldfish for a joke.
Colin Firth 1960– British actor

A self-made man may prefer a self-made name.
Learned Hand 1872–1961 American judge, *on Samuel Goldfish changing his name to Samuel Goldwyn*

A nickname is the heaviest stone that the devil can throw at a man.
William Hazlitt 1778–1830 English essayist

We've put an accent over the first 'a' to make it a bit more exotic, and two 'i's at the end just to make it look a bit different.
Jordan 1978– English model, *on her daughter's name, Princess Tíaamii*

If you should have a boy do not christen him John…'Tis a bad name and goes against a man. If my name had been Edmund I should have been more fortunate.
John Keats 1795–1821 English poet

Just as crystallization of surnames was one of the steps in human civilization, their relinquishment gradually increases as we revert to savagery.
Anthony Powell 1905–2000 English novelist

What's in a name? that which we call a rose
By any other name would smell as sweet.
William Shakespeare 1564–1616 English dramatist

JAQUES: I do not like her name.
ORLANDO: There was no thought of pleasing you when she was christened.
William Shakespeare 1564–1616 English dramatist

Nature

KATHARINE HEPBURN: Nature, Mr Allnutt, is what we are put into this world to rise above.
James Agee 1909–55 American writer, *in the film* The African Queen

Nature does nothing without purpose or uselessly.
Aristotle 384–322 BC Greek philosopher

A culture is no better than its woods.
W. H. Auden 1907–73 English poet

The subtlety of nature is greater many times over than the subtlety of the senses and understanding.
Francis Bacon 1561–1626 English courtier

The tree which moves some to tears of joy is in the eyes of others only a green thing that stands in the way.
William Blake 1757–1827 English poet

All things are artificial, for nature is the art of God.
Sir Thomas Browne 1605–82 English writer

I love not man the less, but nature more.
Lord Byron 1788–1824 English poet

What a book a devil's chaplain might write on the clumsy, wasteful, blundering, low, and horridly cruel works of nature!
Charles Darwin 1809–82 English naturalist

You may drive out nature with a pitchfork, yet she'll be constantly running back.
Horace 65–8 BC Roman poet

In her [Nature's] inventions nothing is lacking, and nothing is superfluous.
Leonardo da Vinci 1452–1519 Italian painter

It is far from easy to judge whether she [Nature] has
proved a kind parent to man or a harsh step-mother.
 Pliny the Elder AD 23–79 Roman senator

And this our life, exempt from public haunt,
Finds tongues in trees, books in the running brooks,
Sermons in stones, and good in everything.
 William Shakespeare 1564–1616 English dramatist

Nature, red in tooth and claw.
 Alfred, Lord Tennyson 1809–92 English poet

Nature is not a temple, but a workshop, and man's the
workman in it.
 Ivan Turgenev 1818–83 Russian novelist

One impulse from a vernal wood
May teach you more of man,
Of moral evil and of good,
Than all the sages can.
 William Wordsworth 1770–1850 English poet

News ⇒ Journalism

Tell it not in Gath, publish it not in the streets of
Askelon.
 Bible

How beautiful upon the mountains are the feet of him
that bringeth good tidings.
 Bible

When a dog bites a man, that is not news, because it
happens so often. But if a man bites a dog, that is news.
 John B. Bogart 1848–1921 American journalist

Ill news hath wings, and with the wind doth go,
Comfort's a cripple and comes ever slow.
 Michael Drayton 1563–1631 English poet

News

What news on the Rialto?
William Shakespeare 1564–1616 English dramatist

The nature of bad news infects the teller.
William Shakespeare 1564–1616 English dramatist

✳ Night →Day

Lighten our darkness, we beseech thee, O Lord; and by
thy great mercy defend us from all perils and dangers of
this night.
Book of Common Prayer 1662

I cannot walk through the suburbs in the solitude of the
night without thinking that the night pleases us because
it suppresses idle details, just as our memory does.
Jorge Luis Borges 1899–1986 Argentinian writer

The Sun's rim dips; the stars rush out;
At one stride comes the dark.
Samuel Taylor Coleridge 1772–1834 English poet

The curfew tolls the knell of parting day,
The lowing herd wind slowly o'er the lea,
The ploughman homeward plods his weary way,
And leaves the world to darkness and to me.
Thomas Gray 1716–71 English poet

The cares that infest the day
Shall fold their tents, like the Arabs,
And as silently steal away.
Henry Wadsworth Longfellow 1807–82 American poet

Night came down, and enfolded the earth in her dusky
wings.
Virgil 70–19 BC Roman poet

Old Age ✳

Age will not be defied.
Francis Bacon 1561–1626 English courtier

To me old age is always fifteen years older than I am.
Bernard Baruch 1870–1965 American financier

The days of our age are threescore years and ten; and though men be so strong that they come to fourscore years: yet is their strength then but labour and sorrow; so soon passeth it away, and we are gone.
Bible

If I'd known I was gonna live this long, I'd have taken better care of myself.
Eubie Blake 1883–1983 American ragtime pianist, *on reaching the age of 100*

What is called the serenity of age is only perhaps a euphemism for the fading power to feel the sudden shock of joy or sorrow.
Arthur Bliss 1891–1975 English composer

The man who works and is not bored is never old.
Pablo Casals 1876–1973 Spanish cellist

Considering the alternative, it's not too bad at all.
Maurice Chevalier 1888–1972 French actor, *when asked what he felt about the advancing years on his 72nd birthday*

Oh, to be seventy again!
Georges Clemenceau 1841–1929 French statesman, *on seeing a pretty girl on his eightieth birthday*

We turn not older with years, but newer every day.
Emily Dickinson 1830–86 American poet

While there's snow on the roof, it doesn't mean the fire has gone out in the furnace.
John G. Diefenbaker 1895–1979 Canadian statesman, *approaching his 80th birthday*

Old Age

I grow old...I grow old...
I shall wear the bottoms of my trousers rolled.
T. S. Eliot 1888–1965 American-born British poet

As Groucho Marx once said, 'Anyone can get old—all
you have to do is to live long enough.'
Elizabeth II 1926– British monarch

Age does not make us childish, as men tell,
It merely finds us children still at heart.
Johann Wolfgang von Goethe 1749–1832 German writer

You will recognize, my boy, the first sign of old age: it is
when you go out into the streets of London and realize
for the first time how young the policemen look.
Seymour Hicks 1871–1949 English actor-manager

Nothing really wrong with him—only anno domini, but
that's the most fatal complaint of all, in the end.
James Hilton 1900–54 English novelist

When I am an old woman I shall wear purple
With a red hat which doesn't go, and doesn't suit me.
Jenny Joseph 1932– English poet

Perhaps being old is having lighted rooms
Inside your head, and people in them, acting.
People you know, yet can't quite name.
Philip Larkin 1922–85 English poet

Will you still need me, will you still feed me,
When I'm sixty four?
John Lennon 1940–80 and **Paul McCartney** 1942– English
pop singers

Old people have one advantage compared with young
ones. They have been young themselves, and young
people haven't been old.
Lord Longford 1905–2001 British politician

Growing old is no more than a bad habit which a busy man has no time to form.
André Maurois 1885–1967 French writer

The unending problem of growing old was not how he changed, but how things did.
Toni Morrison 1931– American novelist

Growing old is like being increasingly penalized for a crime you haven't committed.
Anthony Powell 1905–2000 English novelist

In a dream you are never eighty.
Anne Sexton 1928–74 American poet

How ill white hairs become a fool and jester!
William Shakespeare 1564–1616 English dramatist

Second childishness, and mere oblivion,
Sans teeth, sans eyes, sans taste, sans everything.
William Shakespeare 1564–1616 English dramatist

Every man desires to live long; but no man would be old.
Jonathan Swift 1667–1745 Irish poet and satirist

Do not go gentle into that good night,
Old age should burn and rave at close of day;
Rage, rage against the dying of the light.
Dylan Thomas 1914–53 Welsh poet

Old age is the most unexpected of all things that happen to a man.
Leon Trotsky 1879–1940 Russian revolutionary

Time has shaken me by the hand and death is not far behind.
John Wesley 1703–91 English preacher

When you are old and grey and full of sleep,
And nodding by the fire, take down this book
And slowly read and dream of the soft look

Old Age

Your eyes had once, and of their shadows deep.
W. B. Yeats 1865–1939 Irish poet

✳ Opinion

Why should you mind being wrong if someone can show you that you are?
A. J. Ayer 1910–89 English philosopher

I've never had a humble opinion. If you've got an opinion, why be humble about it?
Joan Baez 1941– American singer

He that complies against his will,
Is of his own opinion still.
Samuel Butler 1612–80 English poet

People seem not to see that their opinion of the world is also a confession of character.
Ralph Waldo Emerson 1803–82 American writer

Every man has a right to utter what he thinks truth, and every other man has a right to knock him down for it. Martyrdom is the test.
Samuel Johnson 1709–84 English lexicographer

There are nine and sixty ways of constructing tribal lays,
And—every—single—one—of—them—is—right!
Rudyard Kipling 1865–1936 English writer

Thank God, in these days of enlightenment and establishment, everyone has a right to his own opinions, and chiefly to the opinion that nobody else has a right to theirs.
Ronald Knox 1888–1957 English writer

New opinions are always suspected, and usually opposed, without any other reason but because they are not already common.
John Locke 1632–1704 English philosopher

Opinion in good men is but knowledge in the making.
John Milton 1608–74 English poet

Some praise at morning what they blame at night;
But always think the last opinion right.
Alexander Pope 1688–1744 English poet

The opinions that are held with passion are always those for which no good ground exists; indeed the passion is the measure of the holder's lack of rational conviction.
Bertrand Russell 1872–1970 British philosopher

Optimism →Hope, Pessimism

The lark's on the wing;
The snail's on the thorn:
God's in his heaven—
All's right with the world!
Robert Browning 1812–89 English poet

I have known him come home to supper with a flood of tears, and a declaration that nothing was now left but a jail; and go to bed making a calculation of the expense of putting bow-windows to the house, 'in case anything turned up,' which was his favourite expression.
Charles Dickens 1812–70 English novelist, *of Mr Micawber*

Grab your coat, and get your hat,
Leave your worry on the doorstep,
Just direct your feet
To the sunny side of the street.
Dorothy Fields 1905–74 American songwriter

Optimism

Cheer up! the worst is yet to come!
Philander Chase Johnson 1866–1939

Sin is behovely, but all shall be well and all shall be well
and all manner of thing shall be well.
Julian of Norwich 1343–after 1416 English anchoress

an optimist is a guy
that has never had
much experience.
Don Marquis 1878–1937 American poet

You've got to ac-cent-tchu-ate the positive
Elim-my-nate the negative
Latch on to the affirmative
Don't mess with Mister In-between.
Johnny Mercer 1909–76 American songwriter

For me there's a daffodil in every dustbin.
Eric Sykes 1923– British comedian

In this best of possible worlds…all is for the best.
Voltaire 1694–1778 French writer

✳ Originality

The original writer is not he who refrains from imitating
others, but he who can be imitated by none.
François-René Chateaubriand 1768–1848 French writer

What is originality? Undetected plagiarism.
Dean Inge 1860–1954 English writer

If you steal from one author, it's plagiarism; if you steal
from many, it's research.
Wilson Mizner 1876–1933 American dramatist

It could be said of me that in this book I have only made up a bunch of other men's flowers, providing of my own only the string that ties them together.
    Montaigne 1533–92 French moralist

Posterity weaves no garlands for imitators.
    Friedrich von Schiller 1759–1805 German poet

Painting ✳

Good painters imitate nature, bad ones spew it up.
    Cervantes 1547–1616 Spanish novelist

The sound of water escaping from mill-dams, etc., willows, old rotten planks, slimy posts, and brickwork…those scenes made me a painter and I am grateful.
    John Constable 1776–1837 English painter

Remark all these roughnesses, pimples, warts, and everything as you see me; otherwise I will never pay a farthing for it.
    Oliver Cromwell 1599–1658 English statesman, *to Lely, on the painting of his portrait; commonly quoted as 'warts and all'*

All painting, no matter what you're painting, is abstract in that it's got to be organized.
    David Hockney 1937– British artist

Mostly painting is like putting a message in a bottle and flinging it into the sea.
    Howard Hodgkin 1932– British painter

Art does not reproduce the visible; rather, it makes visible.
    Paul Klee 1879–1940 German-Swiss painter

This is not a pipe.
    René Magritte 1898–1967 Belgian surrealist painter, *on a painting of a tobacco pipe*

Painting

You should not paint the chair, but only what someone has felt about it.
Edvard Munch 1863–1944 Norwegian painter

I paint objects as I think them, not as I see them.
Pablo Picasso 1881–1973 Spanish painter

No, painting is not made to decorate apartments. It's an offensive and defensive weapon against the enemy.
Pablo Picasso 1881–1973 Spanish painter

An imitation in lines and colours on any surface of all that is to be found under the sun.
Nicolas Poussin 1594–1665 French painter

I have seen, and heard, much of Cockney impudence before now; but never expected to hear a coxcomb ask two hundred guineas for flinging a pot of paint in the public's face.
John Ruskin 1819–1900 English critic, *on Whistler's* Nocturne in Black and Gold

Every time I paint a portrait I lose a friend.
John Singer Sargent 1856–1925 American painter

Painting is saying 'Ta' to God.
Stanley Spencer 1891–1959 English painter

No, I ask it for the knowledge of a lifetime.
James McNeill Whistler 1834–1903 American-born painter, *in his case against Ruskin, replying to the question: 'For two days' labour, you ask two hundred guineas?'*

※ Parents ⇒Children, The Family

The joys of parents are secret, and so are their griefs and fears.
Francis Bacon 1561–1626 English courtier

Honour thy father and thy mother.
Bible

288

A wise son maketh a glad father: but a foolish son is the heaviness of his mother.
Bible

Having one child makes you a parent; having two you are a referee.
David Frost 1939– English broadcaster

Your children are not your children.
They are the sons and daughters of Life's longing for
   itself.
They came through you but not from you
And though they are with you yet they belong not to you.
Kahlil Gibran 1883–1931 Lebanese-born American writer

They fuck you up, your mum and dad.
They may not mean to, but they do.
They fill you with the faults they had
And add some extra, just for you.
Philip Larkin 1922–85 English poet

Parents can plant magic in a child's mind through certain words spoken with some thrilling quality of voice, some uplift of the heart and spirit.
Robert MacNeil 1931– Canadian writer

Love crawls with the baby, walks with the toddler, runs with the child, then stands aside to let the youth walk into adulthood.
Jo Ann Merrell

Children aren't happy with nothing to ignore,
And that's what parents were created for.
Ogden Nash 1902–71 American humorist

If you bungle raising your children I don't think whatever else you do well matters very much.
Jacqueline Kennedy Onassis 1929–94 American First Lady

Parents

A Jewish man with parents alive is a fifteen-year-old boy, and will remain a fifteen-year-old boy until *they die*!
Philip Roth 1933– American novelist

No matter how old a mother is she watches her middle-aged children for signs of improvement.
Florida Scott-Maxwell 1883–1979 American writer

Parentage is a very important profession, but no test of fitness for it is ever imposed in the interest of the children.
George Bernard Shaw 1856–1950 Irish dramatist

The natural term of the affection of the human animal for its offspring is six years.
George Bernard Shaw 1856–1950 Irish dramatist

Parents learn a lot from their children about coping with life.
Muriel Spark 1918–2006 British novelist

You shouldn't sit in judgment of your parents. We did the best we could while being people too.
John Updike 1932–2009 American writer

Parents are the bones on which children sharpen their teeth.
Peter Ustinov 1921–2004 British actor

My children are ungrateful: they don't care. That is my great reward. They are free.
Fay Weldon 1931– British novelist

Children begin by loving their parents; after a time they judge them; rarely, if ever, do they forgive them.
Oscar Wilde 1854–1900 Irish dramatist

Parties

The sooner every party breaks up the better.
    Jane Austen 1775–1817 English novelist

Like other parties of the kind, it was first silent, then
talky, then argumentative, then disputatious, then
unintelligible, then altogethery, then inarticulate, and then
drunk.
    Lord Byron 1788–1824 English poet

A very merry, dancing, drinking,
Laughing, quaffing, and unthinking time.
    John Dryden 1631–1700 English poet

At every party there are two kinds of people—those who
want to go home and those who don't. The trouble is,
they are usually married to each other.
    Ann Landers 1918–2002 American advice columnist

A successful party is a creative act, and creation is always
painful.
    Phyllis McGinley 1905–78 American poet

At a dinner party one should eat wisely but not too well,
and talk well but not too wisely.
    W. Somerset Maugham 1874–1965 English novelist

May I join you in the doghouse, Rover?
I wish to retire till the party's over.
    Ogden Nash 1902–71 American humorist, *on a children's party*

He showed me his bill of fare to tempt me to dine with
him; poh, said I, I value not your bill of fare, give me
your bill of company.
    Jonathan Swift 1667–1745 Irish poet and satirist

If one plays good music, people don't listen and if one
plays bad music people don't talk.
    Oscar Wilde 1854–1900 Irish dramatist

✳ Parting →Meeting

CORBETT: It's goodnight from me.
BARKER: And it's goodnight from him.
> **Ronnie Barker** 1929–2005 and **Ronnie Corbett** 1930–
> English comedians

I wish everyone, friend or foe, well. That is that. The end.
> **Tony Blair** 1953– British statesman, *leaving the House of Commons*

ARNOLD SCHWARZENEGGER: I'll be back.
> **James Cameron** 1954– Canadian film director, *in the film* The Terminator

Atque in perpetuum, frater, ave atque vale.
And so, my brother, hail, and farewell evermore!
> **Catullus** c.84–c.54 BC Roman poet

You have sat too long here for any good you have been doing. Depart, I say, and let us have done with you. In the name of God, go!
> **Oliver Cromwell** 1599–1658 English statesman, *addressing the Rump Parliament*

Parting is all we know of heaven,
And all we need of hell.
> **Emily Dickinson** 1830–86 American poet

Since there's no help, come let us kiss and part,
Nay, I have done: you get no more of me.
> **Michael Drayton** 1563–1631 English poet

GROUCHO MARX: If you can't leave in a taxi you can leave in a huff. If that's too soon, you can leave in a minute and a huff.
> **Bert Kalmar** 1884–1947 et al., American screenwriters, *in the film* Duck Soup

Leave them while you're looking good.
Anita Loos 1893–1981 American writer

Fare well my dear child and pray for me, and I shall for you and all your friends that we may merrily meet in heaven.
Thomas More 1478–1535 English scholar and saint

Good-night, good-night! parting is such sweet sorrow
That I shall say good-night till it be morrow.
William Shakespeare 1564–1616 English dramatist

The Past ✳

Even a god cannot change the past.
Agathon b. c.445 BC Greek tragic poet

Nostalgia isn't what it used to be.
Anonymous

In every age 'the good old days' were a myth. No one ever thought they were good at the time. For every age has consisted of crises that seemed intolerable to the people who lived through them.
Brooks Atkinson 1894–1984 American writer

Stands the Church clock at ten to three?
And is there honey still for tea?
Rupert Brooke 1887–1915 English poet

The moving finger writes; and, having writ,
Moves on: nor all thy piety nor wit
Shall lure it back to cancel half a line,
Nor all thy tears wash out a word of it.
Edward Fitzgerald 1809–83 English poet

The past is a foreign country: they do things differently there.
L. P. Hartley 1895–1972 English novelist

The Past

By despising all that has preceded us, we teach others to despise ourselves.
William Hazlitt 1778–1830 English essayist

O God! Put back Thy universe and give me yesterday.
Henry Arthur Jones 1851–1929 and **Henry Herman** 1832–94 English dramatists

Yesterday, all my troubles seemed so far away,
Now it looks as though they're here to stay.
Oh I believe in yesterday.
John Lennon 1940–80 and **Paul McCartney** 1942– English pop singers

The past is like a collection of photographs: some are familiar and on constant display, others need searching for in dusty drawers.
John Mortimer 1923–2009 English lawyer

Think of it, soldiers; from the summit of these pyramids, forty centuries look down upon you.
Napoleon I 1769–1821 French emperor

Things ain't what they used to be.
Ted Persons

I tell you the past is a bucket of ashes.
Carl Sandburg 1878–1967 American poet

Those who cannot remember the past are condemned to repeat it.
George Santayana 1863–1952 Spanish-born philosopher

What's gone and what's past help
Should be past grief.
William Shakespeare 1564–1616 English dramatist

O! call back yesterday, bid time return.
William Shakespeare 1564–1616 English dramatist

Patience

I think that today's youth have a tendency to live in the present and work for the future—and to be totally ignorant of the past.
Steven Spielberg 1947– American film director

The past is the only dead thing that smells sweet.
Edward Thomas 1878–1917 English poet

But where are the snows of yesteryear?
François Villon c.1431–after 63 French poet

Patience ✳

We had better wait and see.
Herbert Asquith 1852–1928 British statesman

Our patience will achieve more than our force.
Edmund Burke 1729–97 Irish-born politician

Beware the fury of a patient man.
John Dryden 1631–1700 English poet

Patience is a bitter thing, but its fruit is sweet.
Sadi c.1213–91 Persian poet

Let nothing trouble you, nothing frighten you. All things are passing; God never changes. Patient endurance attains all things.
St Teresa of Ávila 1512–82 Spanish mystic

I am extraordinarily patient, provided I get my own way in the end.
Margaret Thatcher 1925– British stateswoman

The strongest of all warriors are these two—time and patience.
Leo Tolstoy 1828–1910 Russian novelist

✳ Patriotism

What pity is it
That we can die but once to serve our country!
Joseph Addison 1672–1719 English writer

Patriotism is a lively sense of collective responsibility.
Nationalism is a silly cock crowing on its own dunghill.
Richard Aldington 1892–1962 English writer

A steady patriot of the world alone,
The friend of every country but his own.
George Canning 1770–1827 British statesman

Patriotism is not enough. I must have no hatred or
bitterness towards anyone.
Edith Cavell 1865–1915 English nurse, *on the eve of her execution*

Be England what she will,
With all her faults, she is my country still.
Charles Churchill 1731–64 English poet

Our country! In her intercourse with foreign nations, may
she always be in the right; but our country, right or
wrong.
Stephen Decatur 1779–1820 American naval officer

If I had to choose between betraying my country and
betraying my friend, I hope I should have the guts to
betray my country.
E. M. Forster 1879–1970 English novelist

That this House will in no circumstances fight for its
King and Country.
D. M. Graham 1911–99 British broadcaster, *motion for a debate at the Oxford Union, 1933*

I only regret that I have but one life to lose for my country.

Nathan Hale 1755–76 American revolutionary, *prior to his execution by the British for spying*

Dulce et decorum est pro patria mori.

Lovely and honourable it is to die for one's country.

Horace 65–8 BC Roman poet

We don't want to fight, yet by jingo! if we do,
We've got the ships, we've got the men, and got the
  money too.

G. W. Hunt 1829–?1904 English songwriter

Patriotism is the last refuge of a scoundrel.

Samuel Johnson 1709–84 English lexicographer

And so, my fellow Americans: ask not what your country
can do for you—ask what you can do for your country.

John F. Kennedy 1917–63 American statesman

I would die for my country but I would never let my
country die for me.

Neil Kinnock 1942– British politician

My country, right or wrong; if right, to be kept right; and
if wrong, to be set right!

Carl Schurz 1829–1906 American soldier

Breathes there the man, with soul so dead,
Who never to himself hath said,
This is my own, my native land!

Sir Walter Scott 1771–1832 Scottish novelist

You'll never have a quiet world till you knock the
patriotism out of the human race.

George Bernard Shaw 1856–1950 Irish dramatist

I vow to thee, my country—all earthly things above—
Entire and whole and perfect, the service of my love.

Cecil Spring-Rice 1859–1918 British diplomat

Patriotism

The cricket test—which side do they cheer for?...Are you
still looking back to where you came from or where you
are?

Norman Tebbit 1931– British politician, *on the loyalties of
Britain's immigrant population*

✳ Peace

They shall beat their swords into plowshares, and their
spears into pruninghooks: nation shall not lift up sword
against nation, neither shall they learn war any more.

Bible

The peace of God, which passeth all understanding, shall
keep your hearts and minds through Christ Jesus.

Bible

Give peace in our time, O Lord.

Book of Common Prayer 1662

This is the second time in our history that there has
come back from Germany to Downing Street peace with
honour. I believe it is peace for our time.

Neville Chamberlain 1869–1940 British statesman

In His will is our peace.

Dante Alighieri 1265–1321 Italian poet

Lord Salisbury and myself have brought you back peace—
but a peace I hope with honour.

Benjamin Disraeli 1804–81 British statesman

Go placidly amid the noise and the haste, and remember
what peace there may be in silence.

Max Ehrmann 1872–1945 American writer

I think that people want peace so much that one of these days governments had better get out of the way and let them have it.

Dwight D. Eisenhower 1890–1969 American statesman

Kissinger brought peace to Vietnam the same way Napoleon brought peace to Europe: by losing.

Joseph Heller 1923–99 American novelist

Give peace a chance.

John Lennon 1940–80 and **Paul McCartney** 1942– English pop singers

A war can perhaps be won single-handedly. But peace—lasting peace—cannot be secured without the support of all.

Luiz Inácio Lula da Silva 1945– Brazilian statesman

You can't separate peace from freedom because no one can be at peace unless he has his freedom.

Malcolm X 1925–65 American civil rights campaigner

...Peace hath her victories
No less renowned than war.

John Milton 1608–74 English poet

You can't switch on peace like a light.

Mo Mowlam 1949–2005 British politician

Enough of blood and tears. Enough.

Yitzhak Rabin 1922–95 Israeli statesman

They make a wilderness and call it peace.

Tacitus C.AD 56–after 117 Roman historian

Shantih, shantih, shantih.
Peace! Peace! Peace!

The Upanishads c.800–200 BC Hindu sacred treatises

Let him who desires peace, prepare for war.

Vegetius fl. AD 379–95 Roman military writer

✳ Perfection

The pursuit of perfection, then, is the pursuit of sweetness and light.

Matthew Arnold 1822–88 English poet

Pictures of perfection as you know make me sick and wicked.

Jane Austen 1775–1817 English novelist

Faultless to a fault.

Robert Browning 1812–89 English poet

No one ever approaches perfection except by stealth, and unknown to himself.

William Hazlitt 1778–1830 English essayist

Trifles make perfection, and perfection is no trifle.

Michelangelo 1475–1564 Italian artist

The best is the best, though a hundred judges have declared it so.

Arthur Quiller-Couch 1863–1944 English critic

Perfection is finally attained not when there is no longer anything to add but when there is no longer anything to take away, when a body has been stripped down to its nakedness.

Antoine de Saint-Exupéry 1900–44 French novelist

How many things by season seasoned are
To their right praise and true perfection!

William Shakespeare 1564–1616 English dramatist

Finality is death. Perfection is finality.
Nothing is perfect. There are lumps in it.

James Stephens 1882–1950 Irish poet

He is all fault who hath no fault at all:
For who loves me must have a touch of earth.

Alfred, Lord Tennyson 1809–92 English poet

The best is the enemy of the good.
Voltaire 1694–1778 French writer

The intellect of man is forced to choose
Perfection of the life, or of the work.
W. B. Yeats 1865–1939 Irish poet

Pessimism →Despair, Optimism

WOODY ALLEN: I feel that life is—is divided up into the
horrible and the miserable.
Woody Allen 1935- and **Marshall Brickman** 1941-
American film director and American screenwriter, *in the film*
Annie Hall

The optimist proclaims that we live in the best of all
possible worlds; and the pessimist fears this is true.
James Branch Cabell 1879–1958 American writer

I don't consider myself a pessimist. I think of a pessimist
as someone who is waiting for it to rain. And I feel
soaked to the skin.
Leonard Cohen 1934- Canadian singer

If way to the Better there be, it exacts a full look at the
worst.
Thomas Hardy 1840–1928 English novelist

Man hands on misery to man.
It deepens like a coastal shelf.
Get out as early as you can,
And don't have any kids yourself.
Philip Larkin 1922–85 English poet

If we see light at the end of the tunnel,
It's the light of the oncoming train.
Robert Lowell 1917–77 American poet

Pessimism

'Twixt the optimist and pessimist
The difference is droll:
The optimist sees the doughnut
But the pessimist sees the hole.
    McLandburgh Wilson b. 1892

✳ Philosophy

The Socratic manner is not a game at which two can
play.
    Max Beerbohm 1872–1956 English critic

Metaphysics is the finding of bad reasons for what we
believe upon instinct.
    F. H. Bradley 1846–1924 English philosopher

If it was so, it might be; and if it were so, it would be:
but as it isn't, it ain't. That's logic.
    Lewis Carroll 1832–98 English writer

There is nothing so absurd but some philosopher has
said it.
    Cicero 106–43 BC Roman statesman

I refute it *thus*.
    Samuel Johnson 1709–84 English lexicographer, *kicking a
large stone by way of refuting Bishop Berkeley's theory of the
non-existence of matter*

Axioms in philosophy are not axioms until they are
proved upon our pulses.
    John Keats 1795–1821 English poet

The philosophers have only interpreted the world in
various ways; the point is to change it.
    Karl Marx 1818–83 German philosopher

No more things should be presumed to exist than are absolutely necessary.
>   **William of Occam** c.1285–1349 English philosopher, 'Occam's razor', not found in this form in his writings, although he frequently used similar expressions

The unexamined life is not worth living.
>   **Socrates** 469–399 BC Greek philosopher

The safest general characterization of the European philosophical tradition is that it consists of a series of footnotes to Plato.
>   **Alfred North Whitehead** 1861–1947 English philosopher

Philosophy is a battle against the bewitchment of our intelligence by means of language.
>   **Ludwig Wittgenstein** 1889–1951 Austrian-born philosopher

Photography ✳

A photograph is a secret about a secret. The more it tells you the less you know.
>   **Diane Arbus** 1923–71 American photographer

The camera's eye
Does not lie,
But it cannot show
The life within.
>   **W. H. Auden** 1907–73 English poet

Most things in life are moments of pleasure and a lifetime of embarrassment; photography is a moment of embarrassment and a lifetime of pleasure.
>   **Tony Benn** 1925– British politician

In photography you've got to be quick, quick, quick, like an animal and a prey.
>   **Henri Cartier-Bresson** 1908–2004 French photographer

Photography

You press the button, we do the rest.
George Eastman 1854–1932 American inventor, *advertising slogan to launch the Kodak camera, 1888*

The important thing is not the camera but the eye.
Alfred Eisenstaedt 1898–1995 American photographer

Photography deals exquisitely with appearances, but nothing is what it appears to be.
Duane Michals 1932– American photographer

The photographer is like the cod which produces a million eggs in order that one may reach maturity.
George Bernard Shaw 1856–1950 Irish dramatist

My idea of a good picture is one that's in focus and of a famous person doing something unfamous. It's being in the right place at the wrong time.
Andy Warhol 1927–87 American artist

✳ Planning

Be prepared.
Lord Baden-Powell 1857–1941 English soldier, *motto of the Scout Association*

We are ready for any unforeseen event which may or may not happen.
George W. Bush 1946– American statesman

Probability is the very guide of life.
Joseph Butler 1692–1752 English bishop

First things first, second things never.
Shirley Conran 1932– English writer

In preparing for battle I have always found that plans are useless, but planning is indispensable.
Dwight D. Eisenhower 1890–1969 American statesman

I think the necessity of being *ready* increases. Look to it.
Abraham Lincoln 1809–65 American statesman

No plan of operations reaches with any certainty beyond the first encounter with the enemy's main force.
Helmuth von Moltke 1800–91 Prussian military commander, *often quoted as 'no plan survives first contact with the enemy'*

A good plan violently executed *Now* is better than a perfect plan next week.
George S. Patton 1885–1945 American general

There are no small steps in great affairs.
Cardinal de Retz 1613–79 French cardinal

The thing that is important is the thing that is not seen.
Antoine de Saint-Exupéry 1900–44 French novelist

If we had had more time for discussion we should probably have made a great many more mistakes.
Leon Trotsky 1879–1940 Russian revolutionary

Pleasure ✳

One half of the world cannot understand the pleasures of the other.
Jane Austen 1775–1817 English novelist

The great pleasure in life is doing what people say you cannot do.
Walter Bagehot 1826–77 English economist

I'm tired of Love: I'm still more tired of Rhyme.
But Money gives me pleasure all the time.
Hilaire Belloc 1870–1953 British writer

Let us have wine and women, mirth and laughter,
Sermons and soda-water the day after.
Lord Byron 1788–1824 English poet

Pleasure

Life is a matter of passing the time enjoyably. There may be other things in life, but I've been too busy passing my time enjoyably to think very deeply about them.
Peter Cook 1937-95 English comedian

Remorse, the fatal egg by pleasure laid.
William Cowper 1731-1800 English poet

The less we indulge our pleasures the more we enjoy them.
Juvenal c.AD 60-c.130 Roman satirist

Ever let the fancy roam,
Pleasure never is at home.
John Keats 1795-1821 English poet

The greatest pleasure I know, is to do a good action by stealth, and to have it found out by accident.
Charles Lamb 1775-1834 English writer

Who loves not woman, wine, and song
Remains a fool his whole life long.
Martin Luther 1483-1546 German theologian

The Puritan hated bear-baiting, not because it gave pain to the bear, but because it gave pleasure to the spectators.
Lord Macaulay 1800-59 English historian

It is a curious thing that people only ask if you are enjoying yourself when you aren't.
Edith Nesbit 1858-1924 English writer

Pleasure is nothing else but the intermission of pain.
John Selden 1584-1654 English historian

Life would be very pleasant if it were not for its enjoyments.
R. S. Surtees 1805-64 English novelist

All the things I really like to do are either illegal, immoral, or fattening.
Alexander Woollcott 1887-1943 American writer

Poetry

It is barbarous to write a poem after Auschwitz.
Theodor Adorno 1903–69 German philosopher

A poet's hope: to be,
like some valley cheese,
local, but prized elsewhere.
W. H. Auden 1907–73 English poet

Prose is when all the lines except the last go on to the
end. Poetry is when some of them fall short of it.
Jeremy Bentham 1748–1832 English philosopher

The reason Milton wrote in fetters when he wrote of
Angels and God, and at liberty when of Devils and Hell,
is because he was a true Poet, and of the Devil's party
without knowing it.
William Blake 1757–1827 English poet

All poets are mad.
Robert Burton 1577–1640 English clergyman

There's nothing in the world for which a poet will give
up writing, not even when he is a Jew and the language
of his poems is German.
Paul Celan 1920–70 German poet

That willing suspension of disbelief for the moment,
which constitutes poetic faith.
Samuel Taylor Coleridge 1772–1834 English poet

Prose = words in their best order;—poetry = the *best*
words in the best order.
Samuel Taylor Coleridge 1772–1834 English poet

I used to think all poets were Byronic.
They're mostly wicked as a ginless tonic
And wild as pension plans.
Wendy Cope 1945– English poet

Poetry

Immature poets imitate; mature poets steal.
T. S. Eliot 1888–1965 American-born British poet

Poetry is a subject as precise as geometry.
Gustave Flaubert 1821–80 French novelist

Like a piece of ice on a hot stove the poem must ride on its own melting.
Robert Frost 1874–1963 American poet

As soon as war is declared it will be impossible to hold the poets back. Rhyme is still the most effective drum.
Jean Giraudoux 1882–1944 French dramatist

Skilled or unskilled, we all scribble poems.
Horace 65–8 BC Roman poet

[BOSWELL:] Sir, what is poetry?
[JOHNSON:] Why Sir, it is much easier to say what it is not. We all *know* what light is; but it is not easy to *tell* what it is.
Samuel Johnson 1709–84 English lexicographer

If poetry comes not as naturally as the leaves to a tree it had better not come at all.
John Keats 1795–1821 English poet

A poem should not mean
But be.
Archibald MacLeish 1892–1982 American poet

Writing a book of poetry is like dropping a rose petal down the Grand Canyon and waiting for the echo.
Don Marquis 1878–1937 American poet

Rhyme being…but the invention of a barbarous age, to set off wretched matter and lame metre.
John Milton 1608–74 English poet

Most people ignore most poetry
because
most poetry ignores most people.
    Adrian Mitchell 1932–2008 English writer

All a poet can do today is warn.
    Wilfred Owen 1893–1918 English poet

Poets are the unacknowledged legislators of the world.
    Percy Bysshe Shelley 1792–1822 English poet

Poetry is the spontaneous overflow of powerful feelings: it
takes its origin from emotion recollected in tranquillity.
    William Wordsworth 1770–1850 English poet

We make out of the quarrel with others, rhetoric, but of
the quarrel with ourselves, poetry.
    W. B. Yeats 1865–1939 Irish poet

Politicians ⇒Politics

A constitutional statesman is in general a man of
common opinion and uncommon abilities.
    Walter Bagehot 1826–77 English economist

I am not going to spend any time whatsoever in attacking
the Foreign Secretary…If we complain about the tune,
there is no reason to attack the monkey when the organ
grinder is present.
    Aneurin Bevan 1897–1960 British politician

Your representative owes you, not his industry only, but
his judgement; and he betrays, instead of serving you, if
he sacrifices it to your opinion.
    Edmund Burke 1729–97 Irish-born politician

An honest politician is one who when he's bought stays
bought.
    Simon Cameron 1799–1889 American politician

Politicians

A minister who moves about in society is in a position to read the signs of the times even in a festive gathering, but one who remains shut up in his office learns nothing.
Duc de Choiseul 1719–85 French politician

It is the ability to foretell what is going to happen tomorrow, next week, next month, and next year. And to have the ability afterwards to explain why it didn't happen.
Winston Churchill 1874–1965 British statesman, *on the qualifications for becoming a politician*

There are no true friends in politics. We are all sharks circling, and waiting, for traces of blood to appear in the water.
Alan Clark 1928–99 British politician

'Do you pray for the senators, Dr Hale?' 'No, I look at the senators and I pray for the country.'
Edward Everett Hale 1822–1909 American clergyman

Politicians are entitled to change their minds. But when they adjust their principles some explanation is necessary.
Roy Hattersley 1932–   British politician

Politicians are the same all over. They promise to build a bridge where there is no river.
Nikita Khrushchev 1894–1971 Soviet statesman

Forever poised between a cliché and an indiscretion.
Harold Macmillan 1894–1986 British statesman, *on the life of a Foreign Secretary*

What I want is men who will support me when I am in the wrong.
Lord Melbourne 1779–1848 English statesman, *replying to a politician who said 'I will support you as long as you are in the right'*

A statesman is a politician who places himself at the service of the nation. A politician is a statesman who places the nation at his service.

Georges Pompidou 1911–74 French statesman

We all know that Prime Ministers are wedded to the truth, but like other married couples they sometimes live apart.

Saki 1870–1916 Scottish writer

A statesman is a politician who's been dead 10 or 15 years.

Harry S. Truman 1884–1972 American statesman

All those men have their price.

Robert Walpole 1676–1745 English statesman, *of fellow parliamentarians*

Politics ⇒Democracy, Government

In politics the middle way is none at all.

John Adams 1735–1826 American statesman

Man is by nature a political animal.

Aristotle 384–322 BC Greek philosopher

Politics is the art of the possible.

Otto von Bismarck 1815–98 German statesman

A statesman…must wait until he hears the steps of God sounding through events; then leap up and grasp the hem of his garment.

Otto von Bismarck 1815–98 German statesman

Magnanimity in politics is not seldom the truest wisdom; and a great empire and little minds go ill together.

Edmund Burke 1729–97 Irish-born politician

In politics, there is no use looking beyond the next fortnight.

Joseph Chamberlain 1836–1914 British politician

311

Politics

In politics, what begins in fear usually ends in folly.
Samuel Taylor Coleridge 1772–1834 English poet

You campaign in poetry. You govern in prose.
Mario Cuomo 1932– American politician

International life is right-wing, like nature. The social contract is left-wing, like humanity.
Régis Debray 1940– French Marxist theorist

'Two nations; between whom there is no intercourse and no sympathy; who are as ignorant of each other's habits, thoughts, and feelings, as if they were dwellers in different zones, or inhabitants of different planets...' 'You speak of—' said Egremont, hesitatingly, 'THE RICH AND THE POOR.'
Benjamin Disraeli 1804–81 British statesman

Damn your principles! Stick to your party.
Benjamin Disraeli 1804–81 British statesman

I never dared be radical when young
For fear it would make me conservative when old.
Robert Frost 1874–1963 American poet

Politics is not the art of the possible. It consists in choosing between the disastrous and the unpalatable.
J. K. Galbraith 1908–2006 American economist

If I could not go to Heaven but with a party, I would not go there at all.
Thomas Jefferson 1743–1826 American statesman

The great nations have always acted like gangsters, and the small nations like prostitutes.
Stanley Kubrick 1928–99 American film director

Who? Whom?
Lenin 1870–1924 Russian revolutionary, *definition of political science, meaning 'Who will outstrip whom?'*

Politics is a marathon, not a sprint.
Ken Livingstone 1945– British politician

If you want to succeed in politics, you must keep your conscience well under control.
David Lloyd George 1863–1945 British statesman

The opposition of events.
Harold Macmillan 1894–1986 British statesman, *on his biggest problem; popularly quoted as 'Events, dear boy. Events'*

Politics is war without bloodshed while war is politics with bloodshed.
Mao Zedong 1893–1976 Chinese statesman

Political language…is designed to make lies sound truthful and murder respectable, and to give an appearance of solidity to pure wind.
George Orwell 1903–50 English novelist

Socialism can only arrive by bicycle.
José Antonio Viera Gallo 1943– Chilean politician

A week is a long time in politics.
Harold Wilson 1916–95 British statesman

A liberal is a conservative who's been arrested.
Tom Wolfe 1931– American writer

Pollution ⇒Environment

Woe to her that is filthy and polluted, to the oppressing city!
Bible

NOISE, *n*. A stench in the ear…The chief product and authenticating sign of civilization.
Ambrose Bierce 1842–c.1914 American writer

Pollution

Over increasingly large areas of the United States, spring now comes unheralded by the return of the birds, and the early mornings are strangely silent where once they were filled with the beauty of bird song.

Rachel Carson 1907-64 American zoologist

Man has been endowed with reason, with the power to create, so that he can add to what he's been given. But up to now he hasn't been a creator, only a destroyer. Forests keep disappearing, rivers dry up, wild life's become extinct, the climate's ruined and the land grows poorer and uglier every day.

Anton Chekhov 1860–1904 Russian writer

The river Rhine, it is well known,
Doth wash your city of Cologne;
But tell me, Nymphs, what power divine
Shall henceforth wash the river Rhine?

Samuel Taylor Coleridge 1772–1834 English poet

The sea is the universal sewer.

Jacques Cousteau 1910–97 French underwater explorer

Clear the air! clean the sky! wash the wind!

T. S. Eliot 1888–1965 American-born British poet

The sanitary and mechanical age we are now entering makes up for the mercy it grants to our sense of smell by the ferocity with which it assails our sense of hearing. As usual, what we call 'progress' is the exchange of one nuisance for another nuisance.

Havelock Ellis 1859–1939 English sexologist

And all is seared with trade; bleared, smeared with toil;
And wears man's smudge and shares man's smell.

Gerard Manley Hopkins 1844–89 English poet

It goes so heavily with my disposition that this goodly frame, the earth, seems to me a sterile promontory; this most excellent canopy, the air, look you, this brave

o'erhanging firmament, this majestical roof fretted with golden fire, why, it appears no other thing to me but a foul and pestilent congregation of vapours.
William Shakespeare 1564–1616 English dramatist

Poverty ✳

Make poverty history.
Anonymous *campaign slogan, 2005*

Anyone who has ever struggled with poverty knows how extremely expensive it is to be poor.
James Baldwin 1924–87 American writer

Come away; poverty's catching.
Aphra Behn 1640–89 English writer

The poor always ye have with you.
Bible

When I give food to the poor they call me a saint. When I ask why the poor have no food they call me a communist.
Helder Camara 1909–99 Brazilian priest

People don't resent having nothing nearly as much as too little.
Ivy Compton-Burnett 1884–1969 English novelist

The murmuring poor, who will not fast in peace.
George Crabbe 1754–1832 English poet

There is no scandal like rags, nor any crime so shameful as poverty.
George Farquhar 1678–1707 Irish dramatist

I want there to be no peasant in my kingdom so poor that he is unable to have a chicken in his pot every Sunday.
Henri IV 1553–1610 French monarch

Poverty

Oh! God! that bread should be so dear,
And flesh and blood so cheap!

Thomas Hood 1799–1845 English poet

It's easy to be independent when you've got money. But
to be independent when you haven't got a thing—that's
the Lord's test.

Mahalia Jackson 1911–72 American singer

Resolve not to be poor: whatever you have, spend less.
Poverty is a great enemy to human happiness; it certainly
destroys liberty, and it makes some virtues impracticable,
and others extremely difficult.

Samuel Johnson 1709–84 English lexicographer

The misfortunes of poverty carry with them nothing
harder to bear than that it makes men ridiculous.

Juvenal c.AD 60–c.130 Roman satirist

Overcoming poverty is not a gesture of charity. It is an
act of justice.

Nelson Mandela 1918– South African statesman

Poverty is a lot like childbirth—you know it is going to
hurt before it happens, but you'll never know how much
until you experience it.

J. K. Rowling 1965– English novelist

The greatest of evils and the worst of crimes is poverty.

George Bernard Shaw 1856–1950 Irish dramatist

Poverty is no disgrace to a man, but it is confoundedly
inconvenient.

Sydney Smith 1771–1845 English essayist

A hungry man is not a free man.

Adlai Stevenson 1900–65 American politician

Sixteen tons, what do you get?
Another day older and deeper in debt.
Say brother, don't you call me 'cause I can't go

I owe my soul to the company store.
  Merle Travis 1917–83 American singer

Power ☀

Power tends to corrupt and absolute power corrupts absolutely.
  Lord Acton 1834–1902 British historian

All rising to great place is by a winding stair.
  Francis Bacon 1561–1626 English courtier

Every dictator uses religion as a prop to keep himself in power.
  Benazir Bhutto 1953–2007 Pakistani stateswoman

The most potent weapon in the hands of the oppressor is the mind of the oppressed.
  Steve Biko 1946–77 South African anti-apartheid campaigner

A man may build himself a throne of bayonets, but he cannot sit on it.
  Dean Inge 1860–1954 English writer, *quoted by Boris Yeltsin at the time of the failed military coup in Russia, 1991*

Power is the great aphrodisiac.
  Henry Kissinger 1923– American politician

Power? It's like a Dead Sea fruit. When you achieve it, there is nothing there.
  Harold Macmillan 1894–1986 British statesman

Political power grows out of the barrel of a gun.
  Mao Zedong 1893–1976 Chinese statesman

Never doubt that a small group of thoughtful committed citizens can change the world. In fact, it's the only thing that ever has.
  Margaret Mead 1901–78 American anthropologist

Power

Who controls the past controls the future: who controls the present controls the past.

George Orwell 1903–50 English novelist

You only have power over people as long as you don't take *everything* away from them. But when you've robbed a man of *everything* he's no longer in your power—he's free again.

Alexander Solzhenitsyn 1918–2008 Russian novelist

The Pope! How many divisions has *he* got?

Joseph Stalin 1879–1953 Soviet dictator, *on being asked to encourage Catholicism in Russia by way of conciliating the Pope*

The hand that signed the paper felled a city.

Dylan Thomas 1914–53 Welsh poet

✳ Practicality

It's grand, and you canna expect to be baith grand and comfortable.

J. M. Barrie 1860–1937 Scottish writer

Put your trust in God, my boys, and keep your powder dry.

Valentine Blacker 1728–1823 Irish soldier, *'Oliver's Advice', often attributed to Oliver Cromwell himself*

Whenever our neighbour's house is on fire, it cannot be amiss for the engines to play a little on our own.

Edmund Burke 1729–97 Irish-born politician

The colour of the cat doesn't matter as long as it catches the mice.

Deng Xiaoping 1904–97 Chinese statesman

Common sense is the best distributed commodity in the world, for every man is convinced that he is well supplied with it.

René Descartes 1596–1650 French philosopher

Praise

Common sense is nothing more than a deposit of
prejudices laid down in the mind before you reach
eighteen.
  Albert Einstein 1879–1955 German-born theoretical physicist

Praise the Lord and pass the ammunition.
  Howell Forgy 1908–83 American naval chaplain, *at Pearl
  Harbor, while sailors passed ammunition by hand to the deck*

So I really think that American gentlemen are the best
after all, because kissing your hand may make you feel
very very good but a diamond and safire bracelet lasts
forever.
  Anita Loos 1893–1981 American writer

Be nice to people on your way up because you'll meet
'em on your way down.
  Wilson Mizner 1876–1933 American dramatist

Common sense is not so common.
  Voltaire 1694–1778 French writer

Praise ✳

He who discommendeth others obliquely commendeth
himself.
  Sir Thomas Browne 1605–82 English writer

The advantage of doing one's praising for oneself is that
one can lay it on so thick and exactly in the right places.
  Samuel Butler 1835–1902 English novelist

Imitation is the sincerest of flattery.
  Charles Caleb Colton c.1780–1832 English clergyman

How light, how small is the thing which casts down or
restores a mind greedy for praise.
  Horace 65–8 BC Roman poet

Praise

All censure of a man's self is oblique praise. It is in order
to shew how much he can spare.
Samuel Johnson 1709–84 English lexicographer

And even the ranks of Tuscany
Could scarce forbear to cheer.
Lord Macaulay 1800–59 English historian

Damn with faint praise, assent with civil leer,
And without sneering, teach the rest to sneer.
Alexander Pope 1688–1744 English poet

But when I tell him he hates flatterers,
He says he does, being then most flattered.
William Shakespeare 1564–1616 English dramatist

I suppose flattery hurts no one, that is, if he doesn't
inhale.
Adlai Stevenson 1900–65 American politician

❋ Prayer

Pray to the gods only when you're making some effort on
your own behalf, otherwise your prayers are wasted.
Aesop Greek storyteller of the 6th century BC

O Lord! thou knowest how busy I must be this day: if I
forget thee, do not thou forget me.
Jacob Astley 1579–1652 English soldier, *before the Battle of
Edgehill*

The wish for prayer is a prayer in itself.
Georges Bernanos 1888–1948 French writer

Ask, and it shall be given you; seek, and ye shall find;
knock, and it shall be opened unto you.
Bible

And lips say, 'God be pitiful,'
Who ne'er said, 'God be praised.'
   Elizabeth Barrett Browning 1806–61 English poet

He prayeth best, who loveth best
All things both great and small.
   Samuel Taylor Coleridge 1772–1834 English poet

I throw myself down in my Chamber, and I call in, and
invite God, and his Angels thither, and when they are
there, I neglect God and his Angels, for the noise of a fly,
for the rattling of a coach, for the whining of a door.
   John Donne 1572–1631 English poet

To lift up the hands in prayer gives God glory, but a man
with a dungfork in his hand, a woman with a slop-pail,
give him glory too.
   Gerard Manley Hopkins 1844–89 English poet

The prayers of the dying are especially precious to God,
because they will soon be in His presence.
   Basil Hume 1923–99 English cardinal

One single grateful thought raised to heaven is the most
perfect prayer.
   G. E. Lessing 1729–81 German dramatist

Often when I pray I wonder if I am not posting letters to
a non-existent address.
   C. S. Lewis 1898–1963 English literary scholar

The family that prays together stays together.
   Al Scalpone fl. 1947

My words fly up, my thoughts remain below:
Words without thoughts never to heaven go.
   William Shakespeare 1564–1616 English dramatist

I am just going to pray for you at St Paul's, but with no
very lively hope of success.
   Sydney Smith 1771–1845 English essayist

Prayer

> More things are wrought by prayer
> Than this world dreams of.

Alfred, Lord Tennyson 1809–92 English poet

Whatever a man prays for, he prays for a miracle. Every prayer reduces itself to this: Great God, grant that twice two be not four.

Ivan Turgenev 1818–83 Russian novelist

You can't pray a lie.

Mark Twain 1835–1910 American writer

✳ Prejudice →Race

Bigotry may be roughly defined as the anger of men who have no opinions.

G. K. Chesterton 1874–1936 English writer

Being a star has made it possible for me to get insulted in places where the average Negro could never *hope* to go and get insulted.

Sammy Davis Jnr. 1925–90 American entertainer

Minds are like parachutes. They only function when they are open.

James Dewar 1842–1923 Scottish physicist

Human diversity makes tolerance more than a virtue, it makes it a requirement for survival.

René Dubos 1901–82 French-born American microbiologist

This is a local shop for local people.

Jeremy Dyson 1966– et al., British television writers, *catchphrase in* The League of Gentlemen

If my theory of relativity is proven correct, Germany will claim me as a German and France will declare that I am a citizen of the world. Should my theory prove untrue,

France will say that I am a German and Germany will declare that I am a Jew.
Albert Einstein 1879–1955 German-born theoretical physicist

Make hatred hated!
Anatole France 1844–1924 French man of letters

Drive out prejudices through the door, and they will return through the window.
Frederick the Great 1712–86 Prussian monarch

Without the aid of prejudice and custom, I should not be able to find my way across the room.
William Hazlitt 1778–1830 English essayist

When prejudice commands, reason is silent.
Helvétius 1715–71 French philosopher

And wherefore is he wearing such a conscience-stricken air?
Oh they're taking him to prison for the colour of his hair.
A. E. Housman 1859–1936 English poet

Four legs good, two legs bad.
George Orwell 1903–50 English novelist

We should therefore claim, in the name of tolerance, the right not to tolerate the intolerant.
Karl Popper 1902–94 Austrian-born philosopher

When people feel deeply, impartiality is bias.
Lord Reith 1889–1971 British administrator

The only good Indian is a dead Indian.
Philip Henry Sheridan 1831–88 American cavalry commander

Bigotry tries to keep truth safe in its hand
With a grip that kills it.
Rabindranath Tagore 1861–1941 Bengali poet

✳ The Present

Can ye not discern the signs of the times?
Bible

Take therefore no thought for the morrow: for the morrow shall take thought for the things of itself. Sufficient unto the day is the evil thereof.
Bible

Few people can say: I am here. They look for themselves in the past and see themselves in the future.
Georges Braque 1882–1963 French painter

Exhaust the little moment. Soon it dies.
And be it gash or gold it will not come
Again in this identical disguise.
Gwendolyn Brooks 1917–2000 American poet

The rule is, jam to-morrow and jam yesterday—but never jam today.
Lewis Carroll 1832–98 English writer

The present is the funeral of the past,
And man the living sepulchre of life.
John Clare 1793–1864 English poet

Unborn TO-MORROW, and dead YESTERDAY,
Why fret about them if TO-DAY be sweet!
Edward Fitzgerald 1809–83 English poet

Carpe diem, quam minimum credula postero.
Seize the day, put no trust in the future.
Horace 65–8 BC Roman poet

Things are both more trivial than they ever were, and more important than they ever were, and the difference between the trivial and the important doesn't seem to matter. But the nowness of everything is absolutely wondrous.

> **Dennis Potter** 1935–94 English dramatist, *on his approaching death*

What is love? 'tis not hereafter;
Present mirth hath present laughter;
What's to come is still unsure.

> **William Shakespeare** 1564–1616 English dramatist

Our work is for today, yesterday has gone, tomorrow has not yet come. We have only today.

> **Mother Teresa** 1910–97 Roman Catholic nun

The Presidency ⁎

My country has in its wisdom contrived for me the most insignificant office that ever the invention of man contrived or his imagination conceived.

> **John Adams** 1735–1826 American statesman, *of the vice-presidency*

The US presidency is a Tudor monarchy plus telephones.

> **Anthony Burgess** 1917–93 English writer

When I was a boy I was told that anybody could become President. I'm beginning to believe it.

> **Clarence Darrow** 1857–1938 American lawyer

No easy problems ever come to the President of the United States. If they are easy to solve, somebody else has solved them.

> **Dwight D. Eisenhower** 1890–1969 American statesman

All the security around the American president is just to make sure the man who shoots him gets caught.

> **Norman Mailer** 1923–2007 American writer

The Presidency

When the President does it, that means that it is not illegal.
Richard Nixon 1913–94 American statesman

I have got such a bully pulpit!
Theodore Roosevelt 1858–1919 American statesman

The answer to the runaway Presidency is not the messenger-boy Presidency. The American democracy must discover a middle way between making the President a tsar and making him a puppet.
Arthur M. Schlesinger Jr. 1917–2007 American historian

 # Pride

Pride goeth before destruction, and an haughty spirit before a fall.
Bible

For whosoever exalteth himself shall be abased; and he that humbleth himself shall be exalted.
Bible

He that is down needs fear no fall,
He that is low no pride.
He that is humble ever shall
Have God to be his guide.
John Bunyan 1628–88 English writer

URIAH HEEP: We are so very 'umble.
Charles Dickens 1812–70 English novelist

Pride helps us; and pride is not a bad thing when it only urges us to hide our own hurts, not to hurt others.
George Eliot 1819–80 English novelist

I can trace my ancestry back to a protoplasmal primordial atomic globule. Consequently, my family pride is something in-conceivable. I can't help it. I was born sneering.

W. S. Gilbert 1836–1911 English writer

In 1969 I published a small book on Humility. It was a pioneering work which has not, to my knowledge, been superseded.

Lord Longford 1905–2001 British politician

PLEASE ACCEPT MY RESIGNATION. I DON'T WANT TO BELONG TO ANY CLUB THAT WILL ACCEPT ME AS A MEMBER.

Groucho Marx 1890–1977 American film comedian

No one can make you feel inferior without your consent.

Eleanor Roosevelt 1884–1962 American diplomat

Arrogance is a highly under-appreciated character trait.

Sting 1951– English rock singer

As for conceit, what man will do any good who is not conceited? Nobody holds a good opinion of a man who has a low opinion of himself.

Anthony Trollope 1815–82 English novelist

Progress

Belief in progress is a doctrine of idlers and Belgians. It is the individual relying upon his neighbours to do his work.

Charles Baudelaire 1821–67 French poet

Want is one only of five giants on the road of reconstruction…the others are Disease, Ignorance, Squalor and Idleness.

William Henry Beveridge 1879–1963 British economist

Progress

The thing that hath been, it is that which shall be; and that which is done is that which shall be done: and there is no new thing under the sun.
Bible

Man aspires to the stars. But if he can get his sewage and refuse distributed and utilised in orderly fashion he will be doing very well.
Roy Bridger fl. 1959

JOHN CLEESE: What have the Romans ever done for us?
Graham Chapman 1941–89 et al. *in the film* Monty Python's Life of Brian

pity this busy monster, manunkind,
not. Progress is a comfortable disease.
e. e. cummings 1894–1962 American poet

The European talks of progress because by an ingenious application of some scientific acquirements he has established a society which has mistaken comfort for civilization.
Benjamin Disraeli 1804–81 British statesman

Is it progress if a cannibal uses knife and fork?
Stanislaw Lec 1909–66 Polish writer

One step forward two steps back.
Lenin 1870–1924 Russian revolutionary

Oui, cela était autrefois ainsi, mais nous avons changé tout cela.
Yes, in the old days that was so, but we have changed all that.
Molière 1622–73 French comic dramatist

If I have seen further it is by standing on the shoulders of giants.
Isaac Newton 1642–1727 English mathematician

'Change' is scientific, 'progress' is ethical; change is indubitable, whereas progress is a matter of controversy.
Bertrand Russell 1872–1970 British philosopher

The reasonable man adapts himself to the world: the unreasonable one persists in trying to adapt the world to himself. Therefore all progress depends on the unreasonable man.
George Bernard Shaw 1856–1950 Irish dramatist

And he gave it for his opinion, that whoever could make two ears of corn or two blades of grass to grow upon a spot of ground where only one grew before, would deserve better of mankind, and do more essential service to his country than the whole race of politicians put together.
Jonathan Swift 1667–1745 Irish poet and satirist

Without deviation from the norm, progress is not possible.
Frank Zappa 1940–93 American rock musician

Promises

If [human life] depends on anything, it is on this frail cord, flung from the forgotten hills of yesterday to the invisible mountains of tomorrow.
G. K. Chesterton 1874–1936 English writer, *on the promise*

My tongue swore, but my mind's unsworn.
Euripides c.485–c.406 BC Greek dramatist, *lamenting the breaking of an oath*

I believe that it is better to light one candle than promise a million light bulbs.
Stephen Harper 1959– Canadian statesman

Promises

You always pay too much. Particularly for promises. There ain't no such thing as a bargain promise.
Cormac McCarthy 1933- American novelist

A promise made is a debt unpaid.
Robert W. Service 1874–1958 Canadian poet

Promises and pie-crust are made to be broken.
Jonathan Swift 1667–1745 Irish poet and satirist

To promise not to do a thing is the surest way in the world to make a body want to go and do that very thing.
Mark Twain 1835–1910 American writer

✳ Protest

'It's always best on these occasions to do what the mob do.' 'But suppose there are two mobs?' suggested Mr Snodgrass. 'Shout with the largest,' replied Mr Pickwick.
Charles Dickens 1812–70 English novelist

Making noise is an effective means of opposition.
Joseph Goebbels 1897–1945 German Nazi leader

The citizen's first duty is unrest.
Günter Grass 1927- German writer

Even a purely moral act that has no hope of any immediate and visible political effect can gradually and indirectly, over time, gain in political significance.
Václav Havel 1936- Czech statesman

Ev'rywhere I hear the sound of marching, charging feet, boy,
'Cause summer's here and the time is right for fighting in the street, boy.
Mick Jagger 1943- and **Keith Richards** 1943- English rock musicians

One-fifth of the people are against everything all the time.
    Robert Kennedy 1925–68 American politician

A riot is at bottom the language of the unheard.
    Martin Luther King 1929–68 American civil rights leader

Never forget that only dead fish swim with the stream.
    Malcolm Muggeridge 1903–90 British journalist

The lady doth protest too much, methinks.
    William Shakespeare 1564–1616 English dramatist

Minorities…are almost always in the right.
    Sydney Smith 1771–1845 English essayist

I've always had the impression that real militants are like cleaning women, doing a thankless, daily but necessary job.
    François Truffaut 1932–84 French film director

Punctuality ✳

Punctuality is the politeness of kings.
    Louis XVIII 1755–1824 French monarch

People who are late are often so much jollier than the people who have to wait for them.
    E. V. Lucas 1868–1938 English writer

We must leave exactly on time…From now on everything must function to perfection.
    Benito Mussolini 1883–1945 Italian dictator, *to a station-master*

I always multiply deadlines by pi.
    Martin Ryle 1918–84 English astronomer

You come most carefully upon your hour.
    William Shakespeare 1564–1616 English dramatist

Punctuality

Punctuality is the virtue of the bored.
  Evelyn Waugh 1903-66 English novelist

✳ Punishment →Crime

All punishment is mischief: all punishment in itself is evil.
  Jeremy Bentham 1748-1832 English philosopher

He that spareth his rod hateth his son.
  Bible

He that is without sin among you, let him first cast a stone at her.
  Bible

Hanging is too good for him, said Mr Cruelty.
  John Bunyan 1628-88 English writer

Excessive bail shall not be required, nor excessive fines imposed, nor cruel and unusual punishment inflicted.
  Constitution of the United States 1787

Punishment is not for revenge, but to lessen crime and reform the criminal.
  Elizabeth Fry 1780-1845 English prison reformer

Whenever the offence inspires less horror than the punishment, the rigour of penal law is obliged to give way to the common feelings of mankind.
  Edward Gibbon 1737-94 English historian

My object all sublime
I shall achieve in time—
To let the punishment fit the crime—
The punishment fit the crime.
  W. S. Gilbert 1836-1911 English writer

Awaiting the sensation of a short, sharp shock,
From a cheap and chippy chopper on a big black block.
    W. S. Gilbert 1836–1911 English writer

Men are not hanged for stealing horses, but that horses
may not be stolen.
    George Savile, Marquess of Halifax 1633–95 English
    politician

This is the first of punishments, that no guilty man is
acquitted if judged by himself.
    Juvenal c.AD 60–c.130 Roman satirist

In that case, if we are to abolish the death penalty, let the
murderers take the first step.
    Alphonse Karr 1808–90 French writer

The boy learns not to fear sin, but the *punishment* for it,
and thus he learns to lie.
    Charles Kingsley 1819–75 English writer

Society needs to condemn a little more and understand a
little less.
    John Major 1943– British statesman

I went out to Charing Cross, to see Major-general
Harrison hanged, drawn, and quartered; which was done
there, he looking as cheerful as any man could do in that
condition.
    Samuel Pepys 1633–1703 English diarist

Quotations ✳

The surest way to make a monkey of a man is to quote
him.
    Robert Benchley 1889–1945 American humorist

It is a good thing for an uneducated man to read books
of quotations.
    Winston Churchill 1874–1965 British statesman

Quotations

I know heaps of quotations, so I can always make quite a fair show of knowledge.
O. Douglas 1877–1948 Scottish writer

I hate quotation. Tell me what you know.
Ralph Waldo Emerson 1803–82 American writer

An anthology is like all the plums and orange peel picked out of a cake.
Walter Raleigh 1861–1922 English critic

I always have a quotation for everything—it saves original thinking.
Dorothy L. Sayers 1893–1957 English writer

Famous remarks are very seldom quoted correctly.
Simeon Strunsky 1879–1948 American writer

What a good thing Adam had. When he said a good thing he knew nobody had said it before.
Mark Twain 1835–1910 American writer

OSCAR WILDE: How I wish I had said that.
WHISTLER: You will, Oscar, you will.
James McNeill Whistler 1834–1903 American-born painter

Some for renown on scraps of learning dote,
And think they grow immortal as they quote.
Edward Young 1683–1765 English poet

✳ Race ⇒Equality, Prejudice

Black is beautiful.
Anonymous *slogan of American civil rights campaigners, mid-1960s*

You have seen how a man was made a slave; you shall see how a slave was made a man.
Frederick Douglass c.1818–95 American former slave

I herewith commission you to carry out all preparations with regard to...a *total solution* of the Jewish question in those territories of Europe which are under German influence.

Hermann Goering 1893–1946 German Nazi leader

Though it be a thrilling and marvellous thing to be merely young and gifted in such times, it is doubly so, doubly dynamic—to be young, gifted and *black*.

Lorraine Hansberry 1930–65 American dramatist

And if the white man thought that Asians were a low, filthy nation, Asians could still smile with relief—at least, they were not Africans. And if the white man thought that Africans were a low, filthy nation, Africans in southern Africa could still smile—at least, they were not bushmen. They all have their monsters.

Bessie Head 1937–86 South African-born writer

When I look out at this convention, I see the face of America, red, yellow, brown, black, and white. We are all precious in God's sight—the real rainbow coalition.

Jesse Jackson 1941– American clergyman

There are no 'white' or 'coloured' signs on the foxholes or graveyards of battle.

John F. Kennedy 1917–63 American statesman

I have a dream that my four little children will one day live in a nation where they will not be judged by the colour of their skin but by the content of their character.

Martin Luther King 1929–68 American civil rights leader

Our mistreatment was just not right, and I was tired of it.

Rosa Parks 1913–2005 American civil rights activist, *of her refusal to surrender her seat on a segregated bus in Alabama to a white man*

Race

Where today are the Pequot? Where are the Narragansett, the Mohican, the Pokanoket, and many other once powerful tribes of our people? They have vanished before the avarice and oppression of the white man, as snow before the summer sun.

Tecumseh 1768–1813 Shawnee chief

Am I not a man and a brother.

Josiah Wedgwood 1730–95 English potter, *legend on Wedgwood cameo, depicting a kneeling Negro slave in chains*

Growing up, I came up with this name: I'm a Cablinasian.

Tiger Woods 1975– American golfer, *explaining his rejection of 'African-American' as the term to describe his Caucasian, Afro-American, Native American, Thai, and Chinese ancestry*

✳ Railways

This is the Night Mail crossing the Border,
Bringing the cheque and the postal order,
Letters for the rich, letters for the poor,
The shop at the corner, the girl next door.

W. H. Auden 1907–73 English poet

Railways and the Church have their critics, but both are the best ways of getting a man to his ultimate destination.

Revd W. Awdry 1911–97 English writer

The only way of catching a train I have ever discovered is to miss the train before.

G. K. Chesterton 1874–1936 English writer

Railway termini. They are our gates to the glorious and the unknown. Through them we pass out into adventure and sunshine, to them, alas! we return.

E. M. Forster 1879–1970 English novelist

Sir, Saturday morning, although recurring at regular and well-foreseen intervals, always seems to take this railway by surprise.

> **W. S. Gilbert** 1836–1911 English writer, *letter to the station-master at Baker Street, on the Metropolitan line*

That life-quickening atmosphere of a big railway station where everything is something trembling on the brink of something else.

> **Vladimir Nabokov** 1899–1977 Russian novelist

Reading →Books

[Thomas Hobbes] was wont to say that if he had read as much as other men, he should have known no more than other men.

> **John Aubrey** 1626–97 English antiquary

In science, read, by preference, the newest works; in literature, the oldest.

> **Edward Bulwer-Lytton** 1803–73 British novelist

History shows that the less people read, the more books they buy.

> **Albert Camus** 1913–60 French writer

Choose an author as you choose a friend.

> **Wentworth Dillon, Earl of Roscommon** c.1633–85 Irish poet

To her kind lessons I ascribe my early and invincible love of reading, which I would not exchange for the treasures of India.

> **Edward Gibbon** 1737–94 English historian

What do we ever get nowadays from reading to equal the excitement and the revelation in those first fourteen years?

> **Graham Greene** 1904–91 English novelist

Reading

A man ought to read just as inclination leads him; for what he reads as a task will do him little good.
Samuel Johnson 1709–84 English lexicographer

Curiously enough, one cannot *read* a book: one can only reread it. A good reader, a major reader, an active and creative reader is a rereader.
Vladimir Nabokov 1899–1977 Russian novelist

The bookful blockhead, ignorantly read,
With loads of learned lumber in his head.
Alexander Pope 1688–1744 English poet

POLONIUS: What do you read, my lord?
HAMLET: Words, words, words.
William Shakespeare 1564–1616 English dramatist

People say that life is the thing, but I prefer reading.
Logan Pearsall Smith 1865–1946 American writer

Reading is to the mind what exercise is to the body.
Richard Steele 1672–1729 Irish-born essayist

Reality

It's as large as life, and twice as natural!
Lewis Carroll 1832–98 English writer

Reality goes bounding past the satirist like a cheetah laughing as it lopes ahead of the greyhound.
Claud Cockburn 1904–81 British journalist

Reality is that which, when you stop believing in it, doesn't go away.
Philip K. Dick 1928–82 American writer

Human kind
Cannot bear very much reality.
T. S. Eliot 1888–1965 American-born British poet

All theory, dear friend, is grey, but the golden tree of
actual life springs ever green.
Johann Wolfgang von Goethe 1749–1832 German writer

What is rational is actual and what is actual is rational.
G. W. F. Hegel 1770–1831 German philosopher

Each person experiences his own reality, and no one else
can be the judge of what that reality really is.
Shirley Maclaine 1934– American actress

The camera makes everyone a tourist in other people's
reality, and eventually in one's own.
Susan Sontag 1933–2004 American writer

They said, 'You have a blue guitar,
You do not play things as they are.'
The man replied, 'Things as they are
Are changed upon the blue guitar.'
Wallace Stevens 1879–1955 American poet

The nineteenth century dislike of Realism is the rage of
Caliban seeing his own face in the glass.
Oscar Wilde 1854–1900 Irish dramatist

BLANCHE: I don't want realism.
MITCH: Naw, I guess not.
BLANCHE: I'll tell you what I want. Magic!
Tennessee Williams 1911–83 American dramatist

Relationships ✳

Love is like the wild rose-briar;
Friendship like the holly-tree:
The holly is dark when the rose-briar blooms,
But which will bloom most constantly?
Emily Brontë 1818–48 English writer

Relationships

Men love women, women love children; children love hamsters—it's quite hopeless.
Alice Thomas Ellis 1932-2005 English novelist

The ones we choose to love become our anchor
when the hawser of the blood-tie's hacked, or frays.
Tony Harrison 1937- British poet

Three things in human life are important. The first is to be kind. The second is to be kind. And the third is to be kind.
Henry James 1843-1916 American novelist

Marriage may often be a stormy lake, but celibacy is almost always a muddy horsepond.
Thomas Love Peacock 1785-1866 English writer

Human relationships don't belong to engineering, mathematics, chess, which offer problems that can be perfectly solved. Human relationships grow, like trees.
J. B. Priestley 1894-1984 English writer

KATHARINE HEPBURN: The time to make up your mind about people is never.
Donald Ogden Stewart 1894-1980 American humorist, *in the film* The Philadelphia Story

✳ Religion ⇒The Church, God, Prayer

Render therefore unto Caesar the things which are Caesar's; and unto God the things that are God's.
Bible

One religion is as true as another.
Robert Burton 1577-1640 English clergyman

Christians have burnt each other, quite persuaded
That all the Apostles would have done as they did.
Lord Byron 1788-1824 English poet

340

Putting moral virtues at the highest, and religion at the lowest, religion must still be allowed to be a collateral security, at least, to virtue; and every prudent man will sooner trust to two securities than to one.

Lord Chesterfield 1694–1773 English writer

Science without religion is lame, religion without science is blind.

Albert Einstein 1879–1955 German-born theoretical physicist

The various modes of worship, which prevailed in the Roman world, were all considered by the people as equally true; by the philosopher, as equally false; and by the magistrate, as equally useful. And thus toleration produced not only mutual indulgence, but even religious concord.

Edward Gibbon 1737–94 English historian

In all ages of the world, priests have been enemies of liberty.

David Hume 1711–76 Scottish philosopher

I go into the Muslim mosque and the Jewish synagogue and the Christian church and I see one altar.

Jalal ad-Din ar-Rumi 1207–73 Persian poet

Religion's in the heart, not in the knee.

Douglas Jerrold 1803–57 English writer

No compulsion is there in religion.

The Koran

I count religion but a childish toy,
And hold there is no sin but ignorance.

Christopher Marlowe 1564–93 English dramatist

Religion…is the opium of the people.

Karl Marx 1818–83 German philosopher

Religion

Things have come to a pretty pass when religion is allowed to invade the sphere of private life.

Lord Melbourne 1779–1848 English statesman, *on hearing an evangelical sermon*

My country is the world, and my religion is to do good.

Thomas Paine 1737–1809 English political theorist

Is that which is holy loved by the gods because it is holy, or is it holy because it is loved by the gods?

Plato 429–347 BC Greek philosopher

Religion to me has always been the wound, not the bandage.

Dennis Potter 1935–94 English dramatist

A sense of the sacred without a sense of humour becomes leaden.

Robert Runcie 1921–2000 English clergyman

'Men of sense are really but of one religion.'…'Pray, my lord, what religion is that which men of sense agree in?' 'Madam,' says the earl immediately, 'men of sense never tell it.'

Lord Shaftesbury 1621–83 English statesman

We have just enough religion to make us hate, but not enough to make us love one another.

Jonathan Swift 1667–1745 Irish poet and satirist

Orthodoxy is my doxy; heterodoxy is another man's doxy.

William Warburton 1698–1779 English theologian

I went to America to convert the Indians; but oh, who shall convert me?

John Wesley 1703–91 English preacher

So many gods, so many creeds,
So many paths that wind and wind,
While just the art of being kind
Is all the sad world needs.

Ella Wheeler Wilcox 1855–1919 American poet

Retirement ✳

Once I leave, I leave. I am not going to speak to the man on the bridge, and I am not going to spit on the deck.
> **Stanley Baldwin** 1867–1947 British statesman, *on resigning*

I go to Bournemouth in lieu of Paradise.
> **Lord Hugh Cecil** 1869–1956 British politician, *on retiring from Eton*

If anything could have pulled me out of retirement, it would have been an Indiana Jones film. But in the end, retirement is just too damned much fun.
> **Sean Connery** 1930– Scottish actor

The most horrifying thing in the world is to be without an adventure.
> **George Foreman** 1948– American boxer, *considering a comeback at 55*

The transition from Who's Who to Who's He.
> **Eddie George** 1938–2009 English banker

Retirement from the concert hall is like giving up smoking. You have got to finish completely.
> **Beniamino Gigli** 1890–1957 Italian operatic tenor

That [retirement] kind of says giving up to me. It's like going to bed lying down. I can't.
> **Rolf Harris** 1930– Australian artist and singer

When you get done, you get done.
> **Stephen King** 1947– American writer, *announcing his retirement from writing*

Learn to live well, or fairly make your will;
You've played, and loved, and ate, and drunk your fill:
Walk sober off; before a sprightlier age
Comes tittering on, and shoves you from the stage.
> **Alexander Pope** 1688–1744 English poet

Retirement

As to that leisure evening of life, I must say that I do not want it. I can conceive of no contentment of which toil is not to be the immediate parent.
    Anthony Trollope 1815–82 English novelist

I contemplate retirement every evening, and then I forget about it in the morning.
    Peter Ustinov 1921–2004 British actor

✳ Revenge

Revenge is a kind of wild justice, which the more man's nature runs to, the more ought law to weed it out.
    Francis Bacon 1561–1626 English courtier

Vengeance is mine; I will repay, saith the Lord.
    Bible

Sweet is revenge—especially to women.
    Lord Byron 1788–1824 English poet

It may be that vengeance is sweet, and that the gods forbade vengeance to men because they reserved for themselves so delicious and intoxicating a drink. But no one should drain the cup to the bottom. The dregs are often filthy-tasting.
    Winston Churchill 1874–1965 British statesman

Heaven has no rage, like love to hatred turned,
Nor Hell a fury, like a woman scorned.
    William Congreve 1670–1729 English dramatist

The Germans...are going to be squeezed as a lemon is squeezed—until the pips squeak.
    Eric Geddes 1875–1937 British politician

Nobody ever forgets where he buried a hatchet.
    Frank McKinney ('Kin') Hubbard 1868–1930 American humorist

Get your retaliation in first.
Carwyn James 1929–83 Welsh rugby player

Men should be either treated generously or destroyed, because they take revenge for slight injuries—for heavy ones they cannot.
Niccolò Machiavelli 1469–1527 Italian political philosopher

Don't get mad, get everything.
Ivana Trump 1949– Czech model, *advice to wronged wives*

Revolution ✳

Better to abolish serfdom from above than to wait till it begins to abolish itself from below.
Tsar Alexander II 1818–81 Russian monarch

The most radical revolutionary will become a conservative on the day after the revolution.
Hannah Arendt 1906–75 American philosopher

Those who have served the cause of the revolution have ploughed the sea.
Simón Bolívar 1783–1830 Venezuelan statesman

Revolutions are celebrated when they are no longer dangerous.
Pierre Boulez 1925– French composer

Rebellion to tyrants is obedience to God.
John Bradshaw 1602–59 English judge

Would it not be easier
In that case for the government
To dissolve the people
And elect another?
Bertolt Brecht 1898–1956 German dramatist, *on the 1953 uprising in East Germany*

Revolution

All modern revolutions have ended in a reinforcement of the State.

Albert Camus 1913-60 French writer

A desperate disease requires a dangerous remedy.

Guy Fawkes 1570-1606 English conspirator

I will die like a true-blue rebel. Don't waste any time in mourning—organize.

Joe Hill 1879-1915 American labour leader, *farewell telegram prior to his death by firing squad*

The generation which commences a revolution can rarely complete it.

Thomas Jefferson 1743-1826 American statesman

When smashing monuments, save the pedestals—they always come in handy.

Stanislaw Lec 1909-66 Polish writer

Après nous le déluge.
After us the deluge.

Madame de Pompadour 1721-64 French courtesan

J'ai vécu.
I survived.

Abbé Emmanuel Joseph Sieyès 1748-1836 French politician, *when asked what he had done during the French Revolution*

I have seen the future; and it works.

Lincoln Steffens 1866-1936 American journalist, *following a visit to the Soviet Union in 1919*

Bliss was it in that dawn to be alive,
But to be young was very heaven!

William Wordsworth 1770-1850 English poet, *on the French revolution*

Royalty ✳

[A king] is the fountain of honour.
Francis Bacon 1561–1626 English courtier

We must not let in daylight upon magic.
Walter Bagehot 1826–77 English economist

The Sovereign has, under a constitutional monarchy such as ours, three rights—the right to be consulted, the right to encourage, the right to warn.
Walter Bagehot 1826–77 English economist

To be Prince of Wales is not a position. It is a predicament.
Alan Bennett 1934– English writer

A subject and a sovereign are clean different things.
Charles I 1600–49 British monarch

I'd like to be a queen in people's hearts but I don't see myself being Queen of this country.
Diana, Princess of Wales 1961–97 British princess

Everyone likes flattery; and when you come to Royalty you should lay it on with a trowel.
Benjamin Disraeli 1804–81 British statesman

I have found it impossible to carry the heavy burden of responsibility and to discharge my duties as King as I would wish to do without the help and support of the woman I love.
Edward VIII 1894–1972 British monarch, *radio broadcast following his abdication*

I know I have the body of a weak and feeble woman, but I have the heart and stomach of a king, and of a king of England too.
Elizabeth I 1533–1603 English monarch

Royalty

L'État c'est moi.
I am the State.
> **Louis XIV** 1638–1715 French monarch

Royalty is the gold filling in a mouthful of decay.
> **John Osborne** 1929– English dramatist

Uneasy lies the head that wears a crown.
> **William Shakespeare** 1564–1616 English dramatist

Monarchy is only the string that ties the robber's bundle.
> **Percy Bysshe Shelley** 1792–1822 English poet

I will be good.
> **Queen Victoria** 1819–1901 British monarch, *on being shown a chart of the line of succession*

✴ Satisfaction ⇒Discontent

You never know what is enough unless you know what is
more than enough.
> **William Blake** 1757–1827 English poet

A book of verses underneath the bough,
A jug of wine, a loaf of bread—and Thou
Beside me singing in the wilderness—
And wilderness were paradise enow.
> **Edward Fitzgerald** 1809–83 English poet

These are the days when men of all social disciplines and
all political faiths seek the comfortable and the
accepted…in minor modification of the scriptural
parable, the bland lead the bland.
> **J. K. Galbraith** 1908–2006 American economist

I can't get no satisfaction.
> **Mick Jagger** 1943– and **Keith Richards** 1943– English rock
> musicians

If one cannot catch the bird of paradise, better take a wet hen.
Nikita Khrushchev 1894–1971 Soviet statesman

So long as the great majority of men are not deprived of either property or honour, they are satisfied.
Niccolò Machiavelli 1469–1527 Italian political philosopher

He is well paid that is well satisfied.
William Shakespeare 1564–1616 English dramatist

As long as I have a want, I have a reason for living. Satisfaction is death.
George Bernard Shaw 1856–1950 Irish dramatist

Content is disillusioning to behold: what is there to be content about?
Virginia Woolf 1882–1941 English novelist

Science →Life Sciences, Technology

When I find myself in the company of scientists, I feel like a shabby curate who has strayed by mistake into a drawing room full of dukes.
W. H. Auden 1907–73 English poet

Anybody who is not shocked by this subject has failed to understand it.
Niels Bohr 1885–1962 Danish physicist, *of quantum mechanics*

Basic research is what I am doing when I don't know what I am doing.
Werner von Braun 1912–77 German-born rocket engineer

The aim of science is not to open the door to infinite wisdom, but to set a limit to infinite error.
Bertolt Brecht 1898–1956 German dramatist

Science

The scientific method, as far as it is a method, is nothing more than doing one's damnedest with one's mind, no holds barred.
Percy Williams Bridgeman 1882–1961 American physicist

The essence of science: ask an impertinent question, and you are on the way to a pertinent answer.
Jacob Bronowski 1908–74 Polish-born scientist

If an elderly but distinguished scientist says that something is possible he is almost certainly right, but if he says that it is impossible he is very probably wrong.
Arthur C. Clarke 1917–2008 English science fiction writer

In science the credit goes to the man who convinces the world, not to the man to whom the idea first occurs.
Francis Darwin 1848–1925 English botanist

It is more important to have beauty in one's equations than to have them fit experiment.
Paul Dirac 1902–84 British theoetical physicist

I ask you to look both ways. For the road to a knowledge of the stars leads through the atom; and important knowledge of the atom has been reached through the stars.
Arthur Eddington 1882–1944 British astrophysicist

The grand aim of all science [is] to cover the greatest number of empirical facts by logical deduction from the smallest possible number of hypotheses or axioms.
Albert Einstein 1879–1955 German-born theoretical physicist

Nothing is too wonderful to be true, if it be consistent with the laws of nature, and in such things as these, experiment is the best test of such consistency.
Michael Faraday 1791–1867 English scientist

The great tragedy of Science—the slaying of a beautiful hypothesis by an ugly fact.
T. H. Huxley 1825–95 English biologist

It may be so, there is no arguing against facts and experiments.

Isaac Newton 1642–1727 English mathematician, *when told of an experiment which appeared to destroy his theory*

Where observation is concerned, chance favours only the prepared mind.

Louis Pasteur 1822–95 French chemist

A new scientific truth does not triumph by convincing its opponents and making them see the light, but rather because its opponents eventually die, and a new generation grows up that is familiar with it.

Max Planck 1858–1947 German physicist

Science is built up of facts, as a house is built of stones; but an accumulation of facts is no more a science than a heap of stones is a house.

Henri Poincaré 1854–1912 French mathematician

Nature, and Nature's laws lay hid in night.
God said, *Let Newton be!* and all was light.

Alexander Pope 1688–1744 English poet

Aristotle maintained that women have fewer teeth than men; although he was twice married, it never occurred to him to verify this statement by examining his wives' mouths.

Bertrand Russell 1872–1970 British philosopher

All science is either physics or stamp collecting.

Ernest Rutherford 1871–1937 New Zealand physicist

We haven't got the money, so we've got to think!

Ernest Rutherford 1871–1937 New Zealand physicist

Science is for the cultivation of religion, not for worldly enjoyment.

Sadi c.1213–91 Persian poet

Science

It did not last: the Devil howling 'Ho!
Let Einstein be!' restored the status quo.

J. C. Squire 1884–1958 English man of letters, *responding to Pope's lines on Newton*

It is much easier to make measurements than to know exactly what you are measuring.

J. W. N. Sullivan 1886–1937 English writer

✳ Scotland

There are few more impressive sights in the world than a Scotsman on the make.

J. M. Barrie 1860–1937 Scottish writer

Scotland, land of the omnipotent No.

Alan Bold 1943– Scottish poet

My heart's in the Highlands, my heart is not here;
My heart's in the Highlands a-chasing the deer.

Robert Burns 1759–96 Scottish poet

Scots, wha hae wi' Wallace bled,
Scots, wham Bruce has aften led,
Welcome to your gory bed,—
Or to victorie.

Robert Burns 1759–96 Scottish poet

From the lone shieling of the misty island
Mountains divide us, and the waste of seas—
Yet still the blood is strong, the heart is Highland,
And we in dreams behold the Hebrides!

John Galt 1779–1839 Scottish writer

The noblest prospect which a Scotchman ever sees, is the high road that leads him to England!

Samuel Johnson 1709–84 English lexicographer

If one wanted a rough-and-ready generalization to express
the difference between a Glasgow man and an Edinburgh
man, one might say that every Edinburgh man considers
himself a little better than his neighbour, and every
Glasgow man just as good as his neighbour.

Edwin Muir 1887–1959 Scottish poet

O Caledonia! stern and wild,
Meet nurse for a poetic child!

Sir Walter Scott 1771–1832 Scottish novelist

Stands Scotland where it did?

William Shakespeare 1564–1616 English dramatist

O flower of Scotland, when will we see your like again,
that fought and died for your wee bit hill and glen
and stood against him, proud Edward's army,
and sent him homeward tae think again.

Roy Williamson 1936–90 Scottish musician

Sculpture ✳

Most statues seem sad and introspective,
they hold their breath between coming and going,
They lament their devoured, once shuddering stone.

Dannie Abse 1923– Welsh-born poet

Carving is interrelated masses conveying an emotion: a
perfect relationship between the mind and the colour,
light and weight which is the stone, made by the hand
which feels.

Barbara Hepworth 1903–75 English sculptor

It's amazing what you can do with an E in A-level art,
twisted imagination and a chainsaw.

Damien Hirst 1965– English artist, *after winning the 1995
Turner Prize*

Sculpture

The marble not yet carved can hold the form
Of every thought the greatest artist has.
Michelangelo 1475–1564 Italian artist

The first hole made through a piece of stone is a
revelation.
Henry Moore 1898–1986 English sculptor

✳ The Sea

A willing foe and sea room.
Anonymous *naval toast in the time of Nelson*

They that go down to the sea in ships: and occupy their
business in great waters.
Bible

Don't talk to me about naval tradition. It's nothing but
rum, sodomy, and the lash.
Winston Churchill 1874–1965 British statesman

Water, water, everywhere,
And all the boards did shrink;
Water, water, everywhere,
Nor any drop to drink.
Samuel Taylor Coleridge 1772–1834 English poet

No man will be a sailor who has contrivance enough to
get himself into a jail; for being in a ship is being in a
jail, with the chance of being drowned...A man in a jail
has more room, better food, and commonly better
company.
Samuel Johnson 1709–84 English lexicographer

It is an interesting biological fact that all of us have in
our veins the exact same percentage of salt in our blood
that exists in the ocean, and therefore, we have salt in our
blood, in our sweat, in our tears. We are tied to the

ocean. And when we go back to the sea—whether it is to sail or to watch it—we are going back from whence we came.

John F. Kennedy 1917–63 American statesman

I must go down to the sea again, to the lonely sea and the sky,
And all I ask is a tall ship and a star to steer her by.

John Masefield 1878–1967 English poet

Meditation and water are wedded for ever.

Herman Melville 1819–91 American novelist

The sea hates a coward!

Eugene O'Neill 1888–1953 American dramatist

The sea has such extraordinary moods that sometimes you feel this is the only sort of life—and 10 minutes later you're praying for death.

Philip, Duke of Edinburgh 1921– Greek-born husband of Elizabeth II

Whosoever commands the sea commands the trade; whosoever commands the trade of the world commands the riches of the world, and consequently the world itself.

Walter Ralegh c.1552–1618 English courtier

Full fathom five thy father lies;
Of his bones are coral made:
Those are pearls that were his eyes:
Nothing of him that doth fade,
But doth suffer a sea-change
Into something rich and strange.

William Shakespeare 1564–1616 English dramatist

The sea is as near as we come to another world.

Anne Stevenson 1933– English poet

Rocked in the cradle of the deep.

Emma Hart Willard 1787–1870 American educationist

☀ Secrecy

I shall be but a short time tonight. I have seldom spoken with greater regret, for my lips are not yet unsealed.

Stanley Baldwin 1867–1947 British statesman, *usually quoted as 'My lips are sealed'*

When thou doest alms, let not thy left hand know what thy right hand doeth.

Bible

The truth is out there.

Chris Carter 1957– American screenwriter, *catchphrase;* The X Files

The small man said to the other: 'Where does a wise man hide a pebble?' And the tall man answered in a low voice: 'On the beach.'

G. K. Chesterton 1874–1936 English writer

I know that's a secret, for it's whispered every where.

William Congreve 1670–1729 English dramatist

For secrets are edged tools,
And must be kept from children and from fools.

John Dryden 1631–1700 English poet

I would not open windows into men's souls.

Elizabeth I 1533–1603 English monarch

We dance round in a ring and suppose,
But the Secret sits in the middle and knows.

Robert Frost 1874–1963 American poet

Once the toothpaste is out of the tube, it is awfully hard to get it back in.

H. R. Haldeman 1929–93 American Presidential assistant, *comment on the Watergate affair*

Love and a cough cannot be hid.

George Herbert 1593–1633 English poet

It is public scandal that constitutes offence, and to sin in secret is not to sin at all.

Molière 1622–73 French comic dramatist

A secret may be sometimes best kept by keeping the secret of its being a secret.

Henry Taylor 1800–86 British writer

The Self ✳

Whatever you are is never enough; you must find a way to accept something however small from the other to make you whole.

Chinua Achebe 1930– Nigerian novelist

Some thirty inches from my nose
The frontier of my Person goes,
And all the untilled air between
Is private *pagus* or demesne.

W. H. Auden 1907–73 English poet

Through the Thou a person becomes I.

Martin Buber 1878–1965 Austrian-born philosopher

'You' your joys and your sorrows, your memories and ambitions, your sense of personal identity and free will, are in fact no more than the behaviour of a vast assembly of nerve cells and their associated molecules.

Francis Crick 1916–2004 English biophysicist

I am the master of my fate:
I am the captain of my soul.

W. E. Henley 1849–1903 English poet

If I am not for myself who is for me; and being for my own self what am I?

Hillel 'The Elder' c.60–c.9 Jewish scholar

The Self

It is not contrary to reason to prefer the destruction of the whole world to the scratching of my finger.
David Hume 1711–76 Scottish philosopher

He that overvalues himself will undervalue others, and he that undervalues others will oppress them.
Samuel Johnson 1709–84 English lexicographer

Whatever you may be sure of, be sure at least of this, that you are dreadfully like other people.
James Russell Lowell 1819–91 American poet

I am not a number, I am a free man!
Patrick McGoohan 1928–2009 English actor et al. *Number Six, in* The Prisoner

When a man points a finger at someone else, he should remember that four of his fingers are pointing to himself.
Louis Nizer 1902–94 American lawyer

The self is hateful.
Blaise Pascal 1623–62 French scientist and philosopher

Thus God and nature linked the gen'ral frame,
And bade self-love and social be the same.
Alexander Pope 1688–1744 English poet

Personal isn't the same as important.
Terry Pratchett 1948– English novelist

Who is it that can tell me who I am?
William Shakespeare 1564–1616 English dramatist

It is easy—terribly easy—to shake a man's faith in himself. To take advantage of that to break a man's spirit is devil's work.
George Bernard Shaw 1856–1950 Irish dramatist

Whatever people think I am or say I am, that's what I'm not.
Alan Sillitoe 1928– English writer

Rose is a rose is a rose is a rose, is a rose.
Gertrude Stein 1874–1946 American writer

If a man does not keep pace with his companions, perhaps it is because he hears a different drummer. Let him step to the music which he hears, however measured or far away.
Henry David Thoreau 1817–62 American writer

Do I contradict myself?
Very well then I contradict myself,
(I am large, I contain multitudes.)
Walt Whitman 1819–92 American poet

Self-Knowledge ✳

Know thyself.
Anonymous *inscribed on the temple of Apollo at Delphi*

The image of myself which I try to create in my own mind in order that I may love myself is very different from the image which I try to create in the minds of others in order that they may love me.
W. H. Auden 1907–73 English poet

Why beholdest thou the mote that is in thy brother's eye, but considerest not the beam that is in thine own eye?
Bible

The one self-knowledge worth having is to know one's own mind.
F. H. Bradley 1846–1924 English philosopher

O wad some Pow'r the giftie gie us
To see oursels as others see us!
It wad frae mony a blunder free us,
And foolish notion.
Robert Burns 1759–96 Scottish poet

Self-Knowledge

How little do we know that which we are!
How less what we may be!
Lord Byron 1788–1824 English poet

I do not know whether I was then a man dreaming I was
a butterfly, or whether I am now a butterfly dreaming I
am a man.
Chuang-tzu (or Zhuangzi) c.369–286 BC Chinese philosopher

Being totally honest with oneself is a good exercise.
Sigmund Freud 1856–1939 Austrian psychiatrist

I do not know myself, and God forbid that I should.
Johann Wolfgang von Goethe 1749–1832 German writer

All our knowledge is, ourselves to know.
Alexander Pope 1688–1744 English poet

A man who does not trust himself will never really trust
anybody.
Cardinal de Retz 1613–79 French cardinal

This above all: to thine own self be true,
And it must follow, as the night the day,
Thou canst not then be false to any man.
William Shakespeare 1564–1616 English dramatist

There are few things more painful than to recognise one's
own faults in others.
John Wells 1936–98 English satirist

✳ Sex ⇒Love, Marriage

That [sex] was the most fun I ever had without laughing.
Woody Allen 1935– American film director

Don't knock masturbation. It's sex with someone I love.
Woody Allen 1935– American film director

On bisexuality: It immediately doubles your chances for a date on Saturday night.
Woody Allen 1935– American film director

Give me chastity and continency—but not yet!
St Augustine of Hippo AD 354–430 Roman theologian

This trivial and vulgar way of coition; it is the foolishest act a wise man commits in all his life, nor is there any thing that will more deject his cooled imagination, when he shall consider what an odd and unworthy piece of folly he hath committed.
Sir Thomas Browne 1605–82 English writer

It doesn't matter what you do in the bedroom as long as you don't do it in the street and frighten the horses.
Mrs Patrick Campbell 1865–1940 English actress

The pleasure is momentary, the position ridiculous, and the expense damnable.
Lord Chesterfield 1694–1773 English writer

I have never yet seen anyone whose desire to build up his moral power was as strong as sexual desire.
Confucius 551–479 BC Chinese philosopher

Licence my roving hands, and let them go,
Behind, before, above, between, below.
O my America, my new found land,
My kingdom, safeliest when with one man manned.
John Donne 1572–1631 English poet

I'll have what she's having.
Nora Ephron 1941– American screenwriter, *said by woman to waiter, seeing Sally acting an orgasm, in the film* When Harry Met Sally

Personally I know nothing about sex because I've always been married.
Zsa Zsa Gabor 1919– Hungarian-born film actress

Sex

But did thee feel the earth move?
Ernest Hemingway 1899–1961 American novelist

When I hear his steps outside my door I lie down on my bed, close my eyes, open my legs, and think of England.
Lady Hillingdon 1857–1940

I'll come no more behind your scenes, David; for the silk stockings and white bosoms of your actresses excite my amorous propensities.
Samuel Johnson 1709–84 English lexicographer

The only unnatural sex act is that which you cannot perform.
Alfred Kinsey 1894–1956 American sex researcher

'Tisn't beauty, so to speak, nor good talk necessarily. It's just It. Some women'll stay in a man's memory if they once walked down a street.
Rudyard Kipling 1865–1936 English writer

The Duke returned from the wars today and did pleasure me in his top-boots.
Sarah, Duchess of Marlborough 1660–1744

Not tonight, Josephine.
Napoleon I 1769–1821 French emperor

Delight of lust is gross and brief
And weariness treads on desire.
Petronius d. 65 Roman satirist

Love is two minutes fifty-two seconds of squishing noises.
Johnny Rotten 1957– English pop singer

Is it not strange that desire should so many years outlive performance?
William Shakespeare 1564–1616 English dramatist

Someone asked Sophocles, 'How is your sex-life now? Are you still able to have a woman?' He replied, 'Hush, man; most gladly indeed am I rid of it all, as though I had

escaped from a mad and savage master.'
Sophocles c.496-406 BC Greek dramatist

Is that a gun in your pocket, or are you just glad to
see me?
Mae West 1892-1980 American film actress

Sickness ⇒Medicine

A man's illness is his private territory and, no matter how
much he loves you and how close you are, you stay an
outsider. You are healthy.
Lauren Bacall 1924- American actress

If a lot of cures are suggested for a disease, it means that
the disease is incurable.
Anton Chekhov 1860-1904 Russian writer

All diseases run into one, old age.
Ralph Waldo Emerson 1803-82 American writer

It's all about losing your brain without losing your mind.
Michael J. Fox 1961- Canadian actor, *on his fight against
Parkinson's disease*

People mean well and do not see how distancing insistent
cheeriness is, how it denies another's reality, denies a sick
person the space or right to be sick and in pain.
Marilyn French 1929-2009 American writer

My final word, before I'm done,
Is 'Cancer can be rather fun'.
Thanks to the nurses and Nye Bevan
The NHS is quite like heaven
Provided one confronts the tumour
With a sufficient sense of humour.
J. B. S. Haldane 1892-1964 Scottish mathematical biologist

Sickness

Did God who gave us flowers and trees,
Also provide the allergies?
    E. Y. Harburg 1898–1981 American songwriter

Human nature seldom walks up to the word 'cancer'.
    Rudyard Kipling 1865–1936 English writer

Illness is not something a person *has*; it's another way of
being.
    Jonathan Miller 1934– English writer and director

I told you I was ill.
    Spike Milligan 1918–2002 Irish comedian, *inscription on his
gravestone*

The desire to take medicine is perhaps the greatest feature
which distinguishes man from animals.
    William Osler 1849–1919 Canadian-born physician

Cured yesterday of my disease,
I died last night of my physician.
    Matthew Prior 1664–1721 English poet

Illness is the doctor to whom we pay most heed; to
kindness, to knowledge, we make promise only; pain we
obey.
    Marcel Proust 1871–1922 French novelist

I now begin the journey that will lead me into the sunset
of my life.
    Ronald Reagan 1911–2004 American statesman, *statement to
the American people revealing that he had Alzheimer's disease*

You matter because you are you, and you matter to the
last moment of your life. We will do all that we can not
only to help you die peacefully, but also to live until you
die.
    Cicely Saunders 1916–2005 English founder of hospice
movement

Diseases desperate grown,
By desperate appliances are relieved
Or not at all.
     William Shakespeare 1564–1616 English dramatist

I enjoy convalescence. It is the part that makes illness
worth while.
     George Bernard Shaw 1856–1950 Irish dramatist

The biggest disease today is not leprosy or tuberculosis,
but rather the feeling of being unwanted, uncared for and
deserted by everybody.
     Mother Teresa 1910–97 Roman Catholic nun

To know ourselves diseased, is half our cure.
     Edward Young 1683–1765 English poet

Silence ✳

Silence is the virtue of fools.
     Francis Bacon 1561–1626 English courtier

If we had a keen vision and feeling of all ordinary human
life, it would be like hearing the grass grow and the
squirrel's heart beat, and we should die of that roar
which lies on the other side of silence.
     George Eliot 1819–80 English novelist

Thou still unravished bride of quietness,
Thou foster-child of silence and slow time.
     John Keats 1795–1821 English poet

People talking without speaking
People hearing without listening…
'Fools,' said I, 'You do not know
Silence like a cancer grows.'
     Paul Simon 1942– American singer

Silence

The sound of Brahman is OM. At the end of OM is silence. It is a silence of joy.

The Upanishads c.800–200 BC Hindu sacred treatises

✳ Singing →Music

Nothing is capable of being well set to music that is not nonsense.

Joseph Addison 1672–1719 English writer

Today if something is not worth saying, people sing it.

Pierre-Augustin Caron de Beaumarchais 1732–99 French dramatist

The exercise of singing is delightful to Nature, and good to preserve the health of man. It doth strengthen all parts of the breast, and doth open the pipes.

William Byrd 1543–1623 English composer

Swans sing before they die: 'twere no bad thing
Should certain persons die before they sing.

Samuel Taylor Coleridge 1772–1834 English poet

Every tone [of the songs of the slaves] was a testimony against slavery, and a prayer to God for deliverance from chains.

Frederick Douglass c.1818–95 American former slave

In writing songs I've learned as much from Cézanne as I have from Woody Guthrie.

Bob Dylan 1941– American singer

If a man were permitted to make all the ballads, he need not care who should make the laws of a nation.

Andrew Fletcher of Saltoun 1655–1716 Scottish patriot

Opera is when a guy gets stabbed in the back and, instead of bleeding, he sings.

Ed Gardner 1901–63 American comedian

You think that's noise—you ain't heard nuttin' yet!
>   **Al Jolson** 1886–1950 American singer, *in a café, competing with the din from a neighbouring building site*

The Skies ✳

Beautiful! Beautiful! Magnificent desolation.
>   **Buzz Aldrin** 1930– American astronaut, *on landing on the moon*

The heavens declare the glory of God: and the firmament sheweth his handy-work.
>   **Bible**

Slowly, silently, now the moon
Walks the night in her silver shoon.
>   **Walter de la Mare** 1873–1956 English poet

Busy old fool, unruly sun,
Why dost thou thus,
Through windows, and through curtains call on us?
>   **John Donne** 1572–1631 English poet

Eppur si muove.
But it does move.
>   **Galileo Galilei** 1564–1642 Italian astronomer, *after his recantation, that the earth moves around the sun*

It may be that the stars of heaven appear to us fair and pure simply because we are at such a distance from them, and know nothing of their private life.
>   **Heinrich Heine** 1797–1856 German poet

Look at the stars! look, look up at the skies!
O look at all the fire-folk sitting in the air!
The bright boroughs, the circle-citadels there!
>   **Gerard Manley Hopkins** 1844–89 English poet

The Skies

...The evening star,
Love's harbinger.
John Milton 1608–74 English poet

The eternal silence of these infinite spaces [the heavens]
terrifies me.
Blaise Pascal 1623–62 French scientist and philosopher

The moon's an arrant thief,
And her pale fire she snatches from the sun.
William Shakespeare 1564–1616 English dramatist

I have loved the stars too fondly to be fearful of the
night.
Sarah Williams 1837–68 British writer

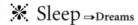 ## Sleep ⇒Dreams

The sleep of a labouring man is sweet.
Bible

...The cool kindliness of sheets, that soon
Smooth away trouble; and the rough male kiss
Of blankets.
Rupert Brooke 1887–1915 English poet

When you're lying awake with a dismal headache, and
repose is taboo'd by anxiety,
I conceive you may use any language you choose to
indulge in, without impropriety.
W. S. Gilbert 1836–1911 English writer

Sleep is when all the unsorted stuff comes flying out as
from a dustbin upset in a high wind.
William Golding 1911–93 English novelist

What hath night to do with sleep?
John Milton 1608–74 English poet

And so to bed.
> **Samuel Pepys** 1633–1703 English diarist

Methought I heard a voice cry, 'Sleep no more!
Macbeth does murder sleep,' the innocent sleep,
Sleep that knits up the ravelled sleave of care.
> **William Shakespeare** 1564–1616 English dramatist

In winter I get up at night
And dress by yellow candle-light.
In summer, quite the other way,—
I have to go to bed by day.
> **Robert Louis Stevenson** 1850–94 Scottish novelist

Early to rise and early to bed makes a male healthy and
wealthy and dead.
> **James Thurber** 1894–1961 American humorist

Tired Nature's sweet restorer, balmy sleep!
> **Edward Young** 1683–1765 English poet

Society ✳

Hunger allows no choice
To the citizen or the police;
We must love one another or die.
> **W. H. Auden** 1907–73 English poet

We started off trying to set up a small anarchist
community, but people wouldn't obey the rules.
> **Alan Bennett** 1934– English writer

The greatest happiness of the greatest number is the
foundation of morals and legislation.
> **Jeremy Bentham** 1748–1832 English philosopher

Society

Society is indeed a contract...it becomes a partnership not only between those who are living, but between those who are living, those who are dead, and those who are to be born.

Edmund Burke 1729–97 Irish-born politician

No man is an Island, entire of it self.

John Donne 1572–1631 English poet

Economics is all about how people make choices. Sociology is all about why they don't have any choices to make.

James Stemble Duesenberry 1918– American economist

Only in the state does man have a rational existence...Man owes his entire existence to the state, and has his being within it alone.

G. W. F. Hegel 1770–1831 German philosopher

In a consumer society there are inevitably two kinds of slaves: the prisoners of addiction and the prisoners of envy.

Ivan Illich 1926–2002 American sociologist

From each according to his abilities, to each according to his needs.

Karl Marx 1818–83 German philosopher

The city is not a concrete jungle, it is a human zoo.

Desmond Morris 1928– English anthropologist

There is no such thing as Society. There are individual men and women, and there are families.

Margaret Thatcher 1925– British stateswoman

The Social Contract is nothing more or less than a vast conspiracy of human beings to lie to and humbug themselves and one another for the general Good. Lies are the mortar that bind the savage individual man into the social masonry.

H. G. Wells 1866–1946 English novelist

Solitude ✳

He who is unable to live in society, or who has no need because he is sufficient for himself, must be either a beast or a god.

Aristotle 384–322 BC Greek philosopher

He [Barrymore] would quote from Genesis the text which says, 'It is not good for man to be alone,' and then add, 'But O my God, what a relief.'

John Barrymore 1882–1942 American actor

It is not good that the man should be alone; I will make him an help meet for him.

Bible

To fly from, need not be to hate, mankind.

Lord Byron 1788–1824 English poet

I want to be alone.

Greta Garbo 1905–90 Swedish actress

If you are idle, be not solitary; if you are solitary, be not idle.

Samuel Johnson 1709–84 English lexicographer

Down to Gehenna or up to the Throne,
He travels the fastest who travels alone.

Rudyard Kipling 1865–1936 English writer

All the lonely people, where do they all come from?

John Lennon 1940–80 and **Paul McCartney** 1942–   English pop singers

Ships that pass in the night, and speak each other in
    passing;
Only a signal shown and a distant voice in the darkness;
So on the ocean of life we pass and speak one another,

Solitude

Only a look and a voice; then darkness again and a
  silence.
Henry Wadsworth Longfellow 1807–82 American poet

Never less alone than when alone.
Samuel Rogers 1763–1855 English poet

Man goes into the noisy crowd to drown his own
clamour of silence.
Rabindranath Tagore 1861–1941 Bengali poet

 Sorrow ⇨Bereavement, Suffering

O my son Absalom, my son, my son Absalom! would
God I had died for thee, O Absalom, my son, my son!
Bible

By the waters of Babylon we sat down and wept: when
we remembered thee, O Sion.
Bible

I tell you, hopeless grief is passionless.
Elizabeth Barrett Browning 1806–61 English poet

We do not expect people to be deeply moved by what is
not unusual. That element of tragedy which lies in the
very fact of frequency, has not yet wrought itself into the
coarse emotion of mankind.
George Eliot 1819–80 English novelist

Nothing that can be said can begin to take away the
anguish and pain of these moments. Grief is the price we
pay for love.
Elizabeth II 1926– British monarch

How small and selfish is sorrow. But it bangs one about
until one is senseless.
Queen Elizabeth, the Queen Mother 1900–2002 British
Queen Consort

Now laughing friends deride tears I cannot hide,
So I smile and say 'When a lovely flame dies,
Smoke gets in your eyes.'
Otto Harbach 1873–1963 American songwriter

Grief is a species of idleness.
Samuel Johnson 1709–84 English lexicographer

Tragedy ought really to be a great kick at misery.
D. H. Lawrence 1885–1930 English writer

No one ever told me that grief felt so like fear.
C. S. Lewis 1898–1963 English literary scholar

Sorrow and silence are strong, and patient endurance is
godlike.
Henry Wadsworth Longfellow 1807–82 American poet

Small sorrows speak; great ones are silent.
Seneca ('the Younger') c.4 BC–AD 65 Roman philosopher

When sorrows come, they come not single spies,
But in battalions.
William Shakespeare 1564–1616 English dramatist

Give sorrow words: the grief that does not speak
Whispers the o'er-fraught heart, and bids it break.
William Shakespeare 1564–1616 English dramatist

Tears, idle tears, I know not what they mean,
Tears from the depth of some divine despair.
Alfred, Lord Tennyson 1809–92 English poet

Pure and complete sorrow is as impossible as pure and
complete joy.
Leo Tolstoy 1828–1910 Russian novelist

Sunt lacrimae rerum et mentem mortalia tangunt.
There are tears shed for things and mortality touches the
heart.
Virgil 70–19 BC Roman poet

Sorrow

Total grief is like a minefield. No knowing when one will touch the tripwire.
Sylvia Townsend Warner 1893–1978 English writer

For of all sad words of tongue or pen,
The saddest are these: 'It might have been!'
John Greenleaf Whittier 1807–92 American poet

Laugh and the world laughs with you;
Weep, and you weep alone;
For the sad old earth must borrow its mirth,
But has trouble enough of its own.
Ella Wheeler Wilcox 1855–1919 American poet

✳ Speechmaking ⇒Conversation

I do not object to people looking at their watches when I am speaking. But I strongly object when they start shaking them to make certain they are still going.
Lord Birkett 1883–1962 English judge

Grasp the subject, the words will follow.
Cato the Elder 234–149 BC Roman statesman

And adepts in the speaking trade
Keep a cough by them ready made.
Charles Churchill 1731–64 English poet

He [Lord Charles Beresford] is one of those orators of whom it was well said, 'Before they get up, they do not know what they are going to say; when they are speaking, they do not know what they are saying; and when they have sat down, they do not know what they have said.'
Winston Churchill 1874–1965 British statesman

When you have nothing to say, say nothing.
Charles Caleb Colton c.1780–1832 English clergyman

Humming, Hawing and Hesitation are the three Graces of contemporary Parliamentary oratory.
Julian Critchley 1930–2000 British politician

When asked what was first in oratory, [he] replied to his questioner, 'action,' what second, 'action,' and again third, 'action'.
Demosthenes c.384–c.322 BC Greek statesman

What worse charge can any one bring against an orator than that his words and his sentiments do not tally?
Demosthenes c.384–c.322 BC Greek statesman

Human speech is like a cracked kettle on which we tap crude rhythms for bears to dance to, while we long to make music that will melt the stars.
Gustave Flaubert 1821–80 French novelist

The finest eloquence is that which gets things done and the worst is that which delays them.
David Lloyd George 1863–1945 British statesman

But all was false and hollow; though his tongue
Dropped manna, and could make the worse appear
The better reason.
John Milton 1608–74 English poet

Be silent, unless your speech is better than silence.
Salvator Rosa 1615–73 Italian painter, *inscription on self portrait*

I do not much dislike the matter, but
The manner of his speech.
William Shakespeare 1564–1616 English dramatist

Friends, Romans, countrymen, lend me your ears.
William Shakespeare 1564–1616 English dramatist

If I reprehend any thing in this world, it is the use of my oracular tongue, and a nice derangement of epitaphs!
Richard Brinsley Sheridan 1751–1816 Irish dramatist

Speechmaking

Do you remember that in classical times when Cicero had
finished speaking, the people said, 'How well he spoke',
but when Demosthenes had finished speaking, they said,
'Let us march.'

Adlai Stevenson 1900–65 American politician

What can be said at all can be said clearly; and whereof
one cannot speak thereof one must be silent.

Ludwig Wittgenstein 1889–1951 Austrian-born philosopher

The reason why we have two ears and only one mouth is
that we may listen the more and talk the less.

Zeno c.335–c.263 BC Greek philosopher

 Sport ⇒Baseball, Cricket, Football, Golf, Tennis

This is a hard tour and hard work wins it. Vive Le Tour.

Lance Armstrong 1971– American cyclist, *on winning his
seventh consecutive Tour de France*

Sports do not build character. They reveal it.

Heywood Hale Broun 1918–2001 American sports
commentator

As the race wore on…his oar was dipping into the water
nearly *twice* as often as any other.

Desmond Coke 1879–1931 English writer, *usually misquoted as
'All rowed fast, but none so fast as stroke'*

The important thing in life is not the victory but the
contest; the essential thing is not to have won but to have
fought well.

Baron Pierre de Coubertin 1863–1937 French sportsman, *on
the Olympic Games*

There is plenty of time to win this game, and to thrash
the Spaniards too.

Francis Drake c.1540–96 English sailor, *receiving news of the
Armada while playing bowls on Plymouth Hoe*

Nice guys. Finish last.
> **Leo Durocher** 1906–91 American baseball coach, *usually quoted as 'Nice guys finish last'*

I hated the easy assumption that girls had to be slower than boys.
> **Dawn Fraser** 1937– Australian swimmer

I skated for pure enjoyment. That's how I wanted my Olympic moment to be.
> **Sarah Hughes** 1985– American skater

We all get cut and we all get stitched up. We get stud marks down our bodies, we break bones and we lose teeth. We play rugby.
> **Martin Johnson** 1970– English rugby player

Only two things does he [the modern citizen] anxiously wish for—bread and circuses.
> **Juvenal** c.AD 60–c.130 Roman satirist

The flannelled fools at the wicket or the muddied oafs at the goals.
> **Rudyard Kipling** 1865–1936 English writer

Chaos umpire sits,
And by decision more embroils the fray.
> **John Milton** 1608–74 English poet

Play up! play up! and play the game!
> **Henry Newbolt** 1862–1938 English writer

Eclipse first, the rest nowhere.
> **Dennis O'Kelly** c.1720–87 Irish racehorse-owner, *comment on a horse race*

Serious sport has nothing to do with fair play. It is bound up with hatred, jealousy, boastfulness, and disregard of all the rules.
> **George Orwell** 1903–50 English novelist

Sport

For when the One Great Scorer comes to mark against
   your name,
He writes—not that you won or lost—but how you
   played the Game.
     Grantland Rice 1880–1954 American sports writer

To play billiards well is a sign of an ill-spent youth.
     Charles Roupell British lawyer

Sure, winning isn't everything. It's the only thing.
     Henry 'Red' Sanders 1905–58 American football coach

✳ Spring

In fact, it is about five o'clock in an evening that the first
hour of spring strikes—autumn arrives in the early
morning, but spring at the close of a winter day.
     Elizabeth Bowen 1899–1973 Anglo-Irish novelist

Whan that Aprill with his shoures soote
The droghte of March hath perced to the roote.
     Geoffrey Chaucer c.1343–1400 English poet

April is the cruellest month, breeding
Lilacs out of the dead land.
     T. S. Eliot 1888–1965 American-born British poet

And since to look at things in bloom
Fifty springs are little room,
About the woodlands I will go
To see the cherry hung with snow.
     A. E. Housman 1859–1936 English poet

Work seethes in the hands of spring,
That strapping dairymaid.
     Boris Pasternak 1890–1960 Russian novelist

Statistics ✳

[The War Office kept three sets of figures:] one to mislead the public, another to mislead the Cabinet, and the third to mislead itself.
Herbert Asquith 1852–1928 British statesman

Statistics are the triumph of the quantitative method, and the quantitative method is the victory of sterility and death.
Hilaire Belloc 1870–1953 British writer

A witty statesman said, you might prove anything by figures.
Thomas Carlyle 1795–1881 Scottish historian

Long and painful experience has taught me one great principle in managing business for other people, viz., if you want to inspire confidence, *give plenty of statistics.*
Lewis Carroll 1832–98 English writer

There are three kinds of lies: lies, damned lies and statistics.
Benjamin Disraeli 1804–81 British statesman

From the fact that there are 400,000 species of beetles on this planet, but only 8,000 species of mammals, he [Haldane] concluded that the Creator, if He exists, has a special preference for beetles.
J. B. S. Haldane 1892–1964 Scottish mathematical biologist

We are just statistics, born to consume resources.
Horace 65-8 BC Roman poet

He uses statistics as a drunken man uses lampposts—for support rather than for illumination.
Andrew Lang 1844–1912 Scottish man of letters

Statistics

If your experiment needs statistics, you ought to have done a better experiment.
Ernest Rutherford 1871–1937 New Zealand physicist

Counting counts only when we have learnt how to count what counts.
Alan Ryan 1940– English academic

The so-called science of poll-taking is not a science at all but a mere necromancy. People are unpredictable by nature, and although you can take a nation's pulse, you can't be sure that the nation hasn't just run up a flight of stairs.
E. B. White 1899–1985 American humorist

※ Strength

The weak have one weapon: the errors of those who think they are strong.
Georges Bidault 1899–1983 French politician

Toughness doesn't have to come in a pinstripe suit.
Dianne Feinstein 1933– American politician

One is never weaker than when one appears to have everybody's support.
Émile Ollivier 1825–1913 French politician

You are the weakest link…goodbye.
Anne Robinson 1944– English television presenter

This is the law of the Yukon, that only the Strong shall thrive;
That surely the Weak shall perish, and only the Fit survive.
Robert W. Service 1874–1958 Canadian poet

O! it is excellent
To have a giant's strength, but it is tyrannous
To use it like a giant.
William Shakespeare 1564–1616 English dramatist

The gods are on the side of the stronger.
Tacitus C.AD 56–after 117 Roman historian

Style ⇒Brevity ✳

Have something to say, and say it as clearly as you can.
That is the only secret of style.
Matthew Arnold 1822–88 English poet

Style is the man.
Comte de Buffon 1707–88 French naturalist

Words easy to be understood do often hit the mark; when
high and learned ones do only pierce the air.
John Bunyan 1628–88 English writer

The Mandarin style…is beloved by literary pundits, by
those who would make the written word as unlike as
possible to the spoken one.
Cyril Connolly 1903–74 English writer

Style is life! It is the very life-blood of thought!
Gustave Flaubert 1821–80 French novelist

When we see a natural style, we are quite surprised and
delighted, for we expected to see an author and we find a
man.
Blaise Pascal 1623–62 French scientist and philosopher

Good design is intelligence made visible.
Frank Pick 1878–1941 British transport administrator

True wit is Nature to advantage dressed,
What oft was thought, but ne'er so well expressed.
Alexander Pope 1688–1744 English poet

Style

Too many flowers...too little fruit.
Sir Walter Scott 1771–1832 Scottish novelist, *of Felicia Hemans's literary style*

Proper words in proper places, make the true definition of a style.
Jonathan Swift 1667–1745 Irish poet and satirist

'Feather-footed through the plashy fen passes the questing vole'...'Yes,' said the Managing Editor. 'That must be good style.'
Evelyn Waugh 1903–66 English novelist

I don't wish to sign my name, though I am afraid everybody will know who the writer is: one's style is one's signature always.
Oscar Wilde 1854–1900 Irish dramatist

☀ Success ⇒Failure, Winning

'Tis not in mortals to command success,
But we'll do more, Sempronius; we'll deserve it.
Joseph Addison 1672–1719 English writer

For what shall it profit a man, if he shall gain the whole world, and lose his own soul?
Bible

Pourvu que ça dure!
Let's hope it lasts!
Laetitia Bonaparte 1750–1836, *on her son Napoleon becoming Emperor, 1804*

The conduct of a losing party never appears right: at least it never can possess the only infallible criterion of wisdom to vulgar judgements—success.
Edmund Burke 1729–97 Irish-born politician

Veni, vidi, vici.
I came, I saw, I conquered.
> **Julius Caesar** 100–44 BC Roman statesman

I have climbed to the top of the greasy pole.
> **Benjamin Disraeli** 1804–81 British statesman

If *A* is a success in life, then *A* equals *x* plus *y* plus *z*.
Work is *x*; *y* is play; and *z* is keeping your mouth shut.
> **Albert Einstein** 1879–1955 German-born theoretical physicist

Success is relative:
It is what we can make of the mess we have made of
  things.
> **T. S. Eliot** 1888–1965 American-born British poet

Success is more dangerous than failure, the ripples break
over a wider coastline.
> **Graham Greene** 1904–91 English novelist

The moral flabbiness born of the exclusive worship of the
bitch-goddess *success*.
> **William James** 1842–1910 American philosopher

In most things success depends on knowing how long it
takes to succeed.
> **Montesquieu** 1689–1755 French political philosopher

Success makes life easier. It doesn't make *living* easier.
> **Bruce Springsteen** 1949– American rock singer

All you need in this life is ignorance and confidence; then
success is sure.
> **Mark Twain** 1835–1910 American writer

It is not enough to succeed. Others must fail.
> **Gore Vidal** 1925– American writer

Suffering

✳ Suffering ⇒Sympathy

Justice inclines her scales so that wisdom comes at the price of suffering.
Aeschylus c.525–456 BC Greek tragedian

Children's talent to endure stems from their ignorance of alternatives.
Maya Angelou 1928– American writer

Even the dreadful martyrdom must run its course
Anyhow in a corner, some untidy spot
Where the dogs go on with their doggy life and the
    torturer's horse
Scratches its innocent behind on a tree.
W. H. Auden 1907–73 English poet

Nothing happens to anybody which he is not fitted by nature to bear.
Marcus Aurelius AD 121–180 Roman emperor

Some people like being burdened. It gives them an interest.
Beryl Bainbridge 1933– English novelist

Where mass hunger reigns, we cannot speak of peace.
Willy Brandt 1913–92 German statesman

The number of casualties will be more than any of us can bear.
Rudolph Giuliani 1944– American politician, *in the aftermath of the terrorist attacks of 11 September 2001*

To each his suff'rings, all are men,
Condemned alike to groan;
The tender for another's pain,
Th' unfeeling for his own.
Thomas Gray 1716–71 English poet

384

The fool learns by suffering.
> **Hesiod** fl. c.700 BC Greek poet

If suffer we must, let's suffer on the heights.
> **Victor Hugo** 1802–85 French writer

Scars have the strange power to remind us that our past is real.
> **Cormac McCarthy** 1933–   American novelist

It is not true that suffering ennobles the character; happiness does that sometimes, but suffering, for the most part, makes men petty and vindictive.
> **W. Somerset Maugham** 1874–1965 English novelist

What does not kill me makes me stronger.
> **Friedrich Nietzsche** 1844–1900 German philosopher

The worst is not,
So long as we can say, 'This is the worst.'
> **William Shakespeare** 1564–1616 English dramatist

He jests at scars, that never felt a wound.
> **William Shakespeare** 1564–1616 English dramatist

I am a man
More sinned against than sinning.
> **William Shakespeare** 1564–1616 English dramatist

Nothing begins, and nothing ends,
That is not paid with moan;
For we are born in other's pain,
And perish in our own.
> **Francis Thompson** 1859–1907 English poet

Those who have courage to love should have courage to suffer.
> **Anthony Trollope** 1815–82 English novelist

O you who have borne even heavier things, God will grant an end to these too.
> **Virgil** 70–19 BC Roman poet

Suffering

Too long a sacrifice
Can make a stone of the heart.
W. B. Yeats 1865–1939 Irish poet

✳ Summer

Sumer is icumen in,
Lhude sing cuccu!
Groweth sed, and bloweth med,
And springeth the wude nu.
Anonymous *'Cuckoo Song'* (c.1250)

June is bustin' out all over.
Oscar Hammerstein II 1895–1960 American songwriter

Summer time an' the livin' is easy,
Fish are jumpin' an' the cotton is high.
Du Bose Heyward 1885–1940 and **Ira Gershwin** 1896–1983
American songwriters

Summer afternoon—summer afternoon…the two most
beautiful words in the English language.
Henry James 1843–1916 American novelist

The way to ensure summer in England is to have it
framed and glazed in a comfortable room.
Horace Walpole 1717–97 English connoisseur

✳ The Supernatural

Up the airy mountain,
Down the rushy glen,
We daren't go a-hunting,
For fear of little men.
William Allingham 1824–89 Irish poet

From ghoulies and ghosties and long-leggety beasties
And things that go bump in the night,
Good Lord, deliver us!

Anonymous *The Cornish or West Country Litany*

I always knew the living talked rot, but it's nothing to the rot the dead talk.

Margot Asquith 1864–1945 British political hostess

Then a spirit passed before my face; the hair of my flesh stood up.

Bible

For we wrestle not against flesh and blood, but against principalities, against powers, against the rulers of the darkness of this world, against spiritual wickedness in high places.

Bible

Black magic operates most effectively in preconscious, marginal areas. Casual curses are the most effective.

William S. Burroughs 1914–97 American novelist

The twilight is the crack between the worlds. It is the door to the unknown.

Carlos Castaneda c.1925–98 American writer

There is no such thing as magic, only acting.

Paul Daniels 1938– British conjuror

THE FAT BOY: I wants to make your flesh creep.

Charles Dickens 1812–70 English novelist

There are fairies at the bottom of our garden!

Rose Fyleman 1877–1957 English writer

Superstition is the poetry of life.

Johann Wolfgang von Goethe 1749–1832 German writer

All argument is against it; but all belief is for it.

Samuel Johnson 1709–84 English lexicographer, *of the existence of ghosts*

The Supernatural

JUDY GARLAND: Toto, I've a feeling we're not in Kansas any more.

Noel Langley 1911–80 et al., American screenwriters, *in the film* The Wizard of Oz

Mr Geller may have psychic powers by means of which he can bend spoons; if so, he appears to be doing it the hard way.

James Randi 1928– Canadian-born American conjuror

Double, double toil and trouble;
Fire burn and cauldron bubble.

William Shakespeare 1564–1616 English dramatist

There are more things in heaven and earth, Horatio,
Than are dreamt of in your philosophy.

William Shakespeare 1564–1616 English dramatist

Superstition sets the whole world in flames; philosophy quenches them.

Voltaire 1694–1778 French writer

✳ Sympathy

Nobody can tell what I suffer! But it is always so. Those who do not complain are never pitied.

Jane Austen 1775–1817 English novelist

For pitee renneth soone in gentil herte.

Geoffrey Chaucer c.1343–1400 English poet

O divine Master, grant that I may not so much seek
To be consoled as to console;
To be understood as to understand.

St Francis of Assisi 1181–1226 Italian monk

Our sympathy is cold to the relation of distant misery.

Edward Gibbon 1737–94 English historian

But yet the pity of it, Iago! O! Iago, the pity of it, Iago!
    William Shakespeare 1564–1616 English dramatist

Honest plain words best pierce the ears of grief.
    William Shakespeare 1564–1616 English dramatist

If you see anybody fallen by the wayside and lying in the ditch, it isn't much good climbing into the ditch and lying by his side.
    Dick Sheppard 1880–1937 British clergyman

When times get rough,
And friends just can't be found
Like a bridge over troubled water
I will lay me down.
    Paul Simon 1942– American singer

Taxes ✳

To tax and to please, no more than to love and to be wise, is not given to men.
    Edmund Burke 1729–97 Irish-born politician

Read my lips: no new taxes.
    George Bush 1924– American statesman

The art of taxation consists in so plucking the goose as to obtain the largest possible amount of feathers with the smallest possible amount of hissing.
    Jean-Baptiste Colbert 1619–83 French statesman

In this world nothing can be said to be certain, except death and taxes.
    Benjamin Franklin 1706–90 American statesman and scientist

All taxes must, at last, fall upon agriculture.
    Edward Gibbon 1737–94 English historian

Taxes

Only the little people pay taxes.
Leona Helmsley c.1920–2007 American hotelier, *reported at her trial for tax evasion*

Excise. A hateful tax levied upon commodities.
Samuel Johnson 1709–84 English lexicographer

Taxation without representation is tyranny.
James Otis 1725–83 American politician

Taxation is just a sophisticated way of demanding money with menaces.
Terry Pratchett 1948– English novelist

Income Tax has made more Liars out of the American people than Golf.
Will Rogers 1879–1935 American actor

There is no art which one government sooner learns of another than that of draining money from the pockets of the people.
Adam Smith 1723–90 Scottish economist

It is the part of the good shepherd to shear his flock, not skin it.
Tiberius 42 BC–AD 37 Roman emperor, *to governors who recommended burdensome taxes*

Pecunia non olet.
Money has no smell.
Vespasian AD 9–79 Roman emperor, *quashing an objection to a tax on public lavatories*

The art of government is to make two-thirds of a nation pay all it possibly can pay for the benefit of the other third.
Voltaire 1694–1778 French writer

Teaching ⇒Education ✳

A teacher affects eternity; he can never tell where his influence stops.
Henry Brooks Adams 1838–1918 American historian

There is no such whetstone, to sharpen a good wit and encourage a will to learning, as is praise.
Roger Ascham 1515–68 English scholar

For precept must be upon precept, precept upon precept; line upon line, line upon line; here a little, and there a little.
Bible

Be a governess! Better be a slave at once!
Charlotte Brontë 1816–55 English novelist

A man who reviews the old so as to find out the new is qualified to teach others.
Confucius 551–479 BC Chinese philosopher

I hope you enjoy the absence of pupils…the total oblivion of them for definite intervals is a necessary condition for doing them justice at the proper time.
James Clerk Maxwell 1831–79 Scottish physicist

We teachers can only help the work going on, as servants wait upon a master.
Maria Montessori 1870–1952 Italian educationist

Men must be taught as if you taught them not,
And things unknown proposed as things forgot.
Alexander Pope 1688–1744 English poet

For every person who wants to teach there are approximately thirty who don't want to learn—much.
W. C. Sellar 1898–1951 and **R. J. Yeatman** 1898–1968 British writers

391

Teaching

Even while they teach, men learn.
Seneca ('the Younger') c.4 BC–AD 65 Roman philosopher

He who can, does. He who cannot, teaches.
George Bernard Shaw 1856–1950 Irish dramatist

Give me a girl at an impressionable age, and she is mine for life.
Muriel Spark 1918–2006 British novelist

Delightful task! to rear the tender thought,
To teach the young idea how to shoot.
James Thomson 1700–48 Scottish poet

Knowledge has to be sucked into the brain, not pushed into it.
Victor Weisskopf 1908–2002 American physicist

✵ Technology ⇒Invention

Science finds, industry applies, man conforms.
Anonymous *guidebook to 1933 Chicago World's Fair*

Give me but one firm spot on which to stand, and I will move the earth.
Archimedes c.287–212 BC Greek mathematician, *on the action of a lever*

I sell here, Sir, what all the world desires to have—POWER.
Matthew Boulton 1728–1809 British engineer, *speaking of his engineering works*

Any sufficiently advanced technology is indistinguishable from magic.
Arthur C. Clarke 1917–2008 English science fiction writer

For a successful technology, reality must take precedence over public relations, for nature cannot be fooled.
Richard Feynman 1918–88 American physicist

Technology...the knack of so arranging the world that we need not experience it.

Max Frisch 1911–91 Swiss writer

Technology happens. It's not good, it's not bad. Is steel good or bad?

Andrew Grove 1936– American businessman

The thing with high-tech is that you always end up using scissors.

David Hockney 1937– British artist

This is not the age of pamphleteers. It is the age of the engineers. The spark-gap is mightier than the pen.

Lancelot Hogben 1895–1975 English scientist

One machine can do the work of fifty ordinary men. No machine can do the work of one extraordinary man.

Elbert Hubbard 1859–1915 American writer

Communism is Soviet power plus the electrification of the whole country.

Lenin 1870–1924 Russian revolutionary

The new electronic interdependence recreates the world in the image of a global village.

Marshall McLuhan 1911–80 Canadian communications scholar

The medium is the message.

Marshall McLuhan 1911–80 Canadian communications scholar

When this circuit learns your job, what are you going to do?

Marshall McLuhan 1911–80 Canadian communications scholar

When you see something that is technically sweet, you go ahead and do it and you argue about what to do about it only after you have had your technical success. That is the way it was with the atomic bomb.

J. Robert Oppenheimer 1904–67 American physicist

One servant is worth a thousand gadgets.

Joseph Alois Schumpeter 1883–1950 American economist

It has been said that an engineer is a man who can do for ten shillings what any fool can do for a pound.

Nevil Shute 1899–1960 British novelist

The Britain that is going to be forged in the white heat of this revolution will be no place for restrictive practices or for outdated methods on either side of industry.

Harold Wilson 1916–95 British statesman, *usually quoted as 'the white heat of the technological revolution'*

✳ Television

Television has brought back murder into the home—where it belongs.

Alfred Hitchcock 1899–1980 British-born film director

Television is simultaneously blamed, often by the same people, for worsening the world and for being powerless to change it.

Clive James 1939– Australian critic

Television brought the brutality of war into the comfort of the living room. Vietnam was lost in the living rooms of America—not the battlefields of Vietnam.

Marshall McLuhan 1911–80 Canadian communications scholar

Television is actually closer to reality than anything in books. The madness of TV is the madness of human life.

Camille Paglia 1947– American writer

Television has made dictatorship impossible, but democracy unbearable.

Shimon Peres 1923– Israeli statesman

He who prides himself on giving what he thinks the public wants is often creating a fictitious demand for lower standards which he will then satisfy.
Lord Reith 1889–1971 British administrator

Nation shall speak peace unto nation.
Montague John Rendall 1862–1950 English headmaster, *motto of the BBC*

Television today has replaced the theatre of the 20th century, the novels of the 19th, the Bible of the 17th, the folktales of the village, the bedtime stories parents told their children.
Jonathan Sacks 1948– British rabbi

It's just like having a licence to print your own money.
Roy Thomson 1894–1976 Canadian-born British newspaper proprietor, *on the profitability of commercial television in Britain*

Never miss a chance to have sex or appear on television.
Gore Vidal 1925– American writer

I hate television. I hate it as much as peanuts. But I can't stop eating peanuts.
Orson Welles 1915–85 American film director

Television contracts the imagination and radio expands it.
Terry Wogan 1938– Irish broadcaster

Temptation ✳

Watch and pray, that ye enter not into temptation: the spirit indeed is willing but the flesh is weak.
Bible

For the good that I would I do not: but the evil which I would not, that I do.
Bible

Temptation

From all the deceits of the world, the flesh, and the devil,
Good Lord, deliver us.
Book of Common Prayer 1662

What's done we partly may compute,
But know not what's resisted.
Robert Burns 1759-96 Scottish poet

Who was it said a temptation resisted is a true measure
of character? Certainly no one in Beverly Hills.
Joan Collins 1933- British actress

The Lord above made liquor for temptation—but
With a little bit of luck...
When temptation comes you'll give right in!
Alan Jay Lerner 1918-86 American songwriter

This extraordinary pride in being exempt from
temptation that you have not yet risen to the level of!
Eunuchs boasting of their chastity!
C. S. Lewis 1898-1963 English literary scholar

If we are to be punished for the sins we have committed,
at least we should be praised for our yearning for the sins
we have not committed.
Jawaharlal Nehru 1889-1964 Indian statesman

        Is this her fault or mine?
The tempter or the tempted, who sins most?
William Shakespeare 1564-1616 English dramatist

There are several good protections against temptations,
but the surest is cowardice.
Mark Twain 1835-1910 American writer

I can resist everything except temptation.
Oscar Wilde 1854-1900 Irish dramatist

Tennis ✳

I call tennis the McDonald's of sport—you go in, they make a quick buck out of you, and you're out.
Pat Cash 1965- Australian tennis player

New Yorkers love it when you spill your guts out there. Spill your guts at Wimbledon and they make you stop and clean it up.
Jimmy Connors 1952- American tennis player

You cannot be serious!
John McEnroe 1959- American tennis player, *said to tennis umpire at Wimbledon*

Do what you love and love what you do and everything else is detail.
Martina Navratilova 1956- Czech-born American tennis player

When we have matched our rackets to these balls,
We will in France, by God's grace, play a set
Shall strike his father's crown into the hazard.
William Shakespeare 1564-1616 English dramatist

If you can keep playing tennis when somebody is shooting a gun down the street, that's concentration. I didn't grow up playing at the country club.
Serena Williams 1981- American tennis player

Thanks ✳

They say late thanks are ever best.
Francis Bacon 1561-1626 English courtier

A joyful and pleasant thing it is to be thankful.
Bible

Thanks

When I'm not thanked at all, I'm thanked enough,
I've done my duty, and I've done no more.
> **Henry Fielding** 1707–54 English novelist

For this relief much thanks.
> **William Shakespeare** 1564–1616 English dramatist

My father spent the last 20 years of his life writing letters.
If someone thanked him for a present, he thanked them
for thanking him and there was no end to the exchange
but death.
> **Evelyn Waugh** 1903–66 English novelist

❋ The Theatre

I go to the theatre to be entertained, I want to be taken
out of myself, I don't want to see lust and rape and incest
and sodomy and so on, I can get all that at home.
> **Alan Bennett** 1934– English writer

There's no business like show business.
> **Irving Berlin** 1888–1989 American songwriter

Things on stage should be as complicated and as simple
as in life. People dine, just dine, while their happiness is
made and their lives are smashed. If in Act 1 you have a
pistol hanging on the wall, then it must fire in the last
act.
> **Anton Chekhov** 1860–1904 Russian writer

JOSEPHINE HULL: Shakespeare is so tiring. You never get a
chance to sit down unless you're a king.
> **George S. Kaufman** 1889–1961 and **Howard Teichmann**
> 1916–87 American dramatists, *in the film* The Solid Gold
> Cadillac

O! for a Muse of fire, that would ascend
The brightest heaven of invention;
A kingdom for a stage, princes to act

And monarchs to behold the swelling scene.
> **William Shakespeare** 1564–1616 English dramatist

It's a sound you can't get in the movies or television…the sound of a wonderful, deep silence that means you've hit them where they live.
> **Shelley Winters** 1922–2006 American actress

Thinking ⇒Ideas, The Mind

Think different.
> **Anonymous** *advertising slogan for Apple Computers*

To change your mind and to follow him who sets you right is to be nonetheless the free agent that you were before.
> **Marcus Aurelius** AD 121–180 Roman emperor

Never express yourself more clearly than you think.
> **Niels Bohr** 1885–1962 Danish physicist

Cogito, ergo sum.
I think, therefore I am.
> **René Descartes** 1596–1650 French philosopher

It is a capital mistake to theorize before you have all the evidence. It biases the judgement.
> **Arthur Conan Doyle** 1859–1930 Scottish-born writer

What was once thought can never be unthought.
> **Friedrich Dürrenmatt** 1921–90 Swiss writer

Reasons are not like garments, the worse for wearing.
> **Robert Devereux, 2nd Earl of Essex** 1566–1601 English courtier

I'll not listen to reason…Reason always means what someone else has got to say.
> **Elizabeth Gaskell** 1810–65 English novelist

Thinking

Logical consequences are the scarecrows of fools and the beacons of wise men.

T. H. Huxley 1825–95 English biologist

I'm Irish. We think sideways.

Spike Milligan 1918–2002 Irish comedian

Doublethink means the power of holding two contradictory beliefs in one's mind simultaneously, and accepting both of them.

George Orwell 1903–50 English novelist

I don't mind your thinking slowly: I mind your publishing faster than you think.

Wolfgang Pauli 1900–58 Austrian-born American physicist

You can't think rationally on an empty stomach, and a whole lot of people can't do it on a full stomach either.

Lord Reith 1889–1971 British administrator

Most people would sooner die than think—in fact they do so.

Bertrand Russell 1872–1970 British philosopher

How comes it to pass, then, that we appear such cowards in reasoning, and are so afraid to stand the test of ridicule?

Lord Shaftesbury 1671–1713 English statesman

Yond Cassius has a lean and hungry look;
He thinks too much: such men are dangerous.

William Shakespeare 1564–1616 English dramatist

The real question is not whether machines think but whether men do.

B. F. Skinner 1904–90 American psychologist

The important thing is not to think much but to love much.

St Teresa of Ávila 1512–82 Spanish mystic

Time �֎

Every instant of time is a pinprick of eternity.
Marcus Aurelius AD 121–180 Roman emperor

VLADIMIR: That passed the time.
ESTRAGON: It would have passed in any case.
VLADIMIR: Yes, but not so rapidly.
Samuel Beckett 1906–89 Irish writer

Time is a great teacher but unfortunately it kills all its pupils.
Hector Berlioz 1803–69 French composer

I am Time grown old to destroy the world,
Embarked on the course of world annihilation.
Bhagavad Gita 250 BC–AD 250 Hindu poem

To every thing there is a season, and a time to every purpose under the heaven:
A time to be born, and a time to die...
A time to weep, and a time to laugh; a time to mourn, and a time to dance.
Bible

Men talk of killing time, while time quietly kills them.
Dion Boucicault 1820–90 Irish dramatist

What's not destroyed by Time's devouring hand?
Where's Troy, and where's the Maypole in the Strand?
James Bramston c.1694–1744 English clergyman

I recommend to you to take care of minutes: for hours will take care of themselves.
Lord Chesterfield 1694–1773 English writer

I shall use the phrase 'time's arrow' to express this one-way property of time which has no analogue in space.
Arthur Eddington 1882–1944 British astrophysicist

Time

The distinction between past, present and future is only an illusion, however persistent.
Albert Einstein 1879–1955 German-born theoretical physicist

I have measured out my life with coffee spoons.
T. S. Eliot 1888–1965 American-born British poet

Time is…Time was…Time is past.
Robert Greene c.1560–92 English dramatist

There is an ancient Egyptian saying that 'Man fears time, and time fears the pyramids,' but this is no longer true. The pyramids must fear time, too.
Zahi Hawass 1947– Egyptian archaeologist

Time, you old gipsy man,
Will you not stay,
Put up your caravan
Just for one day?
Ralph Hodgson 1871–1962 English poet

In the long run we are all dead.
John Maynard Keynes 1883–1946 English economist

Nothing puzzles me more than time and space; and yet nothing troubles me less, as I never think about them.
Charles Lamb 1775–1834 English writer

But at my back I always hear
Time's wingèd chariot hurrying near:
And yonder all before us lie
Deserts of vast eternity.
Andrew Marvell 1621–78 English poet

Time the devourer of everything.
Ovid 43 BC–c.AD 17 Roman poet

Even such is Time, which takes in trust
Our youth, our joys, and all we have,
And pays us but with age and dust.
Walter Ralegh c.1552–1618 English courtier

Half our life is spent trying to find something to do with the time we have rushed through life trying to save.
Will Rogers 1879–1935 American actor

Three o'clock is always too late or too early for anything you want to do.
Jean-Paul Sartre 1905–80 French philosopher

Ah! the clock is always slow;
It is later than you think.
Robert W. Service 1874–1958 Canadian poet

To-morrow, and to-morrow, and to-morrow,
Creeps in this petty pace from day to day,
To the last syllable of recorded time;
And all our yesterdays have lighted fools
The way to dusty death.
William Shakespeare 1564–1616 English dramatist

Time hath, my lord, a wallet at his back,
Wherein he puts alms for oblivion.
William Shakespeare 1564–1616 English dramatist

As if you could kill time without injuring eternity.
Henry David Thoreau 1817–62 American writer

Time is
Too slow for those who wait,
Too swift for those who fear,
Too long for those who grieve,
Too short for those who rejoice;
But for those who love,
Time is eternity.
Henry Van Dyke 1852–1933 American minister

Sed fugit interea, fugit inreparabile tempus.
But meanwhile it is flying, irretrievable time is flying.
Virgil 70–19 BC Roman poet

Time

Time, like an ever-rolling stream,
Bears all its sons away.
   Isaac Watts 1674–1748 English hymn-writer

✳ Toasts

Here's tae us; wha's like us?
Gey few, and they're a' deid.
   Anonymous

HUMPHREY BOGART: Here's looking at you, kid.
   Julius J. Epstein 1909–2001 et al., American screenwriters, *in
   the film* Casablanca

Lang may yer lum reek!
   Scottish Proverb *long may your chimney smoke*

May you live all the days of your life.
   Jonathan Swift 1667–1745 Irish poet and satirist

✳ The Town ⇒The Country

We do not look in great cities for our best morality.
   Jane Austen 1775–1817 English novelist

If you would be known, and not know, vegetate in a
village; if you would know, and not be known, live in a
city.
   Charles Caleb Colton c.1780–1832 English clergyman

Slums may well be breeding-grounds of crime, but
middle-class suburbs are incubators of apathy and
delirium.
   Cyril Connolly 1903–74 English writer

The materials of city planning are sky, space, trees, steel
and cement in that order and in that hierarchy.
   Le Corbusier 1887–1965 French architect

Transience

I come from suburbia...and I don't ever want to go back. It's the one place in the world that's further away than anywhere else.

Frederic Raphael 1931– British writer

The fields and trees won't teach me anything, and the people in the city do.

Socrates 469–399 BC Greek philosopher

The modern city is a place for banking and prostitution and very little else.

Frank Lloyd Wright 1867–1959 American architect

Transience ✳

Sic transit gloria mundi.

Thus passes the glory of the world.

Anonymous *said at the coronation of a new Pope, while flax is burned*

All flesh is as grass, and all the glory of man as the flower of grass. The grass withereth, and the flower thereof falleth away.

Bible

He who binds to himself a joy
Doth the winged life destroy
But he who kisses the joy as it flies
Lives in Eternity's sunrise.

William Blake 1757–1827 English poet

The reputation which the world bestows
is like the wind, that shifts now here now there,
its name changed with the quarter whence it blows.

Dante Alighieri 1265–1321 Italian poet

Look thy last on all things lovely,
Every hour.

Walter de la Mare 1873–1956 English poet

Transience

Gather ye rosebuds while ye may,
Old Time is still a-flying:
And this same flower that smiles to-day,
To-morrow will be dying.
Robert Herrick 1591–1674 English poet

Like that of leaves is a generation of men.
Homer 8th century BC Greek poet

The butterfly counts not months but moments, and has time enough.
Rabindranath Tagore 1861–1941 Bengali poet

✳ Travel

Travel, in the younger sort, is a part of education; in the elder, a part of experience. He that travelleth into a country before he hath some entrance into the language, goeth to school, and not to travel.
Francis Bacon 1561–1626 English courtier

See one promontory (said Socrates of old), one mountain, one sea, one river, and see all.
Robert Burton 1577–1640 English clergyman

Men travel faster now, but I do not know if they go to better things.
Willa Cather 1873–1947 American novelist

What on earth good accrues from going to the North and South Poles? I never could understand—no one is going there when they can go to Monte Carlo!
John Arbuthnot Fisher 1841–1920 British admiral

A wise traveller never despises his own country.
Carlo Goldoni 1707–93 Italian dramatist

Worth seeing, yes; but not worth going to see.
  Samuel Johnson 1709–84 English lexicographer, *of the Giant's Causeway*

Of all noxious animals, too, the most noxious is a tourist. And of all tourists the most vulgar, ill-bred, offensive and loathsome is the British tourist.
  Francis Kilvert 1840–79 English clergyman

A good traveller has no fixed plans.
  Lao Tzu c.604–c.531 BC Chinese philosopher

A good traveller is one who does not know where he is going to, and a perfect traveller does not know where he came from.
  Lin Yutang 1895–1976 Chinese writer

I have not told even half of the things that I have seen.
  Marco Polo c.1254–c.1324 Italian traveller, *when asked if he wished to deny any of his stories of his travels*

A man travels the world in search of what he needs and returns home to find it.
  George Moore 1852–1933 Irish novelist

In the middle ages people were tourists because of their religion, whereas now they are tourists because tourism is their religion.
  Robert Runcie 1921–2000 English clergyman

To travel hopefully is a better thing than to arrive, and the true success is to labour.
  Robert Louis Stevenson 1850–94 Scottish novelist

There is no land unhabitable nor sea innavigable.
  Robert Thorne d. 1527 English merchant

Travel is fatal to prejudice, bigotry, and narrow-mindedness.
  Mark Twain 1835–1910 American writer

✳ Trust and Treachery

I think the greatest of all human virtues is loyalty. It embraces all the best of the human character: courage, faith, love and charity.
Douglas Bader 1910–82 British airman

He that is surety for a stranger shall smart for it.
Bible

Just for a handful of silver he left us,
Just for a riband to stick in his coat.
Robert Browning 1812–89 English poet, *of Wordsworth accepting the Laureateship*

Anyone can rat, but it takes a certain amount of ingenuity to re-rat.
Winston Churchill 1874–1965 British statesman, *on rejoining the Conservatives twenty years after leaving them for the Liberals*

I know what it is to be a subject, and what to be a Sovereign. Good neighbours I have had, and I have met with bad: and in trust I have found treason.
Elizabeth I 1533–1603 English monarch

Anyone who hasn't experienced the ecstasy of betrayal knows nothing about ecstasy at all.
Jean Genet 1910–86 French writer

Treason doth never prosper, what's the reason?
For if it prosper, none dare call it treason.
John Harington 1561–1612 English courtier

And I said to the man who stood at the gate of the year:
'Give me a light that I may tread safely into the unknown.'
And he replied:
'Go out into the darkness and put your hand into the

Hand of God. That shall be to you better than light and safer than a known way.'
Minnie Louise Haskins 1875–1957 English writer, *quoted by George VI in his Christmas broadcast, 1939*

It is better to suffer wrong than to do it, and happier to be sometimes cheated than not to trust.
Samuel Johnson 1709–84 English lexicographer

Quis custodiet ipsos custodes?
Who is to guard the guards themselves?
Juvenal c.AD 60–c.130 Roman satirist

To betray, you must first belong.
Kim Philby 1912–88 British intelligence officer and Soviet spy

But I'm always true to you, darlin', in my fashion.
Yes I'm always true to you, darlin', in my way.
Cole Porter 1891–1964 American songwriter

I fear the Greeks even when they bring gifts.
Virgil 70–19 BC Roman poet

Truth ⇒Lies

The truth is often a terrible weapon of aggression. It is possible to lie, and even to murder, for the truth.
Alfred Adler 1870–1937 Austrian psychologist

The truth which makes men free is for the most part the truth which men prefer not to hear.
Herbert Agar 1897–1980 American writer

Plato is dear to me, but dearer still is truth.
Aristotle 384–322 BC Greek philosopher

It contains a misleading impression, not a lie. It was being economical with the truth.
Robert Armstrong 1927– British civil servant

Truth

What is truth? said jesting Pilate; and would not stay for an answer.
Francis Bacon 1561–1626 English courtier

This is hard to answer, so I'll tell the truth.
David Ben-Gurion 1886–1973 Israeli statesman

And ye shall know the truth, and the truth shall make you free.
Bible

Great is Truth, and mighty above all things.
Bible (Apocrypha)

A truth that's told with bad intent
Beats all the lies you can invent.
William Blake 1757–1827 English poet

One of the favourite maxims of my father was the distinction between the two sorts of truths, profound truths recognized by the fact that the opposite is also a profound truth, in contrast to trivialities where opposites are obviously absurd.
Niels Bohr 1885–1962 Danish physicist

'Tis strange—but true; for truth is always strange;
Stranger than fiction.
Lord Byron 1788–1824 English poet

What I tell you three times is true.
Lewis Carroll 1832–98 English writer

It is commonly said, and more particularly by Lord Shaftesbury, that ridicule is the best test of truth.
Lord Chesterfield 1694–1773 English writer

When you have eliminated the impossible, whatever remains, *however improbable*, must be the truth.
Arthur Conan Doyle 1859–1930 Scottish-born writer

An exaggeration is a truth that has lost its temper.
Kahlil Gibran 1883–1931 Lebanese-born American writer

Believe those who are seeking the truth; doubt those who find it.

André Gide 1869–1951 French novelist

Truth is not merely what we are thinking, but also why, to whom and under what circumstances we say it.

Václav Havel 1936– Czech statesman

True and False are attributes of speech, not of things. And where speech is not, there is neither Truth nor Falsehood.

Thomas Hobbes 1588–1679 English philosopher

It is the customary fate of new truths to begin as heresies and to end as superstitions.

T. H. Huxley 1825–95 English biologist

In lapidary inscriptions a man is not upon oath.

Samuel Johnson 1709–84 English lexicographer

Honesty is praised and left to shiver.

Juvenal c.AD 60–c.130 Roman satirist

The presence of those seeking the truth is infinitely to be preferred to those who think they've found it.

Terry Pratchett 1948– English novelist

But, my dearest Agathon, it is truth which you cannot contradict; you can without any difficulty contradict Socrates.

Socrates 469–399 BC Greek philosopher

There was things which he stretched, but mainly he told the truth.

Mark Twain 1835–1910 American writer

I can't tell a lie, Pa; you know I can't tell a lie. I did cut it with my hatchet.

George Washington 1732–99 American statesman

The truth is rarely pure, and never simple.

Oscar Wilde 1854–1900 Irish dramatist

Truth

A thing is not necessarily true because a man dies for it.
Oscar Wilde 1854–1900 Irish dramatist

✳ The United States

Good Americans, when they die, go to Paris.
Thomas Gold Appleton 1812–84 American epigrammatist

America! America!
God shed His grace on thee
And crown thy good with brotherhood
From sea to shining sea!
Katherine Lee Bates 1859–1929 American writer

God bless America,
Land that I love,
Stand beside her and guide her
Thru the night with a light from above.
Irving Berlin 1888–1989 American songwriter

We are a nation of communities…a brilliant diversity
spread like stars, like a thousand points of light in a
broad and peaceful sky.
George Bush 1924– American statesman

There is nothing wrong with America that cannot be
fixed by what is right with America.
Bill Clinton 1946– American statesman

Isn't this a billion dollar country?
Charles Foster 1828–1904 American politician, *responding to a
Democratic gibe about a 'million dollar Congress'*

Yes, America is gigantic, but a gigantic mistake.
Sigmund Freud 1856–1939 Austrian psychiatrist

Go West, young man, and grow up with the country.
Horace Greeley 1811–72 American journalist

Give me your tired, your poor,
Your huddled masses yearning to breathe free.
Emma Lazarus 1849–87 American poet

There can be no fifty-fifty Americanism in this country.
There is room here for only 100 per cent. Americanism,
only for those who are Americans and nothing else.
Theodore Roosevelt 1858–1919 American statesman

I like to be in America!
OK by me in America!
Ev'rything free in America
For a small fee in America!
Stephen Sondheim 1930– American songwriter

Overpaid, overfed, oversexed, and over here.
Tommy Trinder 1909–89 British comedian, *of American troops in Britain during the Second World War*

America is a vast conspiracy to make you happy.
John Updike 1932–2009 American writer

The United States themselves are essentially the greatest
poem.
Walt Whitman 1819–92 American poet

America is God's Crucible, the great Melting-Pot where
all the races of Europe are melting and re-forming!
Israel Zangwill 1864–1926 Jewish writer

The Universe ✳

Had I been present at the Creation, I would have given
some useful hints for the better ordering of the universe.
Alfonso 'the Wise', King of Castile 1221–84, *on studying the Ptolemaic system*

'Gad! she'd better!'
Thomas Carlyle 1795–1881 Scottish historian, *on hearing that Margaret Fuller 'accept[ed] the universe'*

The Universe

The eternal mystery of the world is its comprehensibility...The fact that it is comprehensible is a miracle.

Albert Einstein 1879–1955 German-born theoretical physicist, *usually quoted as 'The most incomprehensible fact about the universe is that it is comprehensible'*

Now, my own suspicion is that the universe is not only queerer than we suppose, but queerer than we *can* suppose.

J. B. S. Haldane 1892–1964 Scottish mathematical biologist

If we find the answer to that [why it is that we and the universe exist], it would be the ultimate triumph of human reason—for then we would know the mind of God.

Stephen Hawking 1942– English theoretical physicist

This, now, is the judgement of our scientific age—the third reaction of man upon the universe! This universe is not hostile, nor yet is it friendly. It is simply indifferent.

John H. Holmes 1879–1964 American Unitarian minister

There is a coherent plan to the universe, though I don't know what it's a plan for.

Fred Hoyle 1915–2001 English astrophysicist

From the intrinsic evidence of his creation, the Great Architect of the Universe now begins to appear as a pure mathematician.

James Jeans 1877–1946 Scottish astronomer

The Universe is not obliged to conform to what we consider comfortable or plausible.

Carl Sagan 1934–96 American astronomer

How is it that hardly any major religion has looked at science and concluded, 'This is better than we thought! The Universe is much bigger than our prophets said,

grander, more subtle, more elegant'?
Carl Sagan 1934-96 American astronomer

The world is everything that is the case.
Ludwig Wittgenstein 1889–1951 Austrian-born philosopher

Violence ✳

Keep violence in the mind
Where it belongs.
Brian Aldiss 1925– English writer

Pale Ebenezer thought it wrong to fight,
But Roaring Bill (who killed him) thought it right.
Hilaire Belloc 1870–1953 British writer

All they that take the sword shall perish with the sword.
Bible

I say violence is necessary. It is as American as cherry pie.
H. Rap Brown 1943– American Black Power leader

    Who overcomes
By force, hath overcome but half his foe.
John Milton 1608–74 English poet

If you strike a child take care that you strike it in anger,
even at the risk of maiming it for life. A blow in cold
blood neither can nor should be forgiven.
George Bernard Shaw 1856–1950 Irish dramatist

Where force is necessary, there it must be applied boldly,
decisively and completely. But one must know the
limitations of force; one must know when to blend force
with a manoeuvre, a blow with an agreement.
Leon Trotsky 1879–1940 Russian revolutionary

Violence

The quietly pacifist peaceful
always die
to make room for men
who shout.
Alice Walker 1944– American poet

✳ Wales

It profits a man nothing to give his soul for the whole
world…But for Wales—!
Robert Bolt 1924–95 English dramatist

The English have forgot that they ever conquered the
Welsh, but some ages will elapse before the Welsh forget
that the English have conquered them.
George Borrow 1803–81 English writer

Who dare compare the English, the most degraded of all
the races under heaven, with the Welsh?
Giraldus Cambrensis 1146?–1220? Welsh historian

The land of my fathers, how fair is thy fame.
Evan James 1809–78 Welsh bard

Everyday when I wake up, I thank the Lord I'm Welsh.
Cerys Matthews 1969– Welsh singer

Though it appear a little out of fashion,
There is much care and valour in this Welshman.
William Shakespeare 1564–1616 English dramatist

The land of my fathers. My fathers can have it.
Dylan Thomas 1914–53 Welsh poet

The Welsh remain the only race whom you can vilify
without being called a racist.
A. N. Wilson 1950– English writer

War ⇒The Army ✳

When war enters a country
It produces lies like sand.
  Anonymous

We make war that we may live in peace.
    Aristotle 384–322 BC Greek philosopher

The bomber will always get through. The only defence is
in offence, which means that you have to kill more
women and children more quickly than the enemy if you
want to save yourselves.
    Stanley Baldwin 1867–1947 British statesman

Not worth the healthy bones of a single Pomeranian
grenadier.
    Otto von Bismarck 1815–98 German statesman, *of possible
    German involvement in the Balkans*

This policy cannot succeed through speeches, and
shooting-matches, and songs; it can only be carried out
through blood and iron.
    Otto von Bismarck 1815–98 German statesman

C'est magnifique, mais ce n'est pas la guerre.
It is magnificent, but it is not war.
      Pierre Bosquet 1810–61 French general, *on the charge of the
      Light Brigade at Balaclava, 1854*

They have gone too long without a war here. Where is
morality to come from in such a case, I ask? Peace is
nothing but slovenliness, only war creates order.
    Bertolt Brecht 1898–1956 German dramatist

As you know, God is usually on the side of the big
squadrons against the small.
    Comte de Bussy-Rabutin 1618–93 French soldier and poet

War

In war, whichever side may call itself the victor, there are no winners, but all are losers.

Neville Chamberlain 1869–1940 British statesman

We shall fight on the beaches, we shall fight on the landing grounds, we shall fight in the fields and in the streets, we shall fight in the hills; we shall never surrender.

Winston Churchill 1874–1965 British statesman

Let us therefore brace ourselves to our duty, and so bear ourselves that, if the British Empire and its Commonwealth lasts for a thousand years, men will still say, 'This was their finest hour.'

Winston Churchill 1874–1965 British statesman

Never in the field of human conflict was so much owed by so many to so few.

Winston Churchill 1874–1965 British statesman

Laws are silent in time of war.

Cicero 106–43 BC Roman statesman

War is nothing but a continuation of politics with the admixture of other means.

Karl von Clausewitz 1780–1831 Prussian military theorist, *commonly rendered 'War is the continuation of politics by other means'*

War is too serious a matter to entrust to military men.

Georges Clemenceau 1841–1929 French statesman

ROBERT DUVALL: I love the smell of napalm in the morning. It smells like victory.

Francis Ford Coppola 1939– American film director, *in the film* Apocalypse Now

War is the most exciting and dramatic thing in life. In fighting to the death you feel terribly relaxed when you manage to come through.

Moshe Dayan 1915–81 Israeli statesman

I am not only a pacifist but a militant pacifist. I am willing to fight for peace. Nothing will end war unless the people themselves refuse to go to war.

Albert Einstein 1879–1955 German-born theoretical physicist

There never was a good war, or a bad peace.

Benjamin Franklin 1706–90 American statesman and scientist

If we are attacked we can only defend ourselves with guns not with butter.

Joseph Goebbels 1897–1945 German Nazi leader

Would you rather have butter or guns?…preparedness makes us powerful. Butter merely makes us fat.

Hermann Goering 1893–1946 German Nazi leader

War is hell, and all that, but it has a good deal to recommend it. It wipes out all the small nuisances of peace-time.

Ian Hay 1876–1952 Scottish writer

Always mystify, mislead, and surprise the enemy, if possible.

Thomas Jonathan 'Stonewall' Jackson 1824–63 American general, *his strategic motto during the Civil War*

Among the calamities of war may be jointly numbered the diminution of the love of truth, by the falsehoods which interest dictates and credulity encourages.

Samuel Johnson 1709–84 English lexicographer, *possibly the source of 'When war is declared, Truth is the first casualty'; attributed also to Hiram Johnson*

It is well that war is so terrible. We should grow too fond of it.

Robert E. Lee 1807–70 American general

He knew that the essence of war is violence, and that moderation in war is imbecility.

Lord Macaulay 1800–59 English historian

War

Rule 1, on page 1 of the book of war, is: 'Do not march on Moscow'...[Rule 2] is: 'Do not go fighting with your land armies in China.'
Lord Montgomery of Alamein 1887–1976 British field marshal

Probably the battle of Waterloo *was* won on the playing-fields of Eton, but the opening battles of all subsequent wars have been lost there.
George Orwell 1903–50 English novelist

My subject is War, and the pity of War.
The Poetry is in the pity.
Wilfred Owen 1893–1918 English poet

Little girl...Sometime they'll give a war and nobody will come.
Carl Sandburg 1878–1967 American poet

Once more unto the breach, dear friends, once more;
Or close the wall up with our English dead!
In peace there's nothing so becomes a man
As modest stillness and humility:
But when the blast of war blows in our ears,
Then imitate the action of the tiger.
William Shakespeare 1564–1616 English dramatist

There is many a boy here to-day who looks on war as all glory, but, boys, it is all hell.
William Tecumseh Sherman 1820–91 American general

War is capitalism with the gloves off.
Tom Stoppard 1937– British dramatist

The battle of Waterloo was won on the playing fields of Eton.
Duke of Wellington 1769–1852 British general

Next to a battle lost, the greatest misery is a battle gained.
Duke of Wellington 1769–1852 British general

Wealth ⇒Money ✳

Riches are a good handmaid, but the worst mistress.
Francis Bacon 1561–1626 English courtier

It is easier for a camel to go through the eye of a needle, than for a rich man to enter into the kingdom of God.
Bible

Greed is all right…Greed is healthy. You can be greedy and still feel good about yourself.
Ivan F. Boesky 1937– American businessman

A very rich person should leave his kids enough to do anything but not enough to do nothing.
Warren Buffett 1930– American businessman

The man who dies…rich dies disgraced.
Andrew Carnegie 1835–1919 American industrialist

Let me tell you about the very rich. They are different from you and me.
F. Scott Fitzgerald 1896–1940 American novelist, *to which Ernest Hemingway replied, 'Yes, they have more money'*

In every well-governed state, wealth is a sacred thing; in democracies it is the only sacred thing.
Anatole France 1844–1924 French man of letters

We are all Adam's children but silk makes the difference.
Thomas Fuller 1654–1734 English physician

The greater the wealth, the thicker will be the dirt.
J. K. Galbraith 1908–2006 American economist

If you can actually count your money, then you are not really a rich man.
J. Paul Getty 1892–1976 American industrialist

Wealth

We are not here to sell a parcel of boilers and vats, but the potentiality of growing rich, beyond the dreams of avarice.

Samuel Johnson 1709–84 English lexicographer, *at the sale of Thrale's brewery*

I've been rich and I've been poor: rich is better.

Beatrice Kaufman 1895–1945 American writer

Will the people in the cheaper seats clap your hands? All the rest of you, if you'll just rattle your jewellery.

John Lennon 1940–80 English pop singer, *at a Royal Variety Performance*

Let us be frank about it: most of our people have never had it so good.

Harold Macmillan 1894–1986 British statesman

A kiss on the hand may be quite continental,
But diamonds are a girl's best friend.

Leo Robin 1900–84 American songwriter

The chief enjoyment of riches consists in the parade of riches.

Adam Smith 1723–90 Scottish economist

How many things I can do without!

Socrates 469–399 BC Greek philosopher, *on looking at a multitude of goods exposed for sale*

It was very prettily said, that we may learn the little value of fortune by the persons on whom heaven is pleased to bestow it.

Richard Steele 1672–1729 Irish-born essayist

Luxury has been railed at for two thousand years, in verse and in prose, and it has always been loved.

Voltaire 1694–1778 French writer

I am grateful for the blessings of wealth, but it hasn't changed who I am. My feet are still on the ground. I'm just wearing better shoes.

Oprah Winfrey 1954– American talk show hostess

Weather ✳

What dreadful hot weather we have! It keeps one in a continual state of inelegance.

Jane Austen 1775–1817 English novelist

The rain, it raineth on the just
And also on the unjust fella:
But chiefly on the just, because
The unjust steals the just's umbrella.

Lord Bowen 1835–94 English judge

Every time it rains, it rains
Pennies from heaven.
Don't you know each cloud contains
Pennies from heaven?

Johnny Burke 1908–64 American songwriter

I believe we should all behave quite differently if we lived in a warm, sunny climate all the time.

Noël Coward 1899–1973 English dramatist

This is a London particular…A fog, miss.

Charles Dickens 1812–70 English novelist

A woman rang to say she heard there was a hurricane on the way. Well don't worry, there isn't.

Michael Fish 1944– British weather forecaster, *weather forecast on the night before serious gales in southern England*

The weather is like the Government, always in the wrong.

Jerome K. Jerome 1859–1927 English writer

Weather

When two Englishmen meet, their first talk is of the weather.
   Samuel Johnson 1709–84 English lexicographer

It is impossible to live in a country which is continually under hatches...Rain! Rain! Rain!
   John Keats 1795–1821 English poet

No one can tell me,
Nobody knows,
Where the wind comes from,
Where the wind goes.
   A. A. Milne 1882–1956 English writer

The first fall of snow is not only an event, but it is a magical event. You go to bed in one kind of world and wake up to find yourself in another quite different, and if this is not enchantment, then where is it to be found?
   J. B. Priestley 1894–1984 English writer

The fog comes
on little cat feet.
   Carl Sandburg 1878–1967 American poet

So foul and fair a day I have not seen.
   William Shakespeare 1564–1616 English dramatist

There is no such thing as bad weather. All weather is good because it is God's.
   St Teresa of Ávila 1512–82 Spanish mystic

Rain is grace; rain is the sky condescending to the earth; without rain, there would be no life.
   John Updike 1932–2009 American writer

The best sun we have is made of Newcastle coal.
   Horace Walpole 1717–97 English connoisseur

It was the wrong kind of snow.
   Terry Worrall British railway spokesman, *popular summary of his explanation of disruption on British Rail*

Weddings ✳

If it were not for the presents, an elopement would be
preferable.
> **George Ade** 1866–1944 American humorist

Now you will feel no rain, for each of you will be shelter
for the other. Now you will feel no cold, for each of you
will be warmth for the other.
> **Anonymous** *from the saying known as the 'Apache Blessing'*

As the bridegroom rejoiceth over the bride.
> **Bible**

Wilt thou love her, comfort her, honour, and keep her in
sickness and in health; and, forsaking all other, keep thee
only unto her, so long as ye both shall live?
> **Book of Common Prayer** 1662

It's pretty easy. Just say 'I do' whenever anyone asks you a
question.
> **Richard Curtis** 1956– British scriptwriter, *advice to a
> prospective bridegroom, in the film* Four Weddings and a
> Funeral

I'm getting married in the morning,
Ding dong! The bells are gonna chime.
Pull out the stopper;
Let's have a whopper;
But get me to the church on time!
> **Alan Jay Lerner** 1918–86 American songwriter

       The trouble
with being best man is, you don't get a chance to
   prove it.
> **Les A. Murray** 1938– Australian poet

Happy is the bride that the sun shines on.
> **Proverb**

✳ Winning

The race is not to the swift, nor the battle to the strong.
> **Bible**

You ask, what is our aim? I can answer in one word:
Victory, victory at all costs, victory in spite of all terror;
victory, however long and hard the road may be; for
without victory, there is no survival.
> **Winston Churchill** 1874–1965 British statesman

Victory has a hundred fathers, but no-one wants to
recognise defeat as his own.
> **Count Galeazzo Ciano** 1903–44 Italian politician

STEERFORTH: Ride on! Rough-shod if need be, smooth-
shod if that will do, but ride on! Ride on over all
obstacles, and win the race!
> **Charles Dickens** 1812–70 English novelist

Winning is everything. The only ones who remember you
when you come second are your wife and your dog.
> **Damon Hill** 1960– English motor-racing driver

The moment of victory is much too short to live for that
and nothing else.
> **Martina Navratilova** 1956– Czech-born American tennis
> player

Winning isn't everything. It's the money you make doing
it that's everything.
> **Lee Trevino** 1939– American golfer

We are not interested in the possibilities of defeat; they
do not exist.
> **Queen Victoria** 1819–1901 British monarch

Winter ✳

The English winter—ending in July,
To recommence in August.
    Lord Byron 1788–1824 English poet

No shade, no shine, no butterflies, no bees,
No fruits, no flowers, no leaves, no birds,—
November!
    Thomas Hood 1799–1845 English poet

The most serious charge which can be brought against
New England is not Puritanism but February.
    Joseph Wood Krutch 1893–1970 American critic and
    naturalist

Winter is icummen in,
Lhude sing Goddamm,
Raineth drop and staineth slop,
And how the wind doth ramm!
    Ezra Pound 1885–1972 American poet

    O, Wind,
If Winter comes, can Spring be far behind?
    Percy Bysshe Shelley 1792–1822 English poet

Let no man boast himself that he has got through the
perils of winter till at least the seventh of May.
    Anthony Trollope 1815–82 English novelist

Woman's Role →Men and Women ✳

If all men are born free, how is it that all women are
born slaves?
    Mary Astell 1668–1731 English poet

Woman's Role

The freedom women were supposed to have found in the Sixties largely boiled down to easy contraception and abortion: things to make life easier for men, in fact.

Julie Burchill 1960- English journalist

I could have stayed home and baked cookies and had teas. But what I decided was to fulfil my profession, which I entered before my husband was in public life.

Hillary Rodham Clinton 1947- American lawyer

One is not born a woman: one becomes one.

Simone de Beauvoir 1908-86 French novelist

I am a woman and my business is to hold things together.

F. Scott Fitzgerald 1896-1940 American novelist

Today the problem that has no name is how to juggle work, love, home and children.

Betty Friedan 1921-2006 American feminist

I didn't fight to get women out from behind the vacuum cleaner to get them onto the board of Hoover.

Germaine Greer 1939- Australian feminist

My mother said it was simple to keep a man, you must be a maid in the living room, a cook in the kitchen and a whore in the bedroom. I said I'd hire the other two and take care of the bedroom bit.

Jerry Hall 1956- American model

A woman's preaching is like a dog's walking on his hinder legs. It is not done well; but you are surprised to find it done at all.

Samuel Johnson 1709-84 English lexicographer

The first blast of the trumpet against the monstrous regiment of women.

John Knox c.1505-72 Scottish Protestant reformer

But if God had wanted us to think just with our wombs, why did He give us a brain?
    Clare Booth Luce 1903–87 American writer and politician

The Queen is most anxious to enlist every one who can speak or write to join in checking this mad, wicked folly of 'Woman's Rights', with all its attendant horrors, on which her poor feeble sex is bent, forgetting every sense of womanly feeling and propriety.
    Queen Victoria 1819–1901 British monarch

Womanist is to feminist as purple to lavender.
    Alice Walker 1944– American poet

I do not wish them [women] to have power over men; but over themselves.
    Mary Wollstonecraft 1759–97 English feminist

Women ⇒Men and Women

The weaker sex, to piety more prone.
    William Alexander, Earl of Stirling c.1567–1640 Scottish poet

All the privilege I claim for my own sex…is that of loving longest, when existence or when hope is gone.
    Jane Austen 1775–1817 English novelist

Who can find a virtuous woman? for her price is far above rubies.
    Bible

Good women always think it is their fault when someone else is being offensive. Bad women never take the blame for anything.
    Anita Brookner 1928– British novelist

In her first passion woman loves her lover,
In all the others all she loves is love.
    Lord Byron 1788–1824 English poet

Women

The prime truth of woman, the universal mother...that if a thing is worth doing, it is worth doing badly.

G. K. Chesterton 1874–1936 English writer

She knows her man, and when you rant and swear,
Can draw you to her *with a single hair.*

John Dryden 1631–1700 English poet

The happiest women, like the happiest nations, have no history.

George Eliot 1819–80 English novelist

What does a woman want?

Sigmund Freud 1856–1939 Austrian psychiatrist

Women are people who shop. Shopping is the festival of the female oppressed.

Germaine Greer 1939– Australian feminist

Being a woman is of special interest only to aspiring male transsexuals. To actual women, it is merely a good excuse not to play football.

Fran Lebowitz 1946– American writer

She's the sort of woman who lives for others—you can always tell the others by their hunted expression.

C. S. Lewis 1898–1963 English literary scholar

A woman will always sacrifice herself if you give her the opportunity. It is her favourite form of self-indulgence.

W. Somerset Maugham 1874–1965 English novelist

Woman was God's second blunder.

Friedrich Nietzsche 1844–1900 German philosopher

Woman is the nigger of the world.

Yoko Ono 1933– Japanese poet

The greatest glory of a woman is to be least talked about by men.

Pericles c.495–429 BC Greek statesman

Every woman adores a Fascist,
The boot in the face, the brute
Brute heart of a brute like you.
Sylvia Plath 1932–63 American poet

She floats, she hesitates; in a word, she's a woman.
Jean Racine 1639–99 French tragedian

O Woman! in our hours of ease,
Uncertain, coy, and hard to please…
When pain and anguish wring the brow,
A ministering angel thou!
Sir Walter Scott 1771–1832 Scottish novelist

Frailty, thy name is woman!
William Shakespeare 1564–1616 English dramatist

Here's to the maiden of bashful fifteen
Here's to the widow of fifty
Here's to the flaunting, extravagant quean;
And here's to the housewife that's thrifty.
Richard Brinsley Sheridan 1751–1816 Irish dramatist

The great and almost only comfort about being a woman
is that one can always pretend to be more stupid than
one is and no one is surprised.
Freya Stark 1893–1993 English traveller

We are becoming the men we wanted to marry.
Gloria Steinem 1934– American journalist

From birth to 18 a girl needs good parents. From 18 to 35,
she needs good looks. From 35 to 55, good personality.
From 55 on, she needs good cash.
Sophie Tucker 1884–1966 American vaudeville artist

When once a woman has given you her heart, you can
never get rid of the rest of her body.
John Vanbrugh 1664–1726 English architect and dramatist

Words

✳ Words →Language, Meaning

The Greeks had a word for it.
  Zoë Akins 1886–1958 American writer

There is no use indicting words, they are no shoddier
than what they peddle.
  Samuel Beckett 1906–89 Irish writer

'When *I* use a word,' Humpty Dumpty said in a rather
scornful tone, 'it means just what I choose it to mean—
neither more nor less.'
  Lewis Carroll 1832–98 English writer

It cannot in the opinion of His Majesty's Government be
classified as slavery in the extreme acceptance of the word
without some risk of terminological inexactitude.
  Winston Churchill 1874–1965 British statesman

A man who could make so vile a pun would not scruple
to pick a pocket.
  John Dennis 1657–1734 English writer

       Words strain,
Crack and sometimes break, under the burden,
Under the tension, slip, slide, perish,
Decay with imprecision, will not stay in place,
Will not stay still.
  T. S. Eliot 1888–1965 American-born British poet

The chief merit of language is clearness, and we know
that nothing detracts so much from this as do unfamiliar
terms.
  Galen AD 129–199 Greek physician

And once sent out, a word takes wing beyond recall.
  Horace 65–8 BC Roman poet

Lexicographer. A writer of dictionaries, a harmless drudge.
  Samuel Johnson 1709–84 English lexicographer

I am not yet so lost in lexicography as to forget that words are the daughters of earth, and that things are the sons of heaven. Language is only the instrument of science, and words are but the signs of ideas.
Samuel Johnson 1709–84 English lexicographer

Words ought to be a little wild, for they are the assault of thoughts upon the unthinking.
John Maynard Keynes 1883–1946 English economist

Words are, of course, the most powerful drug used by mankind.
Rudyard Kipling 1865–1936 English writer

In my youth there were words you couldn't say in front of a girl; now you can't say 'girl'.
Tom Lehrer 1928– American humorist

Woord is but wynd; leff woord and tak the dede.
John Lydgate c.1370–c.1451 English poet

Whatever we have words for, that we have already got beyond.
Friedrich Nietzsche 1844–1900 German philosopher

Syllables govern the world.
John Selden 1584–1654 English historian

Work ⇒Careers

In the sweat of thy face shalt thou eat bread.
Bible

For the labourer is worthy of his hire.
Bible

Work is love made visible.
Kahlil Gibran 1883–1931 Lebanese-born American writer

Work

That state is a state of slavery in which a man does what he likes to do in his spare time and in his working time that which is required of him.

Eric Gill 1882–1940 English sculptor

I have long been of the opinion that if work were such a splendid thing the rich would have kept more of it for themselves.

Bruce Grocott 1940– British politician

I like work: it fascinates me. I can sit and look at it for hours. I love to keep it by me: the idea of getting rid of it nearly breaks my heart.

Jerome K. Jerome 1859–1927 English writer

Why should I let the toad *work*
Squat on my life?
Can't I use my wit as a pitchfork
And drive the brute off?

Philip Larkin 1922–85 English poet

Blessèd are the horny hands of toil!

James Russell Lowell 1819–91 American poet

Work expands so as to fill the time available for its completion.

C. Northcote Parkinson 1909–93 English writer

We spend our midday sweat, our midnight oil;
We tire the night in thought, the day in toil.

Francis Quarles 1592–1644 English poet

It's true hard work never killed anybody, but I figure why take the chance?

Ronald Reagan 1911–2004 American statesman

If you have great talents, industry will improve them: if you have but moderate abilities, industry will supply their deficiency.

Joshua Reynolds 1723–92 English painter

Far and away the best prize that life offers is the chance to work hard at work worth doing.
Theodore Roosevelt 1858–1919 American statesman

Which of us…is to do the hard and dirty work for the rest—and for what pay? Who is to do the pleasant and clean work, and for what pay?
John Ruskin 1819–1900 English critic

One of the symptoms of approaching nervous breakdown is the belief that one's work is terribly important, and that to take a holiday would bring all kinds of disaster.
Bertrand Russell 1872–1970 British philosopher

The labour we delight in physics pain.
William Shakespeare 1564–1616 English dramatist

Work was like a stick. It had two ends. When you worked for the knowing you gave them quality; when you worked for a fool you simply gave him eye-wash.
Alexander Solzhenitsyn 1918–2008 Russian novelist

O God, give me work till the end of my life
And life till the end of my work.
Annie S. Swan 1859–1943 Scottish-born novelist

Work saves us from three great evils: boredom, vice and need.
Voltaire 1694–1778 French writer

Writing ⇒Literature, Style

If you can't annoy somebody with what you write, I think there's little point in writing.
Kingsley Amis 1922–95 English novelist

Let other pens dwell on guilt and misery. I quit such odious subjects as soon as I can.
Jane Austen 1775–1817 English novelist

Writing

Writers, like teeth, are divided into incisors and grinders.
Walter Bagehot 1826–77 English economist

Manuscripts don't burn.
Mikhail Bulgakov 1891–1940 Russian writer

Beneath the rule of men entirely great
The pen is mightier than the sword.
Edward Bulwer-Lytton 1803–73 British novelist

When in doubt have a man come through the door with a gun in his hand.
Raymond Chandler 1888–1959 American writer

A writer must be as objective as a chemist: he must abandon the subjective line; he must know that dung-heaps play a very reasonable part in a landscape, and that evil passions are as inherent in life as good ones.
Anton Chekhov 1860–1904 Russian writer

We must beat the iron while it is hot, but we may polish it at leisure.
John Dryden 1631–1700 English poet

The writer's only responsibility is to his art. He will be completely ruthless if he is a good one...If a writer has to rob his mother, he will not hesitate; the *Ode on a Grecian Urn* is worth any number of old ladies.
William Faulkner 1897–1962 American novelist

The test of a round character is whether it is capable of surprising in a convincing way. If it never surprises, it is flat. If it does not convince, it is flat pretending to be round.
E. M. Forster 1879–1970 English novelist

Only connect!...Only connect the prose and the passion.
E. M. Forster 1879–1970 English novelist

The business of the poet and novelist is to show the sorriness underlying the grandest things, and the grandeur underlying the sorriest things.

Thomas Hardy 1840–1928 English novelist

The most essential gift for a good writer is a built-in, shock-proof shit detector. This is the writer's radar and all great writers have had it.

Ernest Hemingway 1899–1961 American novelist

No man but a blockhead ever wrote, except for money.

Samuel Johnson 1709–84 English lexicographer

Read over your compositions, and where ever you meet with a passage which you think is particularly fine, strike it out.

Samuel Johnson 1709–84 English lexicographer

A writer's ambition should be…to trade a hundred contemporary readers for ten readers in ten years' time and for one reader in a hundred years.

Arthur Koestler 1905–83 Hungarian-born writer

When my sonnet was rejected, I exclaimed, 'Damn the age; I will write for Antiquity!'

Charles Lamb 1775–1834 English writer

There is no need for the writer to eat a whole sheep to be able to tell you what mutton tastes like. It is enough if he eats a cutlet. But he should do that.

W. Somerset Maugham 1874–1965 English novelist

What in me is dark
Illumine, what is low raise and support;
That to the height of this great argument
I may assert eternal providence,
And justify the ways of God to men.

John Milton 1608–74 English poet

Writing

The last thing one knows in constructing a work is what to put first.
Blaise Pascal 1623-62 French scientist and philosopher

But those who cannot write, and those who can,
All rhyme, and scrawl, and scribble, to a man.
Alexander Pope 1688–1744 English poet

And, as imagination bodies forth
The forms of things unknown, the poet's pen
Turns them to shapes, and gives to airy nothing
A local habitation and a name.
William Shakespeare 1564–1616 English dramatist

Learn to write well, or not to write at all.
John Sheffield 1648–1721 English politician

Writing is not a profession but a vocation of unhappiness.
Georges Simenon 1903–89 Belgian novelist

Not that the story need be long, but it will take a long while to make it short.
Henry David Thoreau 1817–62 American writer

How vain it is to sit down to write when you have not stood up to live.
Henry David Thoreau 1817–62 American writer

I have written my work, not as an essay which is to win the applause of the moment, but as a possession for all time.
Thucydides c.455–c.400 BC Greek historian

I come from a backward place: your duty is supplied by life around you. One guy plants bananas; another plants cocoa; I'm a writer, I plant lines.
Derek Walcott 1930–   West Indian writer

A woman must have money and a room of her own if she is to write fiction.
Virginia Woolf 1882–1941 English novelist

Never forget what I believe was observed to you by Coleridge, that every great and original writer, in proportion as he is great and original, must himself create the taste by which he is to be relished.
William Wordsworth 1770–1850 English poet

Youth ⇒The Generation Gap

I'm not young enough to know everything.
J. M. Barrie 1860–1937 Scottish writer

Youth is something very new: twenty years ago no one mentioned it.
Coco Chanel 1883–1971 French couturière

It is better to waste one's youth than to do nothing with it at all.
Georges Courteline 1858–1929 French writer

Youth is happy because it has the ability to see beauty.
Franz Kafka 1883–1924 Czech novelist

20 to 40 is the fillet steak of life. After that it's all short cuts.
Philip Larkin 1922–85 English poet

A boy's will is the wind's will
And the thoughts of youth are long, long thoughts.
Henry Wadsworth Longfellow 1807–82 American poet

Youth is vivid rather than happy, but memory always remembers the happy things.
Bernard Lovell 1913– British astronomer

Whom the gods love dies young.
Menander 342–c.292 BC Greek comic dramatist

Youth

The atrocious crime of being a young man...I shall
neither attempt to palliate nor deny.
William Pitt 1708-78 British statesman

Being young is greatly overestimated...Any failure seems
so total. Later on you realize you can have another go.
Mary Quant 1934- English fashion designer

> My salad days,
When I was green in judgement.
William Shakespeare 1564-1616 English dramatist

Maturity is a high price to pay for growing up.
Tom Stoppard 1937- British dramatist

The force that through the green fuse drives the flower
Drives my green age.
Dylan Thomas 1914-53 Welsh poet

Make me young, make me young, make me young!
Kurt Vonnegut 1922-2007 American novelist

The only way to stay young is to avoid old people.
James D. Watson 1928- American biologist

Heaven lies about us in our infancy!
Shades of the prison-house begin to close
Upon the growing boy.
William Wordsworth 1770-1850 English poet

Index of Authors

Index of Authors

Index of Authors

Index of Authors

445

Index of Authors

Index of Authors

Index of Authors

Index of Authors

Index of Authors

Index of Authors

Index of Authors

Index of Authors

Index of Authors

Index of Authors

Index of Authors

Haskins, Minnie Louise
Trust

Hattersley, Roy
Football, Politicians

Havel, Václav
Hope, Protest, Truth

Hawass, Zahi
Time

Hawking, Stephen
Computers, Mathematics, Universe

Hawkins, Justin
Effort

Hay, Ian
Humour, War

Hazlitt, William
Country, Hatred, Manners, Names, Past, Perfection, Prejudice

Head, Bessie
Race

Heaney, Seamus
Ireland

Hearst, William Randolph
Journalism

Hegel, G. W. F.
Reality, Society

Heine, Heinrich
Censorship, Skies

Heisenberg, Werner
Mistakes

Heller, Joseph
Madness, Peace

Hellman, Lillian
Conscience, Cynicism

Helmsley, Leona
Taxes

Héloise
Lovers

Helvétius
Prejudice

Hemingway, Ernest
Courage, Failure, Sex, Writing

Henley, W. E.
Determination, Self

Henri IV
Cynicism, Poverty

Henry, O.
Deceit

Henry, Patrick
Liberty

Hepworth, Barbara
Drawing, Sculpture

Heraclitus
Change, Character

Herbert, A. P.
Country

Herbert, George
Drink, Hope, Secrecy

Herman, Henry see
Jones, Henry Arthur
and Herman, Henry

Herrick, Robert
Clothes, Marriage, Transience

Hervey, Lord
Lies

Herzberg, Frederick
Management

Herzog, Maurice
Mountains

Hesiod
Effort, Suffering

Hesse, Hermann
Hatred, Home

Heston, Charlton
Apology

Hewart, Lord
Justice

Heyward, Du Bose
and **Gershwin, Ira**
Summer

Hicks, J. R.
Business

Hicks, Seymour
Old Age

Hightower, Jim
Moderation

Hill, Aaron
Courage

Hill, Damon
Winning

Hill, Joe
Revolution

Hill, Napoleon
Money

Hill, Pattie S.
Birthdays

Hillary, Edmund
Mountains

Hillel 'The Elder'
Self

Hillingdon, Lady
Sex

Hilton, James
Old Age

Hippocrates
Art, Manners, Medicine

Hirst, Damien
Sculpture

Hitchcock, Alfred
Acting, Cinema, Fear, Television

Hitler, Adolf
Leadership, Lies

Hobbes, Thomas
Life, Truth

Hockney, David
Criticism, Painting, Technology

Index of Authors

Index of Authors

Index of Authors

Index of Authors

Index of Authors

Index of Authors

Index of Authors

Index of Authors

Index of Authors

Index of Authors

Index of Authors

Index of Authors

Rootes, Lord
Cars

Rosa, Salvator
Speechmaking

Rossetti, Christina
Memory

Rostand, Jean
Life Sciences,
Murder

Rosten, Leo
Children

Roth, Eric
Life

Roth, Philip
Parents

Rotten, Johnny
Sex

Roupell, Charles
Sport

Rousseau, Jean-
Jacques
Books, Liberty

Rowland, Helen
Foolishness, Men

Rowling, J. K.
Ability, Morality,
Poverty

Royden, Maude
Church

Rumbold, Richard
Democracy

Rumsfeld, Donald
Advice, Criticism,
Europe, Ignorance,
Knowledge

Runcie, Robert
Religion, Travel

Runyon, Damon
Money

Rushdie, Salman
Absence, Liberty

Rusk, Dean
Crises

Ruskin, John
Architecture, Art,

Beauty, Books,
Cooperation,
Ignorance,
Mountains,
Painting, Work

Russell, Bertrand
Belief, Boredom,
Censorship, Fathers,
Gossip, Happiness,
Leisure, Opinion,
Progress, Science,
Thinking, Work

Rutherford, Ernest
Science, Statistics

Ryan, Alan
Statistics

Ryle, Martin
Punctuality

Sacks, Jonathan
Television

Sadi
Patience, Science

Sagan, Carl
Earth, Invention,
Universe

Sagan, Françoise
Envy

Saint-Exupéry,
Antoine de
Children, Fear,
Love, Perfection,
Planning

Saint Laurent, Yves
Clothes

Saki
Clothes, Cookery,
Leadership,
Politicians

Salisbury, Lord
Elections

Sallust
Friendship

Samuel, Lord
Libraries

Sandburg, Carl
Babies, Language,
Past, War, Weather

Sanders, Henry
'Red'
Sport

Santayana, George
Past

Sargent, John
Singer
Painting

Sartre, Jean-Paul
Despair, Habit,
Hell, Time

Saunders, Cicely
Sickness

Sayers, Dorothy L.
Men and Women,
Quotations

Scalpone, Al
Prayer

Schelling,
Friedrich von
Architecture

Schiller,
Friedrich von
Happiness,
Intelligence,
Originality

Schlesinger, Arthur
M. Jr.
Presidency

Schnabel, Artur
Music

Schulberg, Budd
Ability

Schumacher, E. F.
Economics,
Environment

Schumpeter, Joseph
Alois
Technology

Schurz, Carl
Patriotism

469

Index of Authors

Index of Authors

Index of Authors

Index of Authors

473

Index of Authors

Index of Authors

475

Index of Authors